D1251008

WITHDRAWN

Taipei

Belhaven World Cities Series

Edited by
Professor R. J. Johnston and Professor P. Knox

Published titles in the series:

Mexico City *Peter Ward*
Lagos *Margaret Peil*
Tokyo *Roman Cybriwsky*
Budapest *György Enyedi and Viktória Szirmai*
Hong Kong *C. P. Lo*
Dublin *Andrew MacLaran*
Vienna *Elisabeth Lichtenberger*
Birmingham *Gordon E. Cherry*
Taipei *Roger Mark Selya*

Forthcoming titles in the series:

Beijing *Victor F. S. Sit*
Brussels *Alexander B. Murphy*
Buenos Aires *David J. Keeling*
Glasgow *Michael Pacione*
Harare *Carole Rakodi*
Havana *Joseph Scarpaci, Roberto Segre and Mario Coyula*
Johannesburg *Keith Beavon*
Lisbon *Jorge Gaspar and Allan Williams*
London *Michael Hebbert*
Melbourne *Kevin O'Connor*
Montreal *Annick Germain and Damaris Rose*
New York City *David A. Johnson*
Paris *Daniel Noin and Paul White*
Randstad *Frans M. Dieleman, Rein B. Jobse and Jan van Weesep*
Rome *John Agnew*
Seoul *Joochul Kim and Sang Chuel Choe*

Other titles are in preparation

Taipei

Roger Mark Selya
University of Cincinnati, Ohio, USA

JOHN WILEY & SONS
Chichester • New York • Brisbane • Toronto • Singapore

Published 1995 by John Wiley & Sons Ltd,
          Baffins Lane, Chichester,
          West Sussex PO19 1UD, England
          Telephone National Chichester (01243) 779777
                    International +44 1243 779777

Other Wiley Editorial Offices

John Wiley & Sons, Inc., 605 Third Avenue,
New York, NY 10158-0012, USA

Jacaranda Wiley Ltd, 33 Park Road, Milton,
Queensland 4064, Australia

John Wiley & Sons (Canada) Ltd, 22 Worcester Road,
Rexdale, Ontario M9W 1L1, Canada

John Wiley & Sons (SEA) Pte Ltd, 37 Jalan Pemimpin #05-04,
Block B, Union Industrial Building, Singapore 2057

Library of Congress Cataloging-in-Publication Data
Selya, Roger Mark.
    Taipei / Roger Mark Selya.
      p. cm. — (Belhaven world cities series)
    Includes bibliographical references and index.
    ISBN 0-471-94981-7
    I. Title. II. Series.
DS799.9.T36S45   1995
951.24'9—dc20   94-31794
                                          CIP

British Library Cataloguing in Publication Data

A catalogue record for this book is available from the British Library

ISBN 0-471-94981-7

Typeset in 10/12pt Sabon from author's disks by
Mayhew Typesetting, Rhayader, Powys
Printed and bound in Great Britain by
Biddles Ltd, Guildford and King's Lynn

For
Barbara, Rena, Micha, and Isaac

Contents

Contents

List of figures

List of figures

List of tables

List of tables

Preface

This book traces the development of Taipei City as a world city. The geographic center of Taipei (pronounced Tai Bay) is located at longitude 121° 32″ 39′ E and latitude 25° 05″ 40′ N (Figure 0.1). The city covers some 27 214 hectares, or 105 square miles (259 square kilometers). Its site characteristics place it in Taipei Basin (Figure 0.2).

The basin is bounded to the north and east by the Tatun volcanic mountains which have heights up to 1000 meters, to the south by the northern foothills of the Central mountain range, and to the west by the Linkou terrace at a height of some 200 meters. The basin itself, once the location of an ancient lake (Ho, 1988; Hsieh, 1964), consists of some 230 meters of sedimentary deposits from the Oliocene to recent times. The hydrology consists of the Tamshui river which is formed by the confluence of three other rivers. The Keelung river flows into the basin from the north in a S–SW direction via a valley separating the Tatun and Central mountains; the Hsintien Creek flows north from the Hsueh Shan of the Central mountain range; the Takokan river is the outlet for the Shihmen dam and has cut a channel along the foot of the Central range entering the basin between the Linkou terrace and the Central mountain range. In all the Tamshui is 188.1 miles long (Hsieh, 1964). Only the Tamshui is navigable.

Administratively, in 1990 Taipei was divided into sixteen *chu* (districts); the changes in the number and configuration of the districts and their respective subdivisions are more fully discussed in Chapter 5, Government and planning. The sixteen *chu* are made up of two separate groups. The first group, referred to as Old Taipei or the Original City Area, includes the ten *chu* of Sungshan, Ta-an, Kuting, Shuangyuan, Lungshan, Chengchung, Chiencheng, Yenping, Tatong, and Chungshan. The second

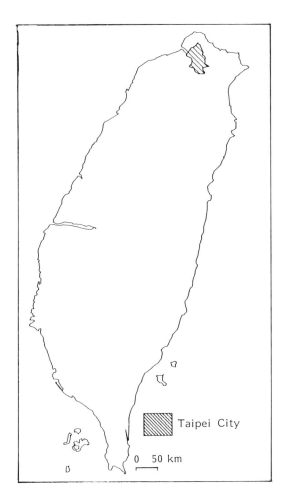

Figure 0.1 Location of Taipei

group includes four townships transferred from Taipei *hsien* (county) (Chingmei, Mucha, Nankang, and Neihu), and the Yangmingshan Administrative District (made up of Shihlin and Peitou), all of which were incorporated into the city in 1968 (Figure 0.3). In this book the sixteen districts (*chu*) are used whenever spatial analysis is presented.

The data for the book are taken from a variety of sources. The most commonly used sources were various years of the annual *Statistical Abstract of Taipei Municipality* and the annual *Taiwan-Fukien Demographic Fact Book, Republic of China*, and the *Industrial and Commercial Census Taiwan-Fukien Area, The Republic of China*, which were conducted in 1954, 1961, 1966, 1971, 1976, 1981, and 1986. These

Figure 0.2 Geology and hydrology

three main sources were supplemented by the specialized reports of the various bureaux and departments of the Taipei City Government. Many thanks to those government officials and staff who shared their materials. Figures P.1 to P.4 are reproduced from the atlas *1991 Greater Taipei Maps* with the kind permission of the Dah Yu Publishing Company, Taipei, Chou Yu-ting, president. Reference items marked with * are Chinese language materials. Unless otherwise indicated all calculations are by the author.

Special thanks are due those individuals who assisted in the preparation of the book. Shirley Philley did the initial bibliographic search. Sarah Ens and Mary Marx drafted maps and charts that I was unable to execute myself. Hung Fu-feng (Jason) made helpful suggestions and answered numerous questions about the details of living in Taipei as a native Taiwanese. The staff of the Library of the College of Design, Art, Architecture, and Planning, University of Cincinnati, and inter-library and reference librarians of the Langsam Library, University of Cincinnati, did yeoman's service in helping to obtain materials. The author is indebted to Ms Claire Walker, Ms Sally Yeung and the entire Wiley production staff for the efficiency and speed with which they transformed the manuscript into book form. Finally, special thanks to my wife, Barbara, and our

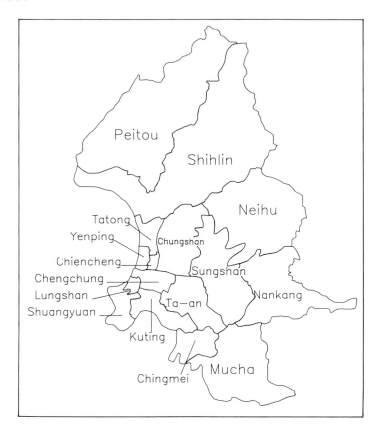

Figure 0.3 Administrative districts

children, Rena, Micha, and Isaac, who endured my absences for fieldwork, and my mood swings and preoccupation as the study evolved.

References

Ho, C. S. (1988) *An Introduction to the Geology of Taiwan. Explanatory Text of the Geologic Map of Taiwan.* Second Edition. Central Geological Survey, Ministry of Economic Affairs, Taipei.

Hsieh, C.-m. (1964) *Taiwan – Ilha Formosa. A Geography in Perspective.* Butterworths, Washington.

Prologue: one city, two reminiscences

15 June 1969. It is hard to believe that I will be leaving for home next week. The ten months here in Taipei dragged on and many times I thought June would never arrive. But somehow I did manage to complete four months of intensive language training and complete the fieldwork for my dissertation. These were no mean accomplishments, especially in light of the many obstacles and frustrations I had to overcome.

Oh sure, the trip to Taipei started off smoothly enough. The flight from Tokyo via Naha was comfortable. The weather in Tokyo had been perfect: a crisp, clear, and cloud free autumn day. I know I should have realized that weather would not follow me to Taipei, but what a shock when I stepped off the plane down the portable steps onto the tarmac in Taipei. I felt as if I had walked into a wall of heat. The terminal was comfortable and passport control took hardly any time. At customs the official, neatly dressed in a starched white uniform, had no trouble in first finding my luggage which had been sent on ahead and then clearing my bags. But then the situation started to deteriorate. When I entered the main arrival hall I was immediately accosted by some two dozen men, each of whom wanted me to spend a night or two at his hotel. Never mind that I already had a confirmed reservation at International House (IH). Once past these rude and boisterous agents, I was on the sidewalk outside again, in the heat. Got to get a cab. No problem – there must have been hundreds of little Taiwan-made cabs waiting to take travelers. So I took the first one in the queue, squeezed my bags, typewriter, and camera case into the trunk and front seat, and off we went. As we left the airport area I began to worry whether I had really landed in Taipei *City*, for as we moved on to city streets all I could see was rice growing in wide fields. In a city? We had gone no more than five blocks when the driver pulled over to the side of the road, drove right up on the sidewalk, and parked in front of a group of small stores. Despite my protests, the driver told me not to worry – just stay in the car. What was the problem? A flat tire, and the tire which was put on as a replacement was in worse shape than the flat it was supposed to replace. I would come to learn that this type of "maintenance" of vehicles was standard operating procedure. After about five minutes, during which time all the neighborhood kids had to come over and try their three English phrases on me, we were on our way again.

The rest of the trip was as disconcerting as the first part. There were factories, stores, and houses in what seemed to be a confusing and inappropriate juxtaposition, and there were more rice fields, with what seemed to be little farm villages sprinkled here and there. Every so often I doubted that we would safely get to IH since the normal rules of driving did not seem to apply: my driver accelerated into red lights, cut corners, and proceeded into intersections when he could see the traffic lights for traffic on our right turn yellow.

By the time we actually arrived at IH I was exhausted, thirsty, and hungry. IH was not what I had expected. It turned out to be a low, two-story, dirty grey building, with what seemed like an mini airplane hanger on one side and tennis courts on the other. Facing IH was a large, noisy squatter housing settlement. Check in proved to be simple and painless, and I was quickly escorted to my single room, which I found dreary, depressing, and dirty. A single, bare light bulb hung down from the center of the ceiling. I was shown where I could get boiled water. I had been warned not to drink tap water and to ask for boiled water since the water in Taiwan was heavily polluted by night soil. Those who disregarded this important advice risked contracting hepatitis. I was lucky – I never contracted it, although many of my friends did. I avoided cholera too, although I put myself at risk of hepatitis by getting a cholera shot at the government health station at the airport. Not one of us managed to escape an occasional bout of gastro-intestinal upset. I discovered the showers and toilets. I can still smell the camphor liberally placed in every stall. In fact this smell became one of the more pleasant ones as far as toilets were concerned. I was appalled by the toilet paper which resembled large sheets of fine grey sandpaper. Within days I discovered where to buy soft paper and carried a supply with me at all times.

I rested before dinner, which I ate at the small restaurant at IH. I immediately developed a long-term loathing for Chinese food. Since the sun set early and there was nothing else to do I tried to get some rest. But the heat, lack of ventilation in my room, and noise from the squatter housing did not lend themselves to sleep. Finally the noise abated and I managed to doze off, thinking that perhaps coming to Taipei was a bad idea and I should get back on a plane and go home.

The next morning I had two important chores to complete. After breakfast I went to the US Information Agency and checked in with the Fulbright office. The senior official, sympathetic to my state of discomfort, assured me that as soon as I moved out of IH everything would be fine. (Move out? Into an apartment? How would I cook? Would I be isolated, with no chance to meet either Chinese or Westerners?) Seeing that this chap was not going to help me much I then moved on to the second chore – to confirm my registration for private Chinese language tutoring at the Mandarin Training Center. In retrospect I realize that I was given a very informal, crude language skills evaluation, assigned a time and instructor and told to return on October 1 for the start of classes. Oh, wow. What was I supposed to do for two and a half weeks?

Well I did fill my time. I was approached by a part-time faculty member at the College of Chinese Culture about sharing an apartment. The quarters he had been provided did not meet his New York city standards. He agreed to find an apartment and furniture and I did move out of IH, but not before finding a third roommate. I explored the neighborhood and attracted a flock of kids on each trip – they thought it a real adventure to follow me and try their English on me. Their parents just stared when I went by. I learned where and how to shop for food. I got used to having an *ammah* come in and clean the apartment and do the laundry. Watching her hang out the washing was a lesson in cultural differences: washing was put out to dry by running bamboo poles through sleeves or legs in garments and then hanging the poles on special hooks on the back balcony. For socks she had a hanger with clothes pins. Since we had no iron, the clothes took on a rather unkempt look. But compared to the laundry service at IH this was a minor inconvenience. The laundry at IH may have been neatly pressed and whiter than white, but its smell was a mixture of unwashed water buffalo and an uncleaned men's room.

Before classes started I met other grad students who had come to Taipei to learn Chinese and do research. I discovered the other two US expatriate communities: the military and businessmen. Neither group seemed interested in us students. They seemed much too busy preserving their own privileges and perpetuating their own jealousies. However, since the Chinese drivers of the military buses could not tell the difference between one American and another, I was able to use the military bus system which was much less crowded than the public system. Its routes were also very circuitous – giving me more opportunities to see different parts of the city. Riding buses and just walking helped me learn the spatial structure of Taipei. As it turns out Taipei is an easy city to get around in. The layout follows the traditional grid patterns of Chinese cities (figures P.1 and P.2). I did have a bit of a problem navigating the road system where the city

0 _____ 500 meters

Figure P.1 Chungcheng district street map (reproduced with permission of the Dah Yu Publishing Company, Taipei)

reached the hilly and mountainous areas, and in the areas that had been rural in the past but had recently been urbanized (figures P.3 and P.4). This knowledge of the city came in very handy when I bought a motorcycle. I also learned how to steal onto the military base and get an occasional U.S. meal. But as for PX privileges, I had to settle for stifling my rage every time I saw an overpriced box of Kellogg's cereal or Hunt's tomato sauce in stores near where military personnel lived – evidence of an active black market.

I also came to realize how much the Chinese military permeated all of Taipei life. There were jeeps and military trucks on every road. Soldiers were everywhere. Some of them "guarded" buildings or important intersections. Many soldiers of all ranks just seemed to be doing daily, personal, household chores. Middle and high school students also looked like soldiers since their uniforms were the same style and color as the military. One newspaper cartoon had a middle school child sitting beside a

Figure P.2 Wanhwa district street map (reproduced with permission of the Dah Yu Publishing Company, Taipei)

general on a bus asking which high school the general attended. Security concerns also permeated civilian and business offices and it was often difficult to get the research materials I needed. On one occasion the Fulbright office had to intervene and on another I managed to get the materials through a used book store. The store manager was able to obtain the materials through a friend although I had to pay a hefty price to get final delivery.

One "perk" of living in Taipei was my discovery of pirated books. I probably read more books on the *New York Times* Best Seller list during my stay than ever before or since. These books were what preserved our sanity – since except for bars and restaurants there was not too much open at night.

Once classes started I fell into a routine and managed to get my work done. The seasons changed and with the advent of winter new smells and

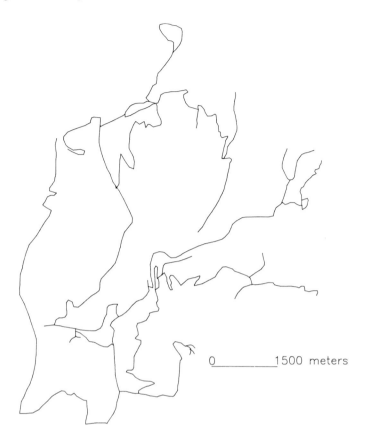

0 _____ 1500 meters

Figure P.3 Shihlin district street map (reproduced with permission of the Dah Yu Publishing Company, Taipei)

sights filled the air. The open sewers steamed and seemed to smell worse when the cooler weather arrived. In the markets winter coats and umbrellas suddenly appeared. Since I am not built like the average Oriental, none of the off the rack Chinese winter jackets fit me so I had to have one custom made. I wore it inside as much as outside – as uncomfortable as our apartment was in the hot weather it was worse in winter since we had no central heating and who could afford to keep an electric space heater going all the time? I did keep a light bulb burning in my closet to prevent mildew. By the time spring arrived most of my research was done and I could enjoy the return of warmer weather and the flowers blooming.

I am sure that I will miss some things about Taipei. There is a certain charm about walking home from the market and having all the women in the neighborhood comment on how well I had done with my shopping.

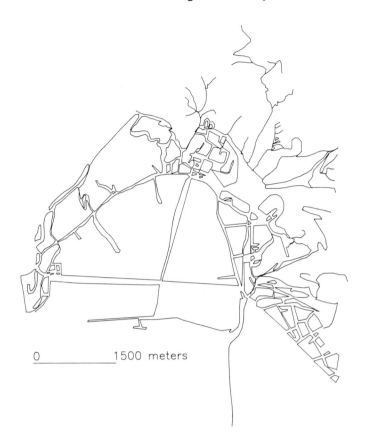

0   1500 meters

Figure P.4   Peitou district street map (reproduced with permission of the Dah Yu Publishing Company, Taipei)

Memorable too is the informality of people coming home from work, eating, changing into their pajamas and then taking an early evening walk. I now take great delight in being able to identify itinerant merchants by their unique calls. My students at National Taiwan University treated me with great respect and took me on many field trips. But there are also things I will not miss. The smells, dirt, and grime which all seem to cling to clothing I will be glad to say good riddance to. I can not get used to being stared at. Even the people in my own alley persist in this habit, perhaps because I have acquired such a deep tan which they find distasteful. (Their attitude has no racial overtones. It merely reflects their low opinion of those forced to do outdoor labor.) The Chinese habit of spitting or picking one's nose in public are also things I will not miss. Some things you can never acculturate to . . .

    28 January 1990. Fieldwork went very well this month and I look forward to returning home tomorrow and starting on the second phase of my research. Much of my success can be traced to the convenience and quality of my accommodation. Again this year I decided to stay at the China Hotel. My room has a small refrigerator and a small, personal hot water maker. Now that there are 24-hour convenience stores I can get quart containers of milk and eat the breakfast cereal I brought with me in my room. I did eat breakfast in the hotel the first day I was here. Toast, tea, a glass of milk and a small glass of orange juice cost almost 10 dollars. In New Taiwan dollars the price was the same as it was in 1969 but no adjustment has been made for the appreciation of the Taiwan currency. Another convenience of the hotel is a small business office center with a typewriter, IBM compatible PC, and a fax. Laundry was a real pleasure to have done. Two blocks behind the hotel, surrounded by large office buildings, is a small, low density, old-fashioned neighborhood with a mix of shops, restaurants, and old Japanese houses. One of the small shops is a laundry with a modern washer and dryer, both of which sit at the entrance to the shop. The shop owner and his family live the old-fashioned way – in the back of the shop.

Transportation is a continuing problem. There are now several bus companies and there are still lots of cabs. But given the slow pace of traffic it is often easier and quicker to walk even moderate distances. The mix of cabs, buses, trucks, and motorcycles has increased the noise to uncomfortable levels. There are hardly any military vehicles on the roads now, although most government offices and bureaux continue to run their own bus services for their employees. The construction of the new Mass Rapid Transit System has added to traffic congestion, noise, and to the overall dirty appearance of the city. Fortunately getting to the new international airport some 30 kilometers southwest of the city is not complicated. There is an express bus which starts at the west bus terminal outside the new railroad station. The bus is even equipped with onboard luggage racks.

As I go about my business no one stares at me, despite my full beard and grey hair. The level of sophistication goes well beyond a nonchalant attitude towards foreigners; people, especially teenagers and young adults, are all dressed in the latest Western fashions, many, it seems, with designer labels. The prices of such clothing seem way out of line with what it costs in the US, but this does not seem to deter the Taipei kids. Eating is more cosmopolitan as well. In addition to Western fast food restaurants, there is a profusion of ethnic restaurants from all over the world. There is even a frozen yogurt store which is doing well. Shops now offer US and European made goods as a matter of course. Prices for luxury items still exceed my budget, but at least there is no black market.

I have had little trouble obtaining materials for my research. Government officials are quite generous with their materials and their staffs very helpful in locating more obscure publications. The ready availability of photocopying is a great improvement over having to hand copy tables of data.

Since information is so much more accessible now I have had time to indulge in what appears to be one of the favorite "sports" among those of us who worked here during the 1960s – exploring our old stomping grounds. In many ways this is a silly game, for surely no one expects a city or neighborhood to remain as it was decades ago. Nevertheless, I hardly recognized Hsin-yi Road. Few if any old Japanese houses remain and large apartment houses and office towers now line the roads. Some of the new buildings are quite beautiful. All the stores have changed and the old market where I shopped daily seems to be abandoned. Why shop in a public market when modern, clean, well-lit supermarkets are open? Parts of the neighborhood had been leveled to make way for an elevated expressway and I was especially disappointed that I could not locate an old artist whose studio provided paintings which line my living room and dining room walls. I did locate my old apartment building with its red gate. But I saw no point in ringing the bell and taking a look around. After all these years who would remember me? There were isolated pockets of old brick buildings and simple family-run stores, but many of these posted notices about their imminent moves.

I went for a walk one night, hoping to see the Chiang Kai-shek Memorial lit up, as it appears in so many tourist brochures. That night however the memorial was dark after sundown and the city at night as dead and dull as it was in 1969. Once the business day ends the city literally goes to sleep. To be fair, there is lots more to do during the daylight hours now with a new zoo and several new museums, and many sophisticated shops to explore.

So Taipei is now a modern, bustling city, and if you close your eyes the sounds are the same as they are in any other large city anywhere in the world. In many ways it has lost its charm. I miss the old speciality stores – the printer who engraved my business cards, the rice store, the quilt store, match making offices, and other colorful establishments. While some of the old wholesale establishments still exist, they are not readily visible on the busy modernized streets. Only the Taiwan smells remain unique . . .

These two reminiscences, synthesized from old letters and field notes, could very well describe two cities thousands of miles apart, rather than the same city some 21 years apart. Some of the differences in the two reminiscences are really indications that the author has changed. I have acquired language and coping skills, as well as a network of contacts who can help in my work. These influence how I use and react to the city.

But Taipei has also changed, and changed in ways that no one in 1969 would have imagined. This book deals with what changes have occurred in Taipei and why these changes took place. One of the most important elements in description and explanation of change is context. As such the opening chapter deals with the special political and economic contexts which formed part of Taipei's environment. Then a series of topical chapters quantitatively describe changes in the population, economy, government, and land use while qualitatively tying these changes to shifts in the rhythm of daily life in Taipei. One chapter deals with some of the adverse effects of all these changes and how government agencies and private organizations are trying to improve the quality of life in Taipei. A further chapter describes how Taipei residents seek ways to rest and restore themselves. The book concludes by exploring how political and business leaders hope to direct future change successfully and ensure the prospects of Taipei as a major cultural, economic, and political center.

1
From colonial backwater to world city

At the end of World War II Taipei had a population of around 600 000 people. As such it ranked 21st in the Chinese urban hierarchy (Pannell, 1973). Under ordinary circumstances it was highly unlikely that Taipei would ever have become anything more than the sleepy, backwater provincial capital that it was in 1945 (Ambruster, 1976; Brunn and Williams, 1983; Chan, 1980; Glenn, 1968). But circumstances were not to be "ordinary" for Taipei. In this chapter the special, necessary political and economic conditions which determined Taipei's evolution from a small provincial capital to a world city are explored.

Political conditions

A series of four political crises weighed heavily on Taipei's role and function as a city. The four crises are retrocession, the strategic retreat of the Kuomintang to Taiwan at the end of the Chinese civil war, diplomatic isolation, and political liberalization and democratization.

Retrocession

The first crisis, the retrocession of Taiwan province to the control of the Republic of China, resulted from the defeat of the Japanese at the end of World War II. Retrocession was promised to China under the terms of the Cairo Conference on 1 December 1943, despite the wording of the Treaty of Shimonoseki under which the government of nineteenth century China ceded Taiwan to Japan. The promise of retrocession was later confirmed in the Potsdam Proclamation of 26 July 1945.

As described by Kerr (1965) and Ballantine (1952), the transition from Japanese colony to Chinese province was not a smooth one. Japanese administrators left abruptly, and the central government of the Republic of China, under the leadership of the Kuomintang (Nationalist) Party, was otherwise occupied with a civil war against the Chinese Communists, and did not have the time, interest, or personnel to arrange properly for a smooth transition of power. Rather, in October 1945, Chiang Kai-shek, the President of the Republic of China, appointed General Chen Yi as administrator general and supreme commander in Taiwan Province. In contrast to the expectations of the Taiwan population, the military government not only did not treat them as equals, but rather saw most Taiwanese of standing under the Japanese colonial government as collaborators. In the economic realm, Chen Yi and his associates quickly assumed control of Japanese assets and reorganized them as official monopolies, thus placing some 90 percent of all economic enterprises under direct government control and administered by Chinese from the mainland (Ballantine, 1952). The island was systematically stripped of much of its infrastructure and plant, as well as its stores of food and consumer goods. The desire on the part of these mainland carpetbaggers for quick profits soon created a pattern of soaring wholesale and retail prices in Taiwan. The focus on profits and commandeering Taiwan's resources also had unfortunate social consequences. Public health deteriorated and cholera and bubonic plague reappeared, after having been wiped out by the former Japanese health authorities. Educational standards fell and public morals also deteriorated (Ballantine, 1952).

On the political front the Chen regime offended the Taiwan population with the decision not to permit local self-government until December 1949, although the new Chinese constitution was to come into effect on the mainland two years earlier. The deterioration of the political economy reached its nadir in the incident of 27 February 1947 and the subsequent revolt. On that date agents of the Tobacco Monopoly killed a woman who had been hawking cigarettes on which no tax had been paid. The following day a group of Taiwanese marched peacefully to the Tobacco Monopoly headquarters to demand redress. Receiving no satisfaction there the group proceeded to the Governor's Offices. When they reached a wide intersection adjacent to the Governor's Offices they were fired upon by policemen. This prompted a general attack on occupation authorities by the Taiwanese in Taipei and elsewhere. The government responded by imposing martial law. However, since General Chen lacked the personnel to deal with a revolt, he adopted a conciliatory attitude and accepted in principle a series of demands, including an agreement that he would consider various economic and political reforms. At the same time that he entered into these agreements, thereby ensuring the cessation of violence, he also prepared to use the 50 000 reinforcements who were scheduled to arrive on 8 March. What resulted was a massacre, under the guise of suppressing a communist rebellion, designed to eliminate the principal native leaders. By the end of March the island had been cowed into submission.

However, news of these events soon spread and under pressure from the United States, Chiang Kai-shek replaced Chen Yi with a civilian adminis-trator, Wei Tao-ming, a former Chinese ambassador to the United States. Under Wei's administration Taiwan was treated as a province of China, with the same government structure found in the rest of China. Chen Yi's associates were replaced by new appointees, including a good proportion of Taiwanese. Furthermore Wei began restructuring the economy by eliminating monopolies, favoring free enterprises, and beginning joint government/private interest enterprises.

But just as economic conditions on Taiwan ameliorated, external political and military events influenced the course of Taiwan's status. As the Chinese civil war wore on and conditions deteriorated, Chiang Kai-shek began giving Taiwan increasing attention as he hoped to create there, as he had in Szechwan province earlier, a last resort stronghold from which Kuomintang (Nationalist) resistance might be continued. To this end Wei was replaced by General Ch'en Ch'eng on 5 January 1949; shortly thereafter martial law was re-established and a new wave of arrests and executions began of those charged with being communist sympathizers. Economic conditions again worsened and the political gains made under Wei's administration, including trust and confidence in the central government, were forfeited.

Retrocession had marginal effect on the status and function of Taipei as a city. It remained, as it had been under the Japanese, the leading political and economic center on the island, although the perception of the population in regard to the administration housed in Taipei worsened, with longstanding distrust and bitterness as a legacy. In contrast, the second political crisis had a major impact upon virtually every charac-teristic of Taipei.

The strategic retreat of the Kuomintang

The second crisis involved, as anticipated by Chiang Kai-shek, the strategic retreat of the Nationalist government to Taiwan as the Chinese Com-munists emerged victorious in the civil war. In December 1949 Chiang and his government fled to Taiwan and established Taipei City as the provisional capital of the Republic of China, a title it still retains. In subsequent chapters the cultural, demographic, economic, and political ramifications of this new status will be related to Taipei's evolution into a world city. However, there are five immediate functional impacts which will be reviewed here.

The first functional impact of Taipei's new status is that Taipei found itself host to separate governments responsible for three different jurisdictions – national, provincial, and municipal. The possibilities for duplication in services and conflict in authority were all too obvious. In a two stage process attempts were made spatially and administratively to keep the three governments separate. In 1958 the Taiwan provincial government was moved to a new site southeast of the mid-island city of Taichung, in Chunghsing New Village, Nantou *hsien* (county). This site, some 180 kilometers down island from Taipei and so located near the center of the island, was supposed to delineate clearly centers of power. However, this clear separation has never truly evolved for several reasons. First, the provincial government for a long time lacked the trained administrative and technical personnel to carry out all its functions. Therefore projects conceived and developed in Chunghsing New Village commonly had to be approved in Taipei before they could be implemented (Jacoby, 1966). Secondly, government personnel and legislators working in Chunghsing New Village disliked the area, which they perceived rightly as being far removed from the center of power. They therefore worked to establish links or reputations which would permit them to return to Taipei. Finally, the inherent ambiguity of having two governments administer and plan for an area of some 36 000 square kilometers (roughly the combined areas of the states of Connecticut, Massachusetts, and Rhode Island) has never been resolved.

Similarly, the anomaly of having Taipei host to both a central and municipal government has never been fully resolved. In theory the ambiguity was solved in 1966 when Taipei was elevated to the status of a special municipality under the direction and jurisdiction of the executive *Yuan* (branch) of the central government. While this designation was constitutionally warranted by the size of the Taipei population, there have been those who have argued that the change in status was designed more to inhibit the growth of local government and weaken the political basis of popular Taiwanese politicians (Copper, 1990). Furthermore, the official reason for the changed status, to permit the municipal government better to coordinate policies and planning with the national government, has not been fully realized, as we shall see below in Chapters 5 and 6.

The second impact of Taipei's new status was the physical need to headquarter, house, feed, and entertain not only the government and its officials and military establishment, but also the diplomatic community which followed Chiang Kai-shek. Again the resolution of this set of fundamental spatial allocation problems has had long-term land use and social consequences which will be reviewed later. In the short-term the solution to these allocation problems led to native Taiwanese displacement, residential segregation, and squatter settlement development. Some of the short-term problems were resolved by the presence of the U.S. Military Advisory and Assistance Group, with its commissaries and clubs. But the presence and selective use of these facilities produced bitterness on the part of those denied access to them.

The third impact of the new status was both physical and cultural. For along with the government, the military, and the diplomats came the treasures of the National Palace Museum, the National Library, and entire universities. Again these had to be properly headquartered. But beyond the physical needs of these cultural institutions, Taipei found itself suddenly elevated to the status of a major cultural and education center.

The fourth impact was the arrival of the major banking and financial institutions. These institutions, in coordination with the national government, would in time make Taipei a major financial and economic center.

The final impact on Taipei was the arrival of various U.S. government aid and advisory groups which had begun working with the Kuomintang (Nationalist) government to recover from the devastation of World War II. Again in addition to the need for physical space, these institutions lent to Taipei an aura, a mystique, of a vibrant place of not only important Chinese government work, but of multinational and international commitment to the rebuilding of China.

Diplomatic isolation

In short, the change in status for Taipei from a simple provincial capital to the provisional capital of the national government provided the major cultural, economic, financial, and political framework in which Taipei evolved into a world city. However, at one point it appeared that Taipei's future as any type of a political center at all, let alone a world city, was in doubt. This cloudy future was based on the diplomatic crisis which faced the Kuomintang (Nationalist) government in the 1960s and 1970s. The crisis involved the suspension of diplomatic relations by virtually all governments with which the Republic of China had diplomatic relations. The low point in this débâcle was in 1979 when United States' President Jimmy Carter severed diplomatic relations with Taiwan in favor of the People's Republic of China. By the 1990s diplomatic recognition of the Nationalist government was restricted to some two dozen or so governments. Similarly the Republic of China's status as an active player in the international community was weakened in 1971 when the General Assembly of the United Nations decided to seat the delegation from the People's Republic of China as the representatives of China. Not only did

5

the Republic of China lose its seat, but in addition it was denied membership in the United Nations affiliated organizations as well. Other international organizations such as the World Bank also denied the Republic of China membership. Field offices and representatives of all these international organizations thus left Taipei.

Despite pessimism with regard to the future of the Republic of China, these diplomatic setbacks did not prove to be crippling blows to the people or the economy of the Republic of China or to the status of Taipei as a world city. Government officials quietly went about developing alternative means of ensuring that Taiwan would be a major player in the fora of the world. In place of embassies and consulates, trade missions were opened not only to foster economic relations but to act as quasi-official embassies as well. To be sure the People's Republic of China continues to pressure the world community to isolate the Republic of China. For example, when the Republic of China applied for membership of the GATT in 1990, Beijing forcefully argued against Taiwan's membership on the basis that the PRC was still not a member and that it was unseemly that a rebellious province should join the GATT before the main body politic. However, governments and institutions appear to be more accommodating to the desires of the Republic of China to be a fuller participant in world affairs, especially since in the early 1990s the national treasury of the Republic held the world's largest foreign currency reserves. Beijing sees any such accommodation as giving in to economic bribery (Kristof, 1989), but regardless of one's perspective it is clear that the Republic of China has weathered the diplomatic crises of the 1960s and 1970s and by the 1990s had emerged as an even stronger player in the international cultural, economic, and political world. As such, Taipei's place as a major cultural, economic, financial, and tourist center has been strengthened rather than weakened.

Political liberalization and democratization

The last functional impact on Taipei involves the gradual evolution of a democratic political system in the Republic of China. After the death of Chiang Kai-shek in April 1975, the Vice-President, Yen Chia-kan, served until May 1978 when Chiang Ching-kuo, Chiang's son, was elected president. Chiang Ching-kuo served as president until his death in January 1988, when he was succeeded by the Cornell-educated Taiwanese agronomist Lee Tung-hui. What is important about this succession is that it coincided with the evolution of genuinely democratic institutions. For example in 1986, while a special commission discussed the termination of martial law which had been in effect since 1945, opposition parties ran candidates in national and local elections. Although such participation was officially illegal, no action was taken against the opposition parties. Martial law was lifted in 1987. In April 1991 the so-called *Temporary Provisions Effective During the Period of Communist Rebellion* were abrogated by the National Assembly. As with the period of retrocession, the major impact on Taipei's function was mostly psychological. In restoring normalcy to the political process the leadership of the Kuomintang (Nationalist) Party and the Republic of China have signaled a realization that continued progress in modernization now requires that political institutions catch up with the economic progress made since the 1960s.

In sum, the political conditions which permitted Taipei to evolve from a quiet provincial capital into a world city existed because of the lack of clear resolution of the Chinese civil war. The transfer of the Kuomintang (Nationalist) government to Taiwan transformed Taipei into a provisional capital, thereby granting it special status and functions which would not have otherwise existed. The political processes operating on Taipei have not always been conducive to easy or smooth changes. But to the credit of the Kuomintang (Nationalist) leadership, the periods of domestic distrust and tension and international disorientation were ultimately seen as opportunities to change policies so that the long-term viability of the Republic of China, and by extension Taipei as a world city, could be ensured. What is all the more amazing about Taipei's status and concern for its future is that the perception that Taipei is still only the provisional capital of the Republic of China persists. The most recent demonstration of this occurred when in June 1991, Premier Hau Pei-tsun rejected a proposal that government funds be used to refurbish or renovate central government buildings in Taipei. Hau indicated that Sun Yat-sen, the founding father of the Republic of China, had designated Nanking as the capital, and that since Taipei remains but a temporary capital funds designated for government buildings could be better spent on public construction to upgrade Taiwan's infrastructure and economic and social development projects.

Economic conditions

The economic conditions which permitted Taipei to evolve into a world city are generally referred to as the Taiwan economic miracle. The following description of the changes which transformed and modernized the economy of Taiwan is not designed to be a comprehensive survey of the economic development and history of the island since other such comprehensive surveys are readily available (Chang, 1968; Ho, 1978; Li, 1988; Kuo *et al.*, 1981). Rather, this material is intended to highlight and outline the major economic changes which took place and explore alternative explanations for these changes.

Table 1.1 Indicators of economic development

Measure		1952	1989
Employment	% primary	56.1	12.9
	% secondary	16.9	42.2
	% tertiary	27.0	44.9
GNP NT$m		2 019.0	198 036.0
GNP per capita NT$		1 913.0	181 281.0
Origins NDP	% primary	36.0	5.9
	% secondary	18.0	43.5
	% tertiary	46.0	50.6
Exports US$m		116.0	66 201.0
Imports US$m		187.0	52 249.0
Balance of trade		0.62	1.27
Exports	% primary products	91.9	4.6
	% manufactured goods	8.1	95.4
Imports	% agricultural products and raw materials	65.9	72.1
	% capital goods	14.2	16.4
	% consumer goods	19.9	11.5

Source: *Taiwan Statistical Data Book, 1990* (1990).

Change

The most direct way to describe the Taiwan economic miracle is found in Table 1.1. The 16 main indicators of economic development clearly show the transformation of the economy. At the individual level we see a country where per capita income has gone from some US$450 in 1952 to US$6300 in 1989. This increase is a reflection of the major structural changes in the economy. Taiwan has progressed from a basically agricultural economy to an industrial one to a service led one. This economic evolution was driven by a major surge in trade. Although buffeted by the oil crises of 1973 and 1979, Taiwan has been able to maintain a strong positive balance of trade, and by 1989 was ranked as the 16th largest exporter and the 11th largest importer in the world, despite the fact that its population of some 20 million ranked 41st in size. The government of the Republic of China prided itself that the modernization of the economy had been accompanied by an increasing equality of income distribution, thereby seeming to put to rest the notion that growth and equity were mutually exclusive economic goals. Also of interest is the parallel development in the areas of demography and education. Taiwan, during its economic development, passed through both the demographic (Freedman, 1986) and epidemiologic transitions (Tsai, 1980), and has witnessed major improvements in the life expectancy and the educational level of its population.

Explanation of changes

Although these macroeconomic measures of change are important in themselves, for students of economic development the main issue to be explored is the explanation of how change took place. There are seven approaches which can be identified in the quest to explain the economic development of Taiwan.

The *institutional* approach argues that economic development occurred because the political elite made a conscious, public commitment to the need for development. To be sure, when Chiang Kai-shek first arrived in Taiwan he saw the development of Taiwan only in terms of enabling him to recapture the mainland. However, Chiang was persuaded to support the economic development of Taiwan for its own sake for several reasons. First, the idea of fostering economic development could be traced back to the writings of Sun Yat-sen (Gold, 1986, 1991; Myers, 1986). Secondly, Chiang was apparently very sensitive to what he hoped would be his place in history. As such he saw his work on Taiwan as a final chance to accomplish something positive for the Chinese people (Gold, 1986, 1991). Furthermore, Chiang's reading of Chinese history convinced him that there was a strong tradition of state interference in the management of economic activities (Myers, 1986).

Given Chiang's change of mind, it was then possible to begin directing the future course of the Taiwan economy. One major principle used in directing the economy was that the government would retain control over critical industrial output and services such as energy and water (Myers, 1986). In addition there was to be a strict separation of the planning and implementation of government goals. The planning aspects were vested in an apparent succession of inter-ministerial councils: the Economic Stabilization Board, the Council for International Economic Cooperation and Development, the Economic Planning Council, and finally the Council for Economic Planning and Development. In fact regardless of which title was in use, the planning was handled by the same group of highly committed and well trained technocrats; the umbrella organization they worked under changed its name as the aid funds and influence of the United States (to be discussed below) waxed and waned and as the Republic of China's status in international organizations shifted. Furthermore, regardless of what name it bore, the inter-ministerial council was charged with *macro*economic planning. In a series of development plans of various lengths (3, 4, 6, or 10 years were most often used), the broad, general economic and social goals and targets of the government economists were outlined. Often specific sectors of the economy and specific industries within those sectors were singled out for special attention. Actual implementation of the broad goals was left to other organizations such as the Board of Foreign Trade, the Industrial

Development Bureau of the Ministry of Economic Affairs, or the Joint Commission of Rural Development (now the Council on Agricultural Development) (Woronoff, 1986). This separation of planning and implementation actually ensured fuller implementation since it removed the issues of debating and setting priorities from the hands of bureaucrats who might otherwise have different priorities and goals; the bureaucrats charged with implementation had freedom of choice as to how to achieve the overall goals, but could not otherwise modify the goals agreed by the inter-ministerial council.

The goals of these development plans shifted as the economy of Taiwan was restructured. During the 1950s the development plans put heavy emphasis on agricultural development supporting an import substitution industrialization. Through a series of agricultural reforms, which focused on a successful land reform program entitled "Land to Tiller", agricultural production was stabilized to the point where surplus labor could be drawn off from the rural areas, and agriculture could continue to prosper. From 1960 through 1973 the development plans stressed an aggressive export orientation. Since the mid-1970s plans have stressed economic restructuring, industrial upgrading, and high technology. The latter three emphases are seen as necessary to ensure Taiwan's place in the world economy in the face of rising labor costs at home and increasing competition from cheap, labor-intensive industries in other developing countries.

The *environmental* approach stresses the creation of an attractive investment environment by the government in order to attract both domestic and foreign investors. The government enhanced the investment environment in four ways. First, it created an administrative and legal framework which fostered and nurtured investment. Typical investment incentives and protections included the same treatment for foreign and domestic investments, the right of foreign investors to maintain 100 percent ownership of an enterprise, conversion and remittance of all net profits, the chance after one year to apply for repatriation of all invested capital, protection against government expropriation or requisition for 20 years if the foreign investment in an enterprise is 45 percent or more of the total registered capital, and protection of intellectual property rights such as patents, trademarks, and copyrights. General tax holidays, tax deferments, and customs exceptions were offered, as were specific tax breaks for investments for quality control, research and development, pollution control, and energy conservation.

Secondly, the government invested in a series of major infrastructure projects (Table 1.2). In 1974 the government announced the beginning of a series of infrastructure projects labeled the Ten Major Construction Projects. In 1979 this group was followed by the Twelve New Development Projects. In early 1985 the government announced the beginning of the third series of projects, Fourteen Key Projects. These investments, of

Table 1.2   Major infrastructure projects

Ten major construction projects (1973–1980)	
Sun Yat-sen national freeway	North Link railroad
Railroad electrification	Taichung port
Chiang Kai-shek international airport	Suao harbor
Integrated steel mill	Kaohsiung shipyard
Petrochemical industry	Nuclear power plant
Twelve new development projects (1980 onwards)	
Around-the-island railroad	Cultural centers
New cross-island highways expansion	China Steel
Kao-Ping region traffic improvement	Nuclear power project
Pingtung–Oluanpi highway widening	Farm mechanization
New towns and housing projects	Taichung harbour
expansion	Regional drainage
Dike and levee construction	
Fourteen key projects (1985 onwards)	
Third phase expansion, China Steel	Telecommunications
Oil and natural gas	modernization
Expansion of rail system	Taipei underground railroad
Expansion of highways	Taipei Mass Rapid Transit
Flood control/drainage improvement	System
Ecological protection/tourism	Water resources exploitation
Medical care	Municipal solid waste disposal
Important power projects	Grassroots development
	projects

course, were not only designed to improve the infrastructure of Taiwan and therefore its long-term competitiveness, but were also part of the government's concerted effort to build public confidence during the loss of international status in the 1970s and to foster economic expansion in light of the economic slowdown which followed the energy crises of 1973 and 1979 (Gold, 1986).

Thirdly, the government sought to upgrade Taiwan's technology. Technology was acquired via four routes: direct imports, being brought in by foreign investors, attracting Taiwanese engineers and scientists to return home to help develop the technologies required, and by borrowing from multinational corporations. Under the last approach the government set minimum supply standards for local industries and subcontractors. In order to honor these standards multinational corporations investing in Taiwan had to transfer the appropriate technology to their Taiwan suppliers (Myers, 1986).

Finally, the government created industrial estates and export processing zones. These permitted native and foreign investors to have ready access to land, water, sewerage, banking, and administrative help in a legal environment where access to these key elements was often complicated. These zones and estates were strategically located near or in major ports and in rural areas the government sought to develop. Often they were restricted to one type of industry, for example the Hsin-chu Science Based Industrial Park, and the Toufen, Ta-she, and Lin-yuan estates which featured petrochemicals.

There is no question but that these four government strategies succeeded as Taiwan was able to attract some US$1.7 billion from overseas Chinese and some US$9.2 billion from other foreign investors in the period 1952 through 1989.

The *financial* approach deals with how the government created the stable financial environment necessary to attract industrial investment (Liang, 1989). Most fundamentally, the government implemented monetary stabilization policies designed to curb the excessive inflation of the period 1946–48. First the government, through a series of devaluations, adjusted the value of the New Taiwan dollar (NT$). By 1960 the value of the NT$ had stabilized at NT$40=US$1. Secondly, meaningful interest rates were set to ensure that when people deposited savings in time accounts the value of the principal and interest exceeded the rate of inflation. Although it took several years to refine the interest rate and time periods for deposits, the net result was a high rate of savings which permitted banks to loan funds to entrepreneurs. This formal financial market was paralleled by a more family based informal one (Kaye, 1990). Finally the government, with the help of U.S. aid funds, was not only able to balance its budget, but with time was able to use the considerable budget surpluses which developed to finance infrastructure projects (Kuo *et al.*, 1981).

The *world conditions* approach argues that the economic development took place at a time of exceptionally favorable conditions (Myers, 1986). The outbreak of the Korean War brought about a re-evaluation of United States policy towards the Republic of China. The new United States policy emphasized protection of the island republic via the extension of financial and military aid (Gold, 1986; Oshima, 1987). Similarly, the Vietnam War boosted the economy of Taiwan in at least four ways. Taiwan supplied agricultural and industrial goods to the United States military in Vietnam. Taiwan permitted the use of military facilities and depots which generated income for the government. Construction work in Vietnam provided additional income, especially for firms such as the Retired Servicemen Engineering Agency. Finally, Taiwan served as a major rest and recreation center for United States troops serving in Vietnam (Copper, 1990; Gold, 1986). In addition to these opportunities generated by the Cold War, on the world economic front the 1960s were in general years of prosperity and openness so that Taiwan was able to export goods in a relatively free market environment.

The *demographic* approach maintains that population played an important role in the development process (Liu, 1985; Mueller, 1977). It has been argued that population pressure, in the form of a high rate of natural increase and high population density, was a worry to government planners and therefore they adopted economic policies designed to increase incomes as rapidly as possible. A second argument is that the quality of the population played an important role in speeding the rate of economic growth. This occurred because the population was hardworking and valued education. Furthermore, among the refugees from mainland China was a highly experienced and skilled group of entrepreneurs, engineers, and technicians who were drawn into the economic development process. Finally, there was a large number of rural residents who were not only available for work, but given the availability of easy transportation had the means to get to the newly opened factories.

But the demographic approach must also include some of the difficult planning problems which have resulted from the interaction of economic development and population change. A decline in fertility and mortality has led to two serious economic and social challenges – the greying of the Taiwan population (Selya, 1989) and a chronic labor shortage which has spawned a flow of illegal migration to Taiwan (Selya, 1992). Further expansion of the economy will have to accommodate the new services which a rapidly ageing population will need, and solve the chronic labor shortages already present without damaging the cultural fabric of the Republic of China.

The *colonial* approach reasons that the policies of the Japanese colonial government left an important base for future industrialization (Oshima, 1987; Myers, 1986). Despite the pillage of the early retrocession period, Taiwan was left with some factories, transportation, water, and electrical infrastructure, and a basically literate population. Thus the government did not need to start the industrialization and economic modernization process from scratch.

Finally, the *structural* approach contends that the managerial and firm structure of Taiwan industry allows for quick responses to changes in markets and technology (Myers, 1986). In general manufacturing establishments in Taiwan are small, commonly with only an average of 20 or so workers, and correspondingly low assets and revenues (Table 1.3). Although there have been numerous government programs to facilitate mergers and consolidation of establishments, it is felt that the small scale of operations permits manufacturers to switch product lines more quickly in response to changes in market conditions.

No one set of variables under these seven approaches is necessarily unique to the Republic of China. Rather, what seems to be the case is that the particular combination of variables and timing has contributed to the rapid economic development of the Republic of China. All together they constitute the building blocks for the economic miracle.

Table 1.3 Scale of manufacturing

	Mean no. of workers	Mean assets (US$)	Mean revenues (US$)
1966	20.29	76 000	60 148
1986	24.00	246 358	130 833

Source: Industrial and Commercial Census of ROC, 1966, 1986.

Since the mid-1980s some doubts have been raised as to just how long lasting the miracle will be. The doubts go beyond the obvious short-term concerns for world economic conditions and the problems of being highly dependent upon a few concentrated markets for Taiwan's exports. Rather they deal with a series of issues involving the long-term health of the Taiwan economy, especially the viability of the agricultural sector, the difficulty in fostering technology, the deterioration in the quality of life, and the worsening of income equity.

In regard to agriculture there is a growing body of evidence (Bello and Rosenfeld, 1990; Williams, 1988) that suggests that in the process of economic development the agricultural sector of Taiwan has been decimated. Although the land reform was seen as a positive policy, it now appears that planners really had no long-term plans for maintaining a vital, viable agricultural sector. Several discriminatory policies, including mandatory rice sales and a very unfavorable rice for fertilizer barter program, were designed to drain capital assets from rural areas. The rapid growth of industry has definitely drained the rural areas of not only surplus workers but many full-time farm workers from agriculture. Changes in diet and the lowering of tariffs on imported, mainly United States, farm produce have created a situation where many farmers are no longer able to make a profit growing either traditional crops such as rice, or newer crops such as apples or pears. From a macroeconomic perspective a thriving, profitable agricultural sector may not be necessary. But given the central role agriculture, and especially rice cultivation, has played in traditional Chinese civilization, the demise of Taiwan agriculture may have severe cultural and psychological ramifications.

Technology is another economic issue where the Taiwan miracle seems very vulnerable (Bello and Rosenfeld, 1990). Despite government attempts to ensure the availability of the latest technology, much of even the high technology industries relies on the low end of the technology and product line. Notwithstanding successes in manufacturing and exporting personal computers, these units remain basically clones. Their manufacture still depends on imported components and site licenses. The main handicaps to the development of an independent, innovative computer industry include shortage of capital, low rates of research and development, and a lack of high-tech personnel. This latter factor remains true despite some well known cases of reverse "brain drain" and the apparent successes of the Hsin-chu Science Based Industrial Zone. A second example of technological handicaps is the inability of the Taiwan automobile industry to produce a Taiwan designed and manufactured car for mass market exports.

Quality of life issues focus on pollution (Bello and Rosenfeld, 1990; Selya, 1975, 1978), and the relative lack of recreational opportunities. Pollution of all sorts – air, water, noise – exists, although long-term, complete records of specific pollutants are not always available. Newspapers do however publish daily the urban air pollution levels: rarely are they anywhere within safe limits. Furthermore, pollution problems are not limited to urban areas: the widespread use of agricultural chemicals and the resulting air, ground, and water pollution have spawned a new underclass of rural workers who out of desperation work in these polluted environments. Farmers are no longer willing to expose themselves to the dangers of the agricultural chemicals (Bello and Rosenfeld, 1990). Virtually no basic epidemiological surveys have been done on either the behavioral or health consequences of living in a polluted, crowded environment as found in the Republic of China.

Lack of recreational facilities is a quality of life problem with both absolute and relative aspects. There are not a lot of open or green spaces in Taiwan cities. Where they exist they are often crowded, run-down, or inaccessible. The desire to escape the cities for uncrowded, clean, open areas is best exemplified by the massive traffic jams which develop around the bus and railroad stations on weekend and holiday mornings and evenings as people leave and then return to the cities.

One last problem relates to the nature of the economic miracle – income equality. Beginning in 1979, but continuing unabated since 1981, the ratio between the highest fifth's income to that of the lowest fifth has increased. The sources of the widening income gap are easy to define: ability to speculate in the Taipei stock market, and profits earned from land sales. Despite the origins of the growing income gap, it does call into question whether sustained economic growth and income equity are indeed both possible simultaneously. While planners debate this question, social tensions grow, evidenced by increases in crime and drug problems.

In contrast to the problems of technology, quality of life issues have not been of primary concern to planners. The reason for this is not hard to establish. There has been a strong "growthism" ideology among the ruling elite. This ideology maintains that any program or issue which might compromise the promise of present and future high rates of economic return must be either deferred or eliminated. The growth of an urban based middle class, many of whose members were educated in the United

15

States, has started to create pressures to deal more effectively with quality of life issues. Whether the political elite and government planners can respond quickly and fully enough is open to debate. There is no question, however, that quality of life issues are affecting economic decisions in ways which are not likely to please the elite or planners. For example, in Taipei residents of mixed residential/industrial–commercial land use have been able to force polluting factories and businesses out. In some cases the neighbors complained about noise pollution; in others it was air and water pollution which led to the mass complaints. Another telling example was the exodus of the corporate headquarters of ACER, the IBM of Taiwan. ACER chose to leave Taipei City for more open rural/suburban areas because the noise and congestion in their prime location created too many technical and personnel problems.

The importance of Taipei and its status *vis-à-vis* the economic development of the Republic of China are easy to appreciate. As the locus of government and financial power, Taipei's status profited directly. For local entrepreneurs and foreign investors alike, Taipei became synonymous with access to decision makers and those individuals and institutions best placed to direct and oversee foreign trade. Taipei thus became a magnet for services as well as industry. As Taiwan's economy was restructured to reflect changing domestic and international conditions, Taipei again was the locus of both articulating and implementing change. Unfortunately Taipei also came to suffer from, and symbolize, the negative consequences of rapid development. Some of these negative consequences, such as crowding, pollution and traffic congestion, are found virtually everywhere in the Republic of China. Other problems such as crime and escalating house prices seem more restricted to Taipei City itself. Regardless of the geographical extent of the problems, however, the degree to which they can be solved in Taipei will not only determine the future of Taipei City, but the course of Taiwan's future social and economic development.

Summary

The change in status from small provincial capital to world city which Taipei has experienced is directly related to a unique set of political and economic events. At times these events appeared to be beyond the control of either the residents of Taipei or the leadership of the Republic of China. Regardless of the origins and magnitude of the events, they had consequences which continue to go beyond the political and economic to include cultural, demographic, land use, and social challenges and problems. The following chapters describe the specific nature of these challenges and problems, and the solutions to them employed in Taipei City.

References

Ambruster, W. (1976) Letter from Taipei. *Far Eastern Economic Review* 94, Nov. 19, 70.

Ballantine, J. W. (1952) *Formosa. A Problem for United States Foreign Policy*. The Brookings Institution, Washington, D.C.

Bello, W. and S. Rosenfeld (1990) *Dragons in Distress. Asia's Miracle Economies in Crisis*. Institute for Food and Development Policy, San Francisco.

Brunn, S. D. and J. F. Williams (1983) *Cities of the World. World Regional Urban Development*. Harper and Row Publishers, New York.

Chan, J. (1980) *The Intellectual's Image of the City in Taiwan*. Papers of East–West Population Institute, Honolulu.

Chang, K., ed. (1968) *Economic Development in Taiwan*. Cheng Chung Book Company, Taipei.

Copper, J. F. (1990) *Taiwan: Nation-State or Province?* Westview Press, Boulder.

Freedman, R. (1986) Policy Options in Taiwan after the Demographic Transition, *Population and Development Review* 12:1, 77–100.

Glenn, W. (1968) Growing Like Topsy (Taipei), *Far Eastern Economic Review* 61, Aug. 8, 280–89.

Gold, T. B. (1986) *State and Society in the Taiwan Miracle*. M.E. Sharpe, Armonk.

Gold, T. B. (1991) Taiwan: In Search of Identity, pp. 22–47, in *MiniDragons. Fragile Economic Miracles of the Pacific*, S. M. Goldstein, ed., Westview, Boulder.

Ho, S. P. S. (1978) *Economic Development of Taiwan, 1860–1970*. Yale University Press, New Haven.

Jacoby, N. H. (1966) *U.S. Aid to Taiwan. A Study of Foreign Aid, Self-Help, and Development*. Frederick A. Praeger, New York.

Kaye, L. (1990) Pains of Adolescence, *Far Eastern Economic Review* 147, Jan. 25, 50–51.

Kerr, G. W. (1965) *Formosa Betrayed*. Houghton-Mifflin, Boston.

Kristof, N. D. (1989) Taiwan's Way to Win Friends and Undercut China's Sway, *New York Times*, December 3, 6.

Kuo, S. W. Y., G. Ranis, and J. C. H. Fei (1981) *The Taiwan Success Story. Rapid Growth With Improved Distribution in the ROC, 1952–1979*. Westview, Boulder.

Li, K. T. (1988) *The Evolution of Policy Behind Taiwan's Development Success*. Yale University Press, New Haven.

Liang, K.-s. (1989) The Taiwan Economy and Financial Markets, *Industry of Free China* 71:4, 1–9.

Liu, P. K. C. (1985) Human Resource Development and Modern Economic Growth in Taiwan, *Academia Economic Papers* 13:2, 367–406.

Mueller, E. (1977) The Impact of Demographic Factors on Economic Development in Taiwan, *Population and Development Review* 3:1 and 2, 1–22.

Myers, R. H. (1986) Economic Development of ROC on Taiwan, 1965–1981, pp. 13–64, in *Models of Development*, Laurence J. Lau, ed., Institute for Contemporary Studies, San Francisco.

Oshima, H. T. (1987) *Economic Growth in Monsoon Asia. A Comparative Survey*. University of Tokyo Press, Tokyo.

Pannell, C. W. (1973) *T'ai-chung, T'ai-wan: Structure and Function*. University of Chicago, Department of Geography, Research Paper number 144, Chicago.

Selya, R. M. (1975) Air and Water Pollution in Taiwan, *Journal of Developing Areas* 9:2, 177–202.

Selya, R. M. (1978) Economic Development and Environment in Taiwan: The Continuing Conflict, *Transition* 8:4, 1–7.

Selya, R. M. (1989) Greying of the Taiwan Population. Presented at the Annual Meeting, Association of American Geographers, March 22.

Selya, R. M. (1992) Illegal Migration in Taiwan: A Preliminary Overview, *International Migration Review* 26:3, 787–805.

Taiwan Statistical Data Book, 1990 (1990) Council for Economic Planning and Development, Taipei.

Tsai, H.-c. (1980) Changes in the Leading Cause of Death in Taiwan, 1964–1978, *Economic Review* 193, 9–23.

Williams, J. F. (1988) Vulnerability and Change in Taiwan's Agriculture, *Pacific Viewpoint* 29:1, 25–44.

Woronoff, J. (1986) *Asia's "Miracle" Economies*. M. E. Sharpe, Armonk.

2
Historical development, land use, and architecture

First-time, especially Western, visitors to Taipei find the city a confusing place. They see sharp juxtapositions of land use – with luxury villas alongside squatter housing or a noisy, smelly factory. Often there is no separation of work and living space; people frequently work on the street or sidewalks right in front of their homes or shops. Visitors hear a cacophony of sounds: traffic, peddlers, emergency vehicles, children playing, and construction noises make for a deafening background. They smell food cooking, open sewers, pollution from traffic and industry. Much of the apparent strangeness of Taipei can be explained by tracing the historical development of the city. Therefore, although our main interest in Taipei is in its development, growth, and change after the 1960s, this chapter describes the historical background of Taipei, including its origins, its succession of land use patterns, and changing architectural styles.

Historical development

The historical development of Taipei can be divided into four phases: initial settlement, late nineteenth century, the Japanese period, and the republican period. The first three are summarized in Figure 2.1.

Initial settlement

The original occupants of Taipei Basin are thought to have been the Ping-pu tribe of Taiwan aboriginals (Chai, 1967). They once occupied the west

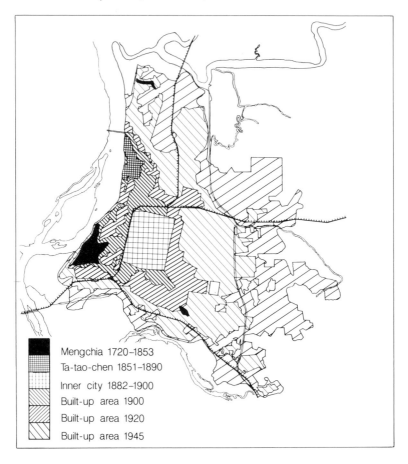

Figure 2.1 Historical development (after Chen, 1956, 6)

side of Taiwan and acted as a barrier or buffer between the Chinese and aboriginals of the mountain areas. The Ping-pu were gradually pushed by the Chinese into higher altitudes of the Central mountains. Over the long term the Ping-pu came to be considered as a civilized tribe and mingled with the Chinese, at times living in the same villages. In so doing they lost their cultural identity. It is generally thought that by 1820 most aborigines had left the Taipei area (Chen, 1956).

The first contacts between the Ping-pu and Chinese settlers in the Taipei area are thought to have occurred in 1709 when a farmer named Chen Lai-cheng from Chuanchow *hsien* (county) in Fukien province received a government land grant covering most of Taipei Basin (Chen, 1956). (Note that the *New Image of Taipei* (1988) dates the arrival to 1599.) Regardless of when in fact Chen did arrive he had been preceded by other Chinese settlers who had established a settlement at Hsinchuang, some 25 kilometers down the Tamshui river. These earlier settlers traded agricultural products such as sweet potatoes and forest products with the Ping-pu at a site near the confluence of the Takokan and Hsintien rivers. A Chinese settlement developed on the east side of the confluence and was named Manka, after the Ping-pu word for canoe or dugout (Wu, 1975). Alternative names for the settlement were Tagana or Menga. The Chinese termed it Mengchia.

Chen, and others who followed him from Chingchiang, Nanan, and Huian districts of Chuanchow *hsien*, continued this trade at Manka. These migrants were referred to as the *san i jen* (three district people). They bartered wine, meat, and clothes for the aboriginals' permission to cultivate the area (Chen, 1956). By 1738 the settlement had prospered and the settlers built a temple in honor of Kuan Yin, the Chinese goddess of mercy who had been their patron saint in Changchou (Wu, 1975). Continued prosperity through the 1740s, 1750s, and 1760s, was accompanied by more temple building. The sites of these temples gave the settlement its major street configurations (Wu, 1975).

Mengchia's importance as a commercial and political settlement received a boost when in 1759 soldiers stationed in Hsinchuang were transferred there (Wu, 1975). By 1800 Mengchia had eclipsed Hsinchuang as a settlement and trading post due to the silting of the upper reaches of the Takokan river, thus making it impossible for large sea-going junks to dock as far upstream as Hsinchuang. In 1808 a naval base was established in Mengchia; a year later the settlement was made the seat of Taipei *hsien* (county) (Hsieh, 1964), and an assistant magistrate assigned (Wu, 1975). The period 1821–1859 represents the peak in the prosperity of Mengchia. Population grew to some 5000 households owing to continued migration from Chuanchow and Changchou *hsien*: a new Chuanchow district, Anshi, began sending migrants too. In addition settlers from the Tungan district of Amoy *hsien*, south of Chuanchow, arrived (Wu, 1975).

The centrality, growth, and prosperity of Mengchia began to decline in 1853. There were five basic causes for the decline (Chen, 1956; Wu, 1975). First, the Tamshui river continued to silt up, and the harbor of Mengchia was thus rendered inaccessible. Secondly, anti-foreign sentiment developed and a leading British tea merchant, John Dodd, moved to the new settlement of Ta-tao-chen, about 2.4 kilometers north of Mengchia along the east bank of the Tamshui river. This new settlement had been established as a direct result of the third and fourth causes, termed the Battles between the Upper and Lower Guilds and the Battles between the Migrants. Both "battles", which lasted from 1851 to 1861, involved the *san i jen* (i.e. "old") versus "new" (i.e. Changchou, Anshi and Tungan) immigrants. Two issues were involved (Wu, 1975). One seems to have been a deliberate attempt on the part of the Chuanchow immigrants to humiliate the migrants from Changchou. What the Chuanchow immigrants did was to call their guild the Upper Guild. By implication, the guild of the other immigrants was the Lower Guild. This humiliation was possible because the word for "Amoy Guild" in the Minnan dialect of Chinese spoken in Fukien is homophonous with "Lower Guild". Considerable animosity developed between the groups because of this "name-calling". The second issue was access to and control of wharf facilities. Apparently from the time of their arrival the Tungan people had tried to gain control of the wharfs so that they could ship their goods without having to accede to the demands of the major Chuanchow clans, the Huangs, Wus, and Lins. Frequent fist fights gradually escalated to outright battles. In 1853 the fighting built up to the point where Chuanchow fighters broke into the district, named Pachiachuang, occupied by the Tungan. A fire was set, during which the Anshi people's Tzu Shih Temple was destroyed. The Tungan were forced to flee down river to a site called Twatutia. There they were joined by immigrants from Changchou. The feuds continued for six more years, with considerable loss of life on both sides. The fifth cause for decline was that in 1884 an outbreak of plague depleted the supply of manpower in Mengchia.

The new settlement at Twatutia, renamed Ta-tao-chen (literally, "big rice open space", i.e. a large field for drying rice), soon became the major trading center for tea and camphor, by then the leading exports of Taiwan (Chang, 1970; Chen, 1956).

Late nineteenth century development

In 1875, the first of many political decisions which would affect the future of Taipei was taken (Chen, 1956). In that year, upon the recommendation of its inspector general, the central government of China established Taipei area as a separate prefecture. The magistrate appointed to administer the new prefecture, Chen Hsin-chu, established his offices in an area southwest of Ta-tao-chen, and to the northeast of Mengchia (Figure 2.1). This area was called the Inner City, and was destined to be the heart of a modernized Taipei (Chen, 1956). In 1878 Chen decided to begin the building of a wall around the Inner City. The wall, which enclosed a rectangular area, was some 5000 meters in length and some six meters high. Chen, other government officials, and "representatives" of the local people contributed some 200 000 tael (ounces) of silver to underwrite the cost of the wall. Five major gates, the East, West, North, Great, and Small South, were built into the wall. The wall itself was surrounded by a moat. Within the wall, streets were laid out in strict grid pattern and land set aside for construction of the mandatory government buildings (yamen, and Examination Hall) and a Confucian temple. Once the new city was completely laid out, the new magistrate, Shen Pao-chen, prohibited the planting of rice within the city limits. Land was then apportioned to the remaining government functions and the surplus land divided into lots and offered to purchasers for building purposes. By 1880 all the formal government buildings were completed, although the final sections of the wall were not since apparently the paddy fields could not take the weight of the walls. In those places temporary bamboo plantings were established (Davidson, 1964).

In 1895 a second important political decision was made which would affect Taipei's future. This time the central government decided to make Taiwan a separate province, with Taipei as its capital (Chen, 1956). Liu Ming-chuan, a lieutenant of the reform-minded Ching official Li Hung-chang, was appointed as the governor-general. Under Liu the streets of Taipei were rearranged, and paved with stone. Streets were to be illuminated once a power plant was built (Chen, 1956); unfortunately due to the cost, street lights had to be eliminated (Davidson, 1964). A new government headquarters (*yamen*) was constructed. A telegraph system was established. Construction began of a railroad from Keelung as far southwest as Hsinchu, with a stop in Taipei.

From the perspective of land use, Liu made several important decisions (Chen, 1956; Wu, 1975). The Inner City was designated as the administrative center, with Ta-tao-chen assigned the role of commercial district. New residential areas were opened southeast of the Inner City. Liu's reforms and building program attracted both Chinese and foreign merchants. The Netherlands, Germany, and the United States also established consulates in Taipei (Chen, 1956).

Unfortunately completion of many of Liu's projects was cut short by two events. First, since Liu was not a genuine Confucian scholar, having risen from a peasant bandit to able commander during the suppression of rebellions in China, he and his reforms were resented by conservative officials. In 1891 they secured his removal. Once he departed many of his programs were permitted to lapse by his successors (Fairbank *et al.*, 1965). Secondly, in 1895 Japan was awarded control of Taiwan as part of the Treaty of Shimonoseki, which ended the Sino-Japanese War of 1894.

The Japanese period

The Japanese retained Taipei as the capital of Taiwan. As such the governor-general had his headquarters in Taipei and former Chinese government organs were left where they were. The Japanese began large-scale building projects including new government buildings, many of which are still in use, a sewerage system, and flood control dikes along the Tamshui river. Attempts were made to improve traffic by redesigning, realigning, and paving roads. One major project was the tearing down of

Figure 2.2 East Gate has been well preserved and used as a focal point for tourism and patriotic parades

the walls of the Inner City in 1900. This was done for both aesthetic and traffic reasons: the walls were badly scarred and were seen as an impediment to improved traffic flow. Where the walls once stood a three lane boulevard was laid down. The Japanese did leave four of the gates from the wall standing: the East, North, Little, and Great South (Figures 2.2 and 2.3).

Some of the structural and design modifications during the Japanese period were the result of a typhoon which struck during August 1911. As a result of the destruction the Japanese were able to build New Park, the botanical gardens and library, and a museum. They also took the opportunity to dismantle the Confucian Temple (Figure 2.4) and move it further north to its current site on Talung Street (Schinz, 1989).

As did Governor-General Liu, the Japanese designated certain areas of the city for particular services (Figure 2.1). Mengchia, renamed Wanhwa, became the designated entertainment district, including brothels (Wu, 1975). Ta-tao-chen continued as the tea center and as a primitive business district (Chen, 1956). Segregated residential patterns were also started by the Japanese. The areas along the river became the area for poor residents (Herr, 1968). The Japanese started new, separate, neighborhoods for themselves to the north and east, such as in Ta-an district (Chen, 1956; Schinz, 1989).

Figure 2.3 North Gate is simpler in design than East Gate. Its proximity to the Central Railroad Station has created traffic congestion which was only partially alleviated by the building of elevated highways

The republican period

The Japanese Period ended abruptly in 1945 with the end of World War II and the retrocession of Taiwan to Chinese control. In some ways the Chinese administration was a continuation of the Japanese one. The old government buildings were taken over; patterns of segregation were maintained with mainland Chinese in place of the Japanese. Squatter housing developed, especially along major east–west roads leading out of the administrative district, such as Hsin-yi Road.

As with the Japanese, land use changes occurred as a result of natural

Figure 2.4 Confucian Temple is the site of biennial celebrations marking the birthday of Confucius

disasters as well as of deliberate government policy. One example of the impact of a natural disaster occurred with Typhoon Wanda, which struck on 1 August 1956. Much of the area adjacent to the Tamshui river was destroyed, so that only total rebuilding of the area was possible (Chen, 1956).

Two of the most important government decisions which had long-term impacts on the development of Taipei were the inclusion of the six townships surrounding Taipei and the decision to build a new international airport in Taoyuan, some 30 kilometers southwest of the city. The new areas gave Taipei much needed growing room and may permit more comprehensive urban planning. It is not clear how well integrated into the Taipei psyche the six townships are, however. Many of the cultural attractions in those areas, such as the National Palace Museum or Taipei Zoo, are frequently described as being in "suburban" Taipei. The same phrase is used when news events are reported from these places.

The decision to build a new international airport had a significant impact on the development of Taipei since it permitted a down-scaling of Sungshan Airport in north central Taipei. With reduced traffic and noise from airport activities, the area just south of the old airport became the focus of intense public and private development during the late 1970s and early 1980s. This was, however, a mixed development, since the increased popularity of the area contributed to the decline of the shopping and entertainment area west of the central railroad station.

Overall, the development of Taipei can be compared to other Chinese and East Asian cities. In terms of Chinese cities, Taipei has been compared to Shanghai, and to Tainan, located in southwestern Taiwan (Schinz, 1989). All three cities started with market areas and harbor settlement. Then military and administrative functions were added, with the resulting extension of the settlement area. Taipei and Tainan also offer significant contrasts in their historical development. Although both had walls, those of Taipei enclosed only administrative and other public buildings, while those of Tainan surrounded the entire built-up area. A second contrast involves the actual layout of the two cities. The Inner City of Taipei was laid out in strict conformance to traditional Chinese geomantic and city planning principles. As such it was regular in shape, had a strict grid system, predetermined locations for public buildings and functions, and included agricultural land (Schinz, 1989; Steinhardt, 1990). All this regularity was imposed on the landscape without regard to topographic differences. In contrast, Tainan was laid out following the most convenient topographic lines.

In terms of other East Asian cities Taipei compares well to Seoul in the sense that early native development was superseded by a Japanese administration which transformed the city to meet the needs of Japanese colonial policy (Brunn and Williams, 1983). Both cities display relics from a past dominated first by a native culture and then by the Japanese. Both cities are still dealing with the landscape and land use legacies from the Japanese period.

Land use

The complexity of land use in Taipei is best approached by discussing the issues involved in describing and explaining it. The key issues are scale, time, and model.

Scale

Since 1949 there have been seven attempts to describe land use in Taipei. The main difference in the approaches has been concerned with scale, with two meanings attached to this concept. One meaning of scale has been to restrict the area of inquiry to Old Taipei, regardless of how large Taipei actually was. The second meaning deals with detail, or level of generalization. The extremes of detail have gone from block by block and street by street information to broad, general land use categories.

27

Chen's approach (1956) was to describe (but not to map) seven broad categories of land use: commercial–residential, administrative, industrial, educational, recreational, and rural. His descriptions of where these land uses are found are very general: commercial–residential was found in the western part of the city, especially in Wanhwa and Ta-tao-chen sections; administrative functions were found in the area of the former Inner City; residential areas are found in four areas: southeast margins of the urbanized areas, the southern outskirts of the city, the northeast, and along the Tamshui river; industrial is described as being dispersed in the commercial districts, in the "suburbs" southwest of Wanhwa, and along the major railroad lines; the location of the educational land use is not spatially defined; recreational land use is described by point locations; the rural areas are in the eastern part of the city. Chen did map the distribution of trade firms located in an area 500 meters east and west, and 3500 meters north and south of the central railroad station.

Huang (1983) has described Taipei as being a city made up of a series of some 300 specialized streets. In so doing he prefers to see Taipei's development as following that advocated by the Ming dynasty (1368–1662), and not that of the Ching dynasty (1662–1912) model preferred by Schinz (1989). Under the Ming, traders within a city were divided into noble and vulgar categories and forced to occupy separate areas within a city. Huang feels that Taipei developed under conditions which were ideal for the speciality street such as a spacious hinterland, easy access, and trademarks were not important. He argues that the speciality street system has five advantages: money is saved on promotional efforts; market concentrations promote increased productivity and efficiency; they are convenient for customers; overhead is reduced; and it is easy to upgrade services. There are also two main drawbacks to such a system: it is often hard to distinguish between shops, and they tend to prolong family style management practices. In terms of understanding land use in Taipei Huang's approach has several drawbacks. First by his own admission, most of the speciality streets are located in Old Taipei. So even though he systematically describes dozens of streets, our knowledge of Taipei is restricted to just a part of the city. Secondly, such an approach deals only with commercial activities, which form but a part of Taipei's economy and land use.

Chang (1970) took a multi-method approach to describing Taipei's land use. Following Chen (1956) he only deals with Old Taipei. Again following Chen he categorized land use into six different classes: residential, public institutions, streets, commercial, industrial and railroad, and parks and playgrounds. He provides quantitative measures of the relative frequency of each land use type as well (Table 2.1). Data for 1990 have been included to show how much land use has shifted. Next Chang compares the frequency of land use in Taipei to that of other large

Table 2.1 Land use categories by percentage of developed area

Category	1966	1990
Residential	39.4	25.4
Streets	11.3	5.1
Commercial	11.2	21.0
Industrial and railroad	9.6	32.3
Parks and playgrounds	2.5	1.3

Sources: Chang (1970); *The Statistical Abstract, Taipei Municipality, 1991* (1992).

metropolitan areas. Finally he provides a land use map of Old Taipei showing seven distinct land use types: commercial–residential, residential, industrial, agricultural, public institutions, and parks and sports. He apparently based his analysis on a 1968 document, *Preliminary (Sketch) Plan for the City of Taipei*, although the original map (Figure 2.5) includes all of Taipei City.

This map shows ten different land uses. There is a main commercial area extending north to south in Wanhwa and Ta-tao-chen, although there is a small, ribbon-like east–west extension of this in the middle of the area. Public institutions appear scattered throughout the area, with a major cluster of such institutions just south and east of the major commercial area. Industrial areas seem confined to the eastern and central parts of the city. Parks and sports are scattered through the city, as are historical and religious buildings. Residential areas surround the commercial and public institutions in Old Taipei and extend east and south to industrial areas. In the northern areas residential areas are scattered along major routes coming into the city, and some are even found in the mountains. The rest of the land below 500 meters appears to be devoted to agriculture.

Lee (1969) takes a much more macro-scale approach to describing land use in Taipei. He sees a series of four concentric land use rings. At the center, occupying most of Old Taipei, is a high population density core with commercial and governmental activities, as well as metal fabrication, dominating the landscape. The area is also categorized by a large difference in the day and night populations. In the second ring, there is a high density residential pattern, which includes some light industry and some handicrafts activities as well. The third ring is the main industrial area, although it also includes major concentrations of residences. In the last ring, low density agricultural activities dominate. Lee argues that over time the core, second, and third rings have grown at the expense of the fourth ring. In fact they have grown so much that they have begun to merge into similar land uses of Keelung City to the northeast.

Hsu and Pannell (1982) present a very simple land use map of central parts of Old Taipei. They define a central business district (CBD) running

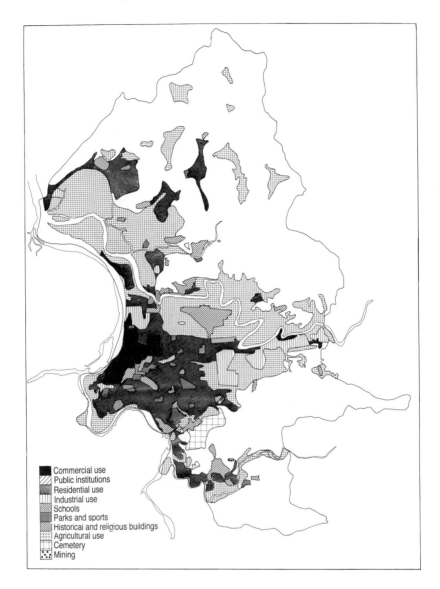

Commercial use
Public institutions
Residential use
Industrial use
Schools
Parks and sports
Historical and religious buildings
Agricultural use
Cemetery
Mining

Figure 2.5 Land use, 1968

several hundred meters east and west of the central railroad station. Due north and south of the CDB are the old major commercial areas of Ta-tao-chen and Mengchia. North of Ta-tao-chen is a major industrial zone, while just south and west of Mengchia is another industrial zone. Southeast of the CBD is a major administrative zone. East of the administrative zone are two industrial centers, separated by a small commercial area. All other areas are left undesignated.

Finally, Williams and Sutherland (1988), working at a scale of 1:42 200, generalize land use into eight basic categories: airport, non-irrigated, irrigated, grass, slope, water, special uses, and built-up areas. The major geographical focus of their work is the central part of Taipei Basin so that Old Taipei dominates their analysis. Furthermore, their land use classes are so broad that it is hard to infer what the major sub-categories of urban land use might be.

Time

The seven land use studies have been presented chronologically. Although they use different methodologies, land use categories, and scales, some broad patterns did appear. Before turning to explanatory models of land use, which will help uncover the reasons for the use of different methodologies and categories, the question of future land use needs to be addressed. A formal discussion of planning as a process is found in Chapter 5.

There have been three main attempts either to forecast land use or to express preferred patterns. Chen (1956) argued that Old Taipei had reached its limit of expansion. He worried that continued growth would make the city vulnerable to air raids, and that residents of a larger Taipei would suffer not only a decline in the moral component of their lives, but also a deterioration in their physical and mental health. He feared too that continued growth of the city would cut it off from provision of food and water. Therefore he urged that limits be placed on the future expansion of the city. He argued that future growth would be better accommodated in a series of small satellite towns some 2.5–3.0 square kilometers in area and housing some 25 000–30 000 residents. According to Chen each town would have its own libraries, theatres, hospitals, town halls, and parks, thereby obviating any need to reside in Taipei City. Existing towns such as Shihlin, Peitou, Hsintien, Hsinchuang, and Luchou were suggested sites for such satellites.

Although the incorporation of Shihlin, Peitou, Chingmei, Mucha, Nankang, and Neihu into Taipei, and the planned annexation of many of the remaining towns to a Greater Taipei (as described in Chapter 5) would seem to have doomed Chen's vision, in fact his concept was incorporated into the first regional plan for northern Taiwan, the *Taipei-Keelung Metropolitan Regional Plan*. The plan envisioned the development of a series of satellite towns in Taipei and Taoyuan *hsien* (county), thus relieving some of the demographic, economic, social, and environmental pressures on Taipei City itself. Some of the satellite towns were to be based on existing towns such as Hsinchuang, Yongho, and Tamshui. At least one new town, Linkou, was also envisioned. The plan was crafted to provide solutions to some of the global problems of Taipei Basin such as agriculture, conservation, housing, flood control, public facilities, recreation, transportation, urban renewal, and utilities.

As with Chen's vision, the plan was soon rendered obsolete and implementation was abandoned for several reasons. First, the elevation of Taipei City to a special municipality took Taipei out of the jurisdiction of the agency which developed the plan, the Urban and Housing Development Committee of the Council for International Economic Cooperation and Development. Secondly, population growth in the entire Taipei Basin did not slow down. Population which the plan had projected to reach 5 million by 1990 (*Taipei-Keelung Metropolitan Regional Plan*, 1968), actually reached this size in 1976. The 1990 population stood at 7.4 million. Economic expansion continued beyond expected levels. Environmental and social conditions further deteriorated. But the most stunning blow to full implementation of the concept of an urban system based on a strong center and a series of satellites was the failure of the central government to build the planned new town at Linkou. The scheme appears to have failed owing to the government's inability to acquire the necessary land. Three issues were involved: the reluctance of the government to use its powers of eminent domain to seize the land from farmers, the inadequate funding of land purchase schemes, and the rapid inflation of land prices in the Linkou area.

The last visions of future land use in Taipei City are found in the *Preliminary (Sketch) Plan for the City of Taipei* (1968) (Figure 2.6) and the 1989 Taipei City master plan (Figure 2.7). The 1968 plan seems to stress the consolidation and extension of land uses. For example, industry was projected to be consolidated in the eastern sections of Ta-an and Nankang, with small compact pockets in the southwestern part of Shihlin and the south central part of Chingmei. The central business district was to be consolidated and extended eastward along Nanking East Road. The administrative center in Chengchung was to be supplemented by administrative areas in Ta-an and Shihlin. Agricultural activities were to be restricted to the southwest of Shihlin and the northern fringes of Sungshan; a small strip was to be kept in Mucha. High density housing was envisioned around the central business district and main administrative area with medium density to the east of the high density areas. Newer parts of Taipei were to be restricted to medium and low density housing. Large areas were to be preserved as either park lands or preservation areas, in part due to their topography which features steep slopes. The large area of Sungshan airport was to be converted to residential use.

The 1989 plan differs significantly from that of 1968. First, instead of one central business district, several commercial districts are established to

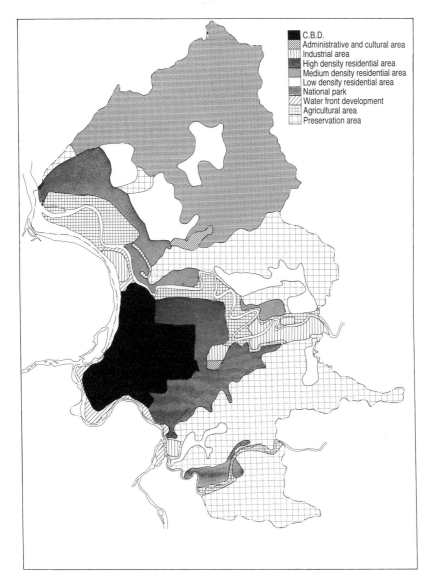

Figure 2.6 Planned land use, 1968

supplement the older central one. The Hsin-yi area is seen as a major business node, with smaller ones distributed so that at least every *chu* has one. Industry is still envisioned in the eastern corridor of Nankang, although there is also an anticipated extension to an area to the northwest in Neihu. The industrial district in Mucha is to be eliminated. Smaller industrial areas are tucked into residential areas in Tatong and Shihlin.

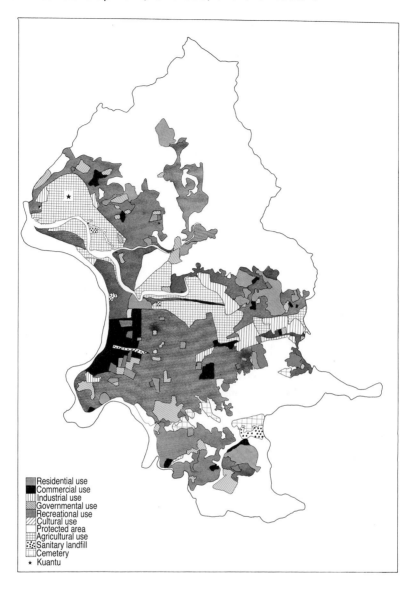

Figure 2.7 Planned land use, 1989

One of these areas, the strip to the west of Chungshan North Road in Tatung, was also cited by Hsu and Pannell (1982) as a good site for future industrial development. Their other suggested industrial sites, along Keelung Road in Hsin-yi and areas in the north of the old area of Ta-tao-chen and the south of old Mengchia, were not selected by the drafters of the 1989 plan for industrial development. Medium density residential

34

areas have been converted to higher residential densities. Educational and cultural areas, such as the municipal zoo in Mucha, are now explicitly identified, as are cemeteries. Garbage dumps are placed in Mucha, Neihu and Shihlin. The number and size of areas allocated to administrative functions have increased. Recreational areas are identified as such. Finally, housing is placed in the one remaining undeveloped area, Kuantu.

Given the rapid rate of growth in Taipei, it is not clear whether or not the 1989 plan is realistic. The reasons for this conclusion are in part historical: all past visions of Taipei have been swept aside by unanticipated local, national, or world political events. In addition, the implementation of plans is subject to both political and economic pressures and exigencies. These are discussed more fully in Chapter 5. In all cases, however, the visions of Taipei reflect changing social values and needs, cultural patterns, and levels of economic development (Chang, 1970).

Model

In all attempts at describing, planning, and explaining changing land use in Taipei, the question of which urban land use model to use has been a central problem. Two main questions are involved: does Taipei have a central business district (CBD), and are Western models and methods of analysis appropriate to Taipei?

In regard to the CBD, two views dominate the literature. Chen (1956) and Chang (1970) assume that Taipei indeed has a CBD. Chen (1956) defines the CBD as the area to the north and south of the Taipei railroad station, although it is not clear how far north and south the area actually extends. However, although he readily accepts that Taipei has a CBD, Chen explicitly rejects all models of urban land use as inappropriate to any analysis of Taipei, since, as with most older cities in China, there was not a complete separation of urban function, let alone a separation of work and residence.

Chang (1970) defines an old CBD as covering roughly the northwest corner of the old walled city, and the area west of the city wall. He argues that the area was consolidated into a CBD between 1920 and 1940. He is less precise in defining the limits of a new CBD. It includes the old CBD but outer limits are not specified; Chang only notes that the old CBD has crept out along the major thoroughfares. According to this approach, the reasons for the expansion of the CBD are easy to identify: redevelopment of the old CBD would require the acquisition of numerous parcels of small plots of land from different owners, followed by demolition of old buildings. Developers of modern office buildings find it much simpler and less expensive to acquire vacant land and build on the wide boulevards radiating out from the old CBD. The closest Chang comes to categorizing

Figure 2.8 The old shophouses in the foreground are being replaced with apartment houses which include retail and office space on the ground floor

urban land use is to compare the expansion of commercial areas to "ribbon-like" development. Chang does not project his study of the CBD to a more formal and complete model of urban land use.

In contrast to this acceptance of the presence of a Taipei CBD, Pannell (1973; 1976) and Hsu and Pannell (1982) substitute the concept of "shophouse core". This designation derives from a major architectural feature of the cities of Taiwan, the shophouse (Figure 2.8). At its simplest the building has some sort of work area on the ground floor, but set back from the street by some three or four meters. In the back of the work area, and/or above the work area and extending out over the sidewalk, are the living quarters for the family. Some of the older office buildings have a similar first floor plan, with offices occupying the entire space of the upper stories. Newer office buildings retain an area of retail space on street level, with offices on upper floors.

According to Hsu and Pannell, the main concentration of these shop-houses is found along Chungshan North Road and the western end of Nanking East Road, that is, north and east of the central railroad station. Functionally this area serves as a CBD since it is the location of higher order services. Hsu and Pannell consider that the older areas of Mengchia and Ta-tao-chen serve as commercial subregions, providing lower order goods and services. During the 1970s the shophouse core was somewhat displaced by the development of a new shopping area along Tunghua North and South Roads, that is, just south of the old Sungshan airport.

In further modeling Taipei, Hsu and Pannell, then define a Major Administrative Area, which they see as occupying the area due east of the shophouse core. However, rather than explain the distribution of land use in Taipei, Hsu and Pannell conclude their analysis of Taipei by defining social areas of the city. Therefore, although their discussion is part of the debate on how to analyze the city, their only contribution is to substitute the CBD with the "shophouse core." Pannell (1976) does use the concept of rent–bid curves in an attempt to explain land use in Taiwanese cities, but rejects the approach owing to the distortion in the curves imposed by the shophouse. Pannell (1973) also argues that some of the land use patterns in Taiwanese cities – such as centralization of primary commerce, intense land use, peak land values, residential areas adjacent to the central zone, and fringe zones of agriculture and industry – are "rational" in Western terms. However, he stops short of naming or using any specific model of land use to analyze Taiwanese cities further.

In complete contrast to these approaches, Sun (1983) absolutely rejects the use of all Western concepts and models – ecological or economic – of urban land use as being appropriate for the analysis of Taiwanese cities. He comes to this view based on three differences between Western and Taiwanese cities. First, he points out that the amount of space devoted to residences is higher in downtown commercial areas of Taiwanese cities than in Western ones. Secondly, he mentions that the physical separation of places of work and residence is generally lacking in Taiwanese cities. Finally, he notes that the integration of shop, factory, and residence on the landscape is not akin to any type of Western spatial organization. He even rejects the notion that a CBD can be defined in Taiwanese cities. He does acknowledge that the presence of both Western firms and a bazaar type community might imply the existence of a CBD; however, the presence of numerous, small retailing centers throughout the city dilutes and nullifies the idea of a true CBD. Expansion of the Taiwanese city is also seen as quite different from that of Western cities. In Taiwan cheap public transportation, and the absence of privately owned cars, precludes according to Sun the development of car oriented, planned shopping facilities. Rather, one finds traditional, and often informal, economic and social services on virtually every corner, even if the firm offering the service appears to be a modern one. The only commonality between Western and Taiwanese cities, according to Sun, is the decline of the population in the core and the growth of the periphery. The similarity, however, is not linked to similar processes of change (Sun, 1983).

One aspect of Taipei's evolution ignored by all those who have dealt with land use is the impact of the incorporation of the six townships from Taipei *hsien*. Each of the six had its own commercial, administrative, and residential areas. As such, if the entire area of Taipei were to be analyzed, not just the original city, it might appear that the multiple nuclei model (Harris and Ullman, 1945) would explain the Taipei situation rather well. However, since the Harris and Ullman model is derived from changes in transportation and accessibility, and not the result of political incorporation of pre-existing economic centers, the usefulness of the model for explaining land use patterns is somewhat limited.

In sum, there appears to be some disagreement about whether or not Taipei had or has a CBD. In contrast there seems to be a consensus that Western models of urban land use are either not appropriate or of limited utility for describing or explaining land use patterns in Taipei. Taipei does not fit any of these models because of historical, cultural, and economic reasons. The commercial, military, and administrative origins of Taipei have left an imprint which includes many of the elements of a traditional planned Chinese city. These elements would include a grid street pattern, the inclusion of agriculturally productive lands, and the dispersion of economic activities. The formal, political incorporation of townships to the north, east, and south of Taipei not only increased the area which must be analyzed, but increased as well the number of land use categories which must be dealt with. All of the new areas contain not only commercial, industrial, and residential land uses, but agricultural ones as well. Often the new areas contain tracts of land which, owing to the topography, have limited use even for recreation. Culturally, the continued merging of the location of work and residence produces a juxtaposition of land uses not readily amenable to Western models. Economic behavior also creates a complicated land use pattern. Frequently developers cannot purchase entire city blocks for redevelopment. The resulting land use pattern is a combination of large, modern structures along a main street, with a small enclave of low density, traditionally mixed buildings squeezed between new structures, or directly behind them. These small enclaves continue to function as microeconomic centers, and provide residence to entrepreneurs as well as a wide range of services such as laundries, restaurants, tailoring, shoe repair, and recreation to traditional customers as well as the tenants of the new buildings. These trapped areas do not fit neatly into the schema of Western land use models.

Architecture

The brief period of Taipei's existence has created a remarkably rich diversity of architectural styles and features. Before describing these, however, two preliminary observations are necessary. First, the different architectural periods are not present on the landscape in proportion to their historical length. Secondly, the architectural mix of Taipei has been subject to frequent derision. For example, Herr (1968) has opined that "no matter how you come to love Taipei, you will never think of it as beautiful." Glenn (1968) has disdainfully referred to the built landscape as a "mongrelizing." He cites the negative aspects of Taipei's environment: its hills are too far off, it has no port, no spacious parks, and few imposing buildings. Glenn attributes the flavor and interest of the city to its noisy vitality – the hawkers' cries and the din of construction. Peterson (1974) argues that it is not the architecture but the people that make Taipei so attractive. Reid (1984) feels that the "ugly duckling" reputation which Taipei earned was a phenomenon of the 1960s. According to this view the drab buildings, dusty streets, open gutters, and battered pedicabs have been replaced by a modern facade which is quite inviting. Note that all of these negative appraisals stand in contrast to the title of "Little Paris" bestowed on Taipei by the Japanese (Naito, 1937/38).

Initial settlement and late nineteenth century

Both periods featured very similar architecture. Commercial buildings tended to be multi-storied and built of red brick, with grey ornamentation. The actual styles of these buildings were quite varied. Chu (1988) catalogued these as including a range from baroque to art deco to impressionism. The dominant architectural style, however, is a mixture of traditional Chinese and colonial rococo. This style, the creation of merchants from Fukien province, is termed "Kulanyu" by Chinese architectural historians (Huang, 1983). Housing tended to reflect current styles on the Chinese mainland. However, already in these periods there was considerable mingling of living and business activities, a pattern which started during the rapid development of trade during the Northern Sung Dynasty (979–1126) (Huang, 1983).

Unfortunately most of the buildings from these periods have not survived. There are pockets of them in Wanhwa, such as Tihua Street, and in the centers of some of the townships in the Taipei basin. The loss of this heritage can be traced to natural and political factors. We have already seen that typhoons in 1911 and 1956 destroyed major parts and altered the land use of the city. Much of the older architecture fell to forces of nature during these typhoons. Since many of these buildings were built of

Figure 2.9 A derelict building dating from late Ching times is still occupied and in need of preservation from natural elements and neglect

poor quality bricks, many of them deteriorated owing to the climate. High levels of air pollution since the 1960s have further endangered the remaining buildings from these periods (Figure 2.9). During the Japanese period, the tearing down of the walls and building of defense structures again diminished the stock of the oldest types of buildings. More recently, the need for urban renewal, and especially street widening, has put the remaining buildings at even higher levels of risk for demolition (Chu, 1988). More will be said on this issue below, when the problem of historic preservation is discussed.

Japanese period

Since it spread over 50 years, the Japanese period contributed significant architectural elements to the landscape. In particular between 1895 and 1945 three types of buildings were constructed.

The first and most obvious type of building was that related to the administration of Taiwan. These buildings were in a "colonial" style, inspired to a large extent by central European baroque and renaissance styles (Schinz, 1989). Typical buildings of this genre include the Foreign Ministry Guest House, the Presidential Office Building (Figure 2.10), the Central Post Office, the Central Railroad Station (Figure 2.11), the main

Figure 2.10   The Presidential Office Building, built by the Japanese to house the offices of the Governor-General, is still in use and is a focal point for the Double Ten (10 October) celebrations

Figure 2.11   Old Central Railroad Station. Its value as a transportation hub was enhanced by the siting of inter-urban bus stations on both extremes and the availability of intra-urban buses and cabs at its entrance

Figure 2.12 Original wards of National Taiwan University College of Medicine. The buildings on the left were added during the 1960s and housed offices and laboratory space

campus of National Taiwan University and its hospital (Figure 2.12), and the Old City Hall (Sun Yat-sen Hall). The latter was the last significant building put up by the Japanese in 1936 (Schinz, 1989). With the exception of the Central Railroad Station, which was replaced by a modern facility in 1990 (Figure 2.13), all of these administrative buildings remain in use.

The second most obvious type of building was the single-family Japanese home. These of course dominated the districts where the Japanese themselves lived. They featured a seven to eight foot brick wall around a Japanese style, tiled room house, complete with tatami mats. In general these are disappearing from the landscape as the process of urban renewal continues. Since these buildings tend to be drafty and open to all sorts of bugs, they are not in high demand. Frequently developers will entice an owner of one of these Japanese homes to sell his land in return for cash and an apartment in a new apartment building to be built on the site. There are, however, several areas such as Ren-ai Road, just east of the main administrative district, and the residential area just south of the administrative district, where this type of home is still found in generally good repair.

A third building type was the multi-storied, steel framed, brick faced buildings which replaced the older Chinese style shop buildings (Figure

Figure 2.13 The new Central Railroad Station is the centerpiece of urban renewal in the CBD

2.8) (Schinz, 1989). Often these buildings were just larger versions of the more traditional shophouse. These buildings are concentrated in the main business areas and for the most part are still in use.

Republican period

Since 1945, building styles have gone through at least three successive stages. During the 1950s and 1960s there was a continuation of the construction of multi-storied, steel framed, brick faced buildings. Some three- and four-story apartment houses were built, as these became symbols of modernity and living in them conveyed a degree of social prestige (Chang, 1970).

By 1978 a second stage evolved. The origins of this stage are derived from two unrelated government policies (Reid, 1984). First, the government rescinded the ban on building new hotels and high rise buildings. Secondly, restrictions on overseas travel were relaxed. The net result was that travellers brought back new tastes in not only fashion, food, and recreation, but in architecture as well. Unfortunately, the resulting building frenzy produced a series of ill-conceived buildings put up for the most part without any attention to zoning laws or architectural aesthetics (Reid, 1984).

Figure 2.14 New facilities of National Taiwan University College of Medicine typify improvements in medical infrastructure over the past decade

The late 1980s marked a third phase. By then professional architects and planners were more outspoken about the need to design buildings which were more than utilitarian, Western inspired, box-like structures. In particular attention is being paid to the incorporation of traditional Chinese motifs, such as tombstone tops, moon windows, lotus flowers, roof tiles, and temple columns, into single-family homes, apartment houses, and public and commercial buildings (Sallinger, 1991). This trend is especially obvious in the construction of infrastructure projects such as the new Central Railroad Station and new National Taiwan University Hospital (Figure 2.14), as well as new culture complexes such as the Chiang Kai-shek Memorial (Figure 2.15), new National Central Library (Figure 2.16), and the Taipei Art Museum.

Historic preservation

If there is one process or theme which dominates the history of Taipei it is that of change in unexpected directions. Successive governments have either imposed or permitted private imprints on the landscape in terms of land use and architecture. During the late 1980s and 1990s another new direction emerged in the form of urban renewal. In many ways the concern for urban renewal is evidence of the economic, political, and social

Figure 2.15 Chiang Kai-shek Memorial and surrounding gardens

development of Taipei. However, it also presents a new challenge. What mechanism should govern the pace and style of renewal? How should landscapes of the past be dealt with?

For the most part, urban renewal appears to be following a rather *laissez-faire* pattern where the government designates areas open to renewal and the free market determines the details. As we shall see in Chapter Five, this approach has many dangers. One of those dangers is that the rich architectural heritage of the earlier Chinese and Japanese periods will be obliterated. Four examples of historic preservation will demonstrate the complexity and dangers of relying on the *laissez-faire* approach to urban renewal in particular, and planning in general.

The first case involves an architectural feature not mentioned above – an elaborate farmstead. As Taipei grew during the late nineteenth century and

Figure 2.16 New National Central Library across the street from Chiang Kai-shek Memorial

under the Japanese, rural areas were incorporated into the urban fabric. The same holds true for the annexation of the six Taipei *hsien* townships incorporated in 1967: they all contained considerable areas of agriculturally productive land. The presence of such agricultural land fits nicely into traditional Chinese city planning theories, as these areas would ensure that a city under siege could not be cut off entirely from its food supply. However, in the post-1960s these rural areas, often little hamlets, came to be surrounded by the range of urban land uses found elsewhere in Taipei. One group of farm buildings, the Lin An-tai estate, was located in the midst of the planned Hsin-yi urban renewal district. This planned development was to be the site of a new commercial zone, with a world trade center at its nucleus, a new Taipei City government complex, and new housing units. Initially planners assumed that the Lin An-tai compound would merely be razed to make room for the new construction. However, public outcries forced a reevaluation of this assumption. It was suggested that the Hsin-yi project could be modified to accommodate the homestead, much like roads in the West, Japan, and Korea have been detoured around historical sites declared to be important enough to preserve (Lee, 1977). An alternative strategy did evolve: the compound would be taken apart and rebuilt elsewhere. One site mentioned as a future home was the new Zoological Garden in Mucha (Lee, 1977).

When the compound was disassembled in 1978 no site had been chosen and so the parts were put in storage, although there was much concern about the effects of prolonged storage on the tile and woodwork (Boraks, 1993). In 1984 a site in Pinchiang Park, north of the old Sungshan Airport, was selected, and by November 1986 the homestead was reopened. The site has been criticized as "less than perfect," because it is nestled against an embankment of the Sun Yat-sen Freeway, and since Sungshan Airport is still used for domestic flights, the boom of airplanes taking off and landing shatters the tranquility of the park (Boraks, 1993). The long-term effects of such a site on the structural and material integrity of the compound are not clear. Nevertheless, public concern was able to bring about a change in policy and one of the best examples of northern Taiwan Minnan (southern Fukien) architecture has been preserved (Lee, 1977).

The second example of the conflict between the need for urban renewal and historic preservation is the case of Tihua Street in particular, and the Wanhwa district in general. In 1988 a decision was made to implement a 15-year-old urban renewal plan which called for widening Tihua Street from 7.8 meters to 23.4 meters (Chu, 1988). Again public outcry was able to halt the bulldozers and a new plan was drawn up within a month. Amongst the pressures for a new, Chinese proposal for historic preservation was the interest of a Japanese consortium in buying the buildings along the street so that they could be dismantled and rebuilt in a park in Japan (Chu, 1988). The plan which was developed called for the preservation of the street as a tourist zone. New gates for the street were built. However, the fundamental problems of preservation of the buildings and improvement of traffic conditions were left unsettled. One solution to the traffic problems was the suggestion of building more parking lots and increasing the bus service (*Free China Journal*, Jan. 17, 1991). Further progress on meeting the conflicting goals of renewal and preservation awaits planning for the renewal of the Hsimen area as an entertainment district, with the removal or consolidation of the long-standing illicit sex and gambling activities of the Wanhwa area (*Free China Journal*, Jan. 17, 1991). It is not clear that merging of multiple planning goals will necessarily bring about an ideal solution to the desire to preserve Wanhwa and its historic streets while at the same time improving the physical infrastructure of the area.

The third and fourth cases of conflicts over historic buildings are complicated by the fact that they are not Chinese, but rather Japanese in origin. The headquarters of the Land Bank of Taiwan was built in 1933; its original occupant was the Taipei branch of the Japanese Dai-Ichi Kanyo Bank (Figure 2.17). Stylistically the building features eight doric columns, and is bedecked with decorative relief sculpture. In addition there are Japanese, Egyptian, and Mayan architectural elements in the building. Private developers have proposed tearing down the building and replacing

Figure 2.17 Land Bank of Taiwan, formerly Dai-Ichi Kanyo Bank, is subject to conflict between developers and advocates of historical preservation

it with a 16- to 23-floor glass and steel structure. Local architects feel that the building is one of about 40 buildings erected during the 50-year Japanese period which should be preserved. One major impediment to the preservation of the building is that it is outside the jurisdiction of the law on preservation of cultural assets. Since this law generally covers buildings over 100 years old, it has not normally been applied to either Aboriginal structures or to those buildings built during the Japanese period (Hsu, 1989). The developers have proposed modifying their plans so that the façade of the bank will be preserved (*Free China Journal*, Mar. 21, 1991). However, a final decision on the fate of the building had not been decided as late as the end of 1991.

The Land Bank building had three advantages which will ensure that its future is publicly debated. First, the building has actually been in use within the past 20 years. Secondly, it is on a list of buildings which local architects feel should be preserved (Hsu, 1989). Thirdly, it is highly visible, being located across from the northern entrance to Taipei New Park on Hsiang Yang Road.

None of these advantages applies to the last of the examples of the need for more attention to historic preservation. The main gate and bell tower of the Tungho Temple are located at the intersection of Linsen South and Ren-ai East Roads, just north of the Chiang Kai-shek Memorial Hall (Figure 2.18). Because it is set back somewhat from the street it is not

Figure 2.18 The gate and bell tower of Tungho Temple are sandwiched in between old shophouses and modern apartment buildings and are not as visible as the Land Bank of Taiwan. Hence the chances for preservation are not good

immediately visible. The building, originally built in 1909, was severely damaged in the 1911 typhoon which devastated so many of the old Chinese buildings, but it was nevertheless rebuilt. By the mid-1960s it was used as squatter housing, with numerous families, chickens, and dogs living in the dilapidated structures. Plans for development of the site were announced in 1991 (*Central Daily News*, Aug. 19, 1991). Although local religious leaders and architects called for restoration of the building, as with the Land Bank its fate is unclear. A temporary reprieve was granted so that the city could reevaluate the value of the building (*Central Daily News*, Aug. 19, 1991).

Summary and conclusion

Much of the strangeness and mysteriousness of Taipei can be readily explained by reference to the city's historical development. This historical background also helps to elucidate the pattern of economic, demographic, political, and cultural change in Taipei. Not surprisingly it also lends insight into the origins of contemporary problems and the likely form their solutions will take. These topics are taken up in the remaining chapters of this book.

References

Boraks, D. (1993) Visit to Lin homestead restores the treasured past, *Free China Journal*, Feb. 16, 5.

Brunn, S. D. and J.F. Williams (1983) *Cities of the World. World Regional Urban Development*. Harper and Row, New York.

Central Daily News (1991) Demolition of the Tongho Temple Bell Tower and Gate Temporarily Postponed. Aug. 19, 7.*

Chai, C.-k. (1967) *Taiwan Aboriginals. A Genetic Study of Tribal Variations.* Harvard University Press, Cambridge.

Chang, S.-d. (1970) Land Use and Intraurban Travel in Taipei, *Proceedings, Association of American Geographers* 2, 40–45.

Chen, C.-s. (1956) *The City of Taipei*. Fu-Min Geographical Institute of Economic Development, Research Report #71, Taipei.

Chu, J. (1988) Way Being Paved to Preserve 100-Year Old Street, *Free China Journal*, Sept. 8, 6.

Davidson, J. W. (1964) *The Island of Formosa. Historical View From 1430 to 1900*. Reprint of 1903 edition, Wen Hsing Publisher, Taipei.

Fairbank, J. K., E. O. Reischauer and A. M. Craig (1965) *East Asia: The Modern Transformation*. Houghton Mifflin Co., Boston.

Free China Journal (1991a) Hsimen, Wanhwa Spotted for Possible Face-Lift, Jan. 17, 3.

Free China Journal (1991b) To Exist or Not to Exist, Mar. 21, 3.

Glenn, W. (1968) Growing Like Topsy, *Far Eastern Economic Review* 61, Aug. 8, 280–289.

Harris, C. D. and E. L. Ullman (1945) The Nature of Cities, *Annals of the American Academy of Political and Social Science* 143, 7–17.

Herr, M. (1968) Taipei: Wicked Cities of the World, Part II, *Holiday* 43, 46–9, 113, 115, 117, 128.

Hsieh, C. M. (1964) Taiwan-ilha Formosa. A Geography in Perspective. Butterworths, Washington, D.C.

Hsu, L. (1989) Historical Preservation of Taiwan Land Bank Urged, *Free China Journal*, June 8, 6.

Hsu, Y.-a. A. and C. W. Pannell (1982) Urbanization and Residential Spatial Structure in Taiwan, *Pacific Viewpoint* 23, 22–52.

Huang, Y.-m. (1983) The Business of the People Congregates on Special City Streets, *Free China Review* 33:4, 4–21.

Lee, C.-l. (1977) The An Tai Lin Family House, *Echo* 6, 19–25, 55.

Lee, T.-m. (1969) Typhoon Zones of Urbanization. An Analysis of the Process of Urbanization, *Journal of Civil Engineering* 11, 62–66, 91 ff.*

Naito, H. (1937/38) *Taiwan. A Unique Colonial Record.* Kokusai Nippon Kyokai, Tokyo.

New Image of Taipei (1988) Municipal Information Office, Taipei.

Pannell, C. W. (1973) *T'ai-Chung, Taiwan: Structure and Function*. The University of Chicago, Department of Geography, Research Paper no. 144, Chicago.

Pannell, C. W. (1976) Cities East and West: Comments on Theory, Form, and Methodology, *Professional Geographer* 28, 233–40.

Peterson, S. W. (1974) Ilha Formosa, *Travel* 141, May, 32–37.

Preliminary (Sketch) Plan for the City of Taipei (1968) Urban and Housing Development Committee, Council for International Economic Cooperation and Development, Taipei.*

Reid, D. P. (1984) *Taiwan*. Prentice-Hall, Englewood Cliffs.

Sallinger, J. (1991) Top Taiwan Architect Sees "Form as Power", *Free China Journal*, February 7, 6.

Schinz, A. (1989) *Cities in China*. Gebruder Borntraeger, Berlin.

The Statistical Abstract of Taipei Municipality, 1991. (1992) Bureau of Budget, Accounting, and Statistics, Taipei Municipal Government, Taipei.

Steinhardt, N. S. (1990) *Chinese Imperial City Planning*. University of Hawaii Press, Honolulu.

Sun, C-s. (1983) Approaching the Study of the Taiwanese City, *Tunghai Journal* 24, 237–259.

Taipei-Keelung Metropolitan Regional Plan (1968) Urban and Housing Development Committee, Council for International Economic Cooperation and Development, Taipei.

Williams, J. F. and C. F. Sutherland (1988) Taipei Basin, Taiwan, Land Use, 1983. *Annals, Association of American Geographers* 78, 358–361, plus map supplement.

Wu, L. (1975) Taipei, Part II: Manka, *Echo* 5:4–5, 5–84.

3
Economy

Without being a primate city, Taipei has been and remains the main economic center of Taiwan. In this chapter the macroeconomic components of Taipei are described and analyzed and then related to the microeconomic aspects of daily life in the city.

Primary activities

At first glance it may appear to be anomalous to include primary economic activities in an analysis of any city, let alone a world city. Yet because of a combination of administrative, historical, and geological reasons, Taipei City continues to have primary economic activities. In Chapter Two the administrative and historical reasons for the presence of primary activities were presented. Briefly, the annexation of the townships of Chingmei, Nankang, Mucha, Neihu, Shihlin, and Peitou in July 1967 had as one of its consequences the inclusion of primary activities, especially agriculture and pisciculture, and mining. Historically, even areas of Old Taipei contained land devoted to agricultural production since this was an integral part of Chinese urban design. All Chinese cities contained areas which were reserved for food production and water supply so that in the event of civil unrest or war the populations of cities could withstand a siege or blockade.

Turning to the geological roots of primary activities, among the Oligocene and Miocene deposits found in Taipei Basin are coal bearing strata (Ho, 1988). Most important of these are the Mushan (which is bituminous) and Shihti (which contains both bituminous and sub-bituminous materials) formations which are found in Nankang and

Chingmei (Ho and Lee, 1963). Other minerals, which are found in Peitou, Chingmei, and Neihu, include ceramic clays, such as fire and refracting, pottery, and bleaching types, and glass sands (Ho and Lee, 1963). The district of Shihlin contains eight commercially workable ore deposits of limonite (Ho and Lee, 1963). Finally at the base of the Tatun Mountains there are numerous geysers and sulphur hot springs (Ho and Lee, 1963). The main concentration of these is in Peitou and has contributed to the growth of Peitou as a resort centre (Hsieh, 1964).

Mining

Primary activities have never made a significant contribution to the economy of Taipei, although in the past they were more important than they are in the 1990s (Table 3.1). At their peak mining employed only some 1.5 percent of the Taipei workforce, and by 1986 the figure had shrunk to 0.5 percent. Furthermore, although coal and other mining companies had offices in every district of Taipei, it was only in Nankang and Chingmei districts that coal was actually mined. During the early 1950s the mines gradually increased their production levels from some 14 000 metric tons to slightly over 40 000 metric tons, thereby reaching and then exceeding the pre-retrocession output levels. At their peak in 1968 the mines produced some 454 387 metric tons of coal, which was however only 9 percent of the total coal output in Taiwan. By the 1990s production had been reduced to virtually zero; the 1986 *Industrial and Commercial Census* indicated that the Taipei coal industry was operating at substantial net losses. Neither the decline nor the losses are surprising. As early as 1963 Ho and Lee argued that for the most part the coal deposits of the Taipei Basin had been exhausted. In addition to the physical depletion of the coal, the geological conditions under which it was mined also contributed to the decline of the coal industry. The Mushan and Shihti deposits were thin, averaging from 0.3 to 0.8 meters thick, spaced far apart, often at a distance of 14 to 23 meters (Ho and Lee, 1963). Furthermore, the Taipei Basin was subject to tectonic disturbances in the Tertiary and Quaternary periods. The net results were that the coal beds were folded, faulted, compressed, and pinched off. Due to these processes the coal itself was often pulverized *in situ* and was therefore of limited economic value (Hsieh, 1964). The dip of the coal beds, from 12 to 40 degrees (Ho and Lee, 1963), made their exploitation both dangerous and expensive. Finally, there have been concerted efforts by the municipal and national governments to cut back on the use of coal as a means of reducing air pollution.

In contrast, the presence of easily exploited, commercial quantities of glass sand and clay has led to the development of glass and pottery

Table 3.1 Employment data

District	1966					1986				
	Ag	Min	Man	Com	Serv	Ag	Min	Man	Com	Serv
Sungshan	2 343	656	8 029	6 414	16 064	1 510	1 452	51 391	67 343	95 349
Ta-an	1 307	470	5 253	7 194	27 705	1 406	746	29 862	50 296	72 249
Kuting	1 006	359	5 699	8 593	20 474	436	312	18 836	23 971	44 227
Shuangyuan	982	335	5 591	6 881	8 565	115	107	22 105	24 511	23 034
Lungshan	92	80	3 555	5 262	6 016	380	59	4 678	8 786	6 180
Chengchung	276	207	2 705	5 524	10 382	228	156	5 016	10 416	12 030
Chiencheng	70	87	2 939	4 379	3 730	216	48	3 565	7 576	3 599
Yenping	91	78	3 016	5 942	4 125	141	31	3 768	7 877	3 767
Tatong	566	166	7 297	6 805	8 162	78	80	15 043	15 940	12 188
Chungshan	2 334	498	8 164	12 117	21 705	298	253	30 436	59 451	50 359
Neihu	2 040	738	1 552	631	3 244	4 387	557	19 416	15 960	27 351
Nankang	826	927	4 053	638	1 943	1 713	696	16 284	8 019	20 244
Chingmei	417	186	1 650	783	3 624	2 413	232	11 794	8 477	23 011
Mucha	1 254	406	567	555	3 810	1 230	435	13 691	14 912	32 161
Shihlin	5 581	278	3 356	2 782	9 830	9 960	562	38 041	35 122	41 079
Peitou	3 930	118	1 379	1 221	7 415	7 714	371	24 348	26 238	37 111

Sources: *1967 Taiwan Demographic Fact Book, Republic of China* (1968); *1986 Taiwan-Fukien Demographic Fact Book, Republic of China* (1987).

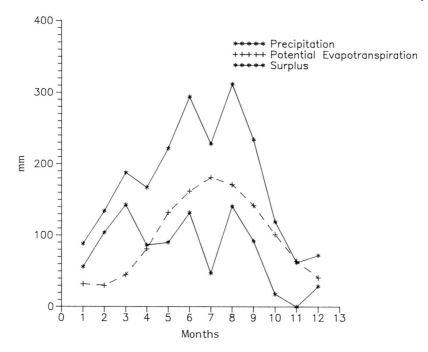

Figure 3.1 Climate

industries which remain viable, especially in Peitou. Frequently the factories have their own show and sales rooms, so that tourists can visit a factory and then immediately purchase items they have found of interest.

Agriculture

Agricultural activities have been an important part of the landscape although, as with mining, their economic importance was slight and declining. In addition to the same administrative, historical, and geological conditions which permitted mining to exist, agriculture has climatic ones as well. The climate of Taipei basin is humid subtropical (Cfa) according to the Koppen system and B2B'1 according to the Thornethwaite system (Hsieh, 1964). Figure 3.1 shows the monthly patterns of precipitation, actual evaporation, and groundwater surplus. In contrast to the rest of Taiwan where there is a winter drought, rainfall does occur from November through March owing to the Winter monsoon. The net result is that on average there is no month in which there is not either adequate rainfall with a surplus or available moisture in ground storage for plants to use. In terms of temperature, with the exception of the elevated parts of the Shihlin and Peitou districts, all months have average temperatures

55

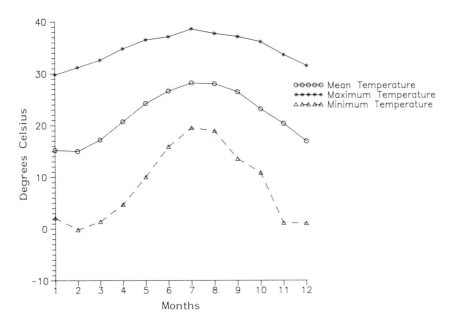

Figure 3.2 Temperature

above freezing point so that the growing season can be extended literally for 12 months (Figure 3.2). Urban agriculture was also possible because idle land was subject to squatter farming (Figure 3.3).

The main crop produced by Taipei farmers was rice. In 1954 in Old Taipei farmers planted some 2247 hectares of rice. At its peak during the 1950s, rice cultivation occupied some 47 percent of the area of Old Taipei. Acreage had actually declined to 1081 hectares when in 1966 the six new districts of Taipei were added. This gave an immediate increase, so that in all some 6340 hectares were under rice cultivation. However, since then the area planted and harvested has declined so that by 1989 only 2014 hectares, or 7.14 percent of the total area of Taipei, were actually cultivated with rice. This decline in acreage is paralleled by a decline in rice production: during the 1950s and 1960s rice output was some 10.8 million kilograms but by 1989, this had declined to some 2.7 million kilograms.

In addition to rice other major crops grown in Taipei included sweet potatoes, maize, edible sugar cane, tea, peanuts, perfume plants, as well as some fruits such as bananas, citrus, and pears. Fish were also raised in ponds. At its peak in 1971 fish culture employed only 45 individuals and supplied just 0.03 percent of the fish handled in the Taipei wholesale fish markets. By the late 1980s maize, sugar cane, peanuts, perfume plants, bananas, and commercial fish were no longer produced and the only

Figure 3.3 Rice was grown on Hsin-yi Road during the 1960s since the government could not implement its road-building program

remaining crop of importance was tea. Whereas the decline of other crops is related to market and other conditions to be discussed below, the continuation of tea is related to direct government intervention. Apparently while mayor of Taipei between 1978 and 1981, President Lee Tung-hui was appalled at the plight of the tea growers in Mucha district. He therefore directed the municipal government to take action to improve the conditions of the farmers. What resulted was the Mucha Scenic Tea Plantation. Under the auspices of the city government the basic infrastructure of the area was improved including new homes and roads, and new strains of tea were introduced. The hope is that the area will become a stop on tourist trips. Visitors can view the tea growing, see the picked teas being processed, sample a cup of tea in a scenic environment, and then purchase teas to take home (Fok, 1990).

Since the actual output of food within Taipei never exceeded 6 percent of the rice or fruit and vegetable demand (Selya, 1977, 1980), its demise is perhaps not to be lamented. However, urban agriculture in Taiwan in general, and in Taipei in particular, did play important roles beyond feeding the population (Selya, 1977). Farmers who abandoned full-time agriculture for positions in either the manufacturing or service sectors of the Taipei economy could not only supplement their incomes by practicing part-time farming, but could always return to farming full time in the event of a recession. As such urban agriculture acted as an important social cushion for the economy, especially during the recessions related to the Arab oil embargo of 1973 and the oil price increases of 1978–79. Urban agriculture also helped to provide green space in an environment which was heavily polluted due to construction, industrialization and transportation. Often crop failures, diseases, or injuries could provide the only early warning of serious environmental problems. The environmental functions of providing green spaces and early warnings are still possible because not all land which was previously farmed has been transferred to urban land uses. Much farm land lies vacant and overgrown, still green and subject to environmental stress which would be readily visible. (In fact one of the problems in recognizing a decline in agriculture based on statistical evidence derives from the fact that the amount of land classified as agricultural does not show marked declines from year to year; the only clear indicator of agricultural decline short of extensive fieldwork is the data showing declines in crop production.)

The demise of urban agriculture in Taipei is related to three main factors. First, as the economy of Taipei grew the opportunity to work outside of agriculture in manufacturing or services, where average salaries were higher, was no doubt tempting. The degree of temptation is perhaps best shown by the persistent demand for labor outside of agriculture: the average unemployment rate was 2.55 percent during the 1970s and 1980s; during the 1990s the rate has continued downward and dropped to 1.8 percent. Secondly, as Taipei's population and economy grew there was increasing pressure to transfer land from agricultural to more urban uses (Figures 3.4, 3.5, 3.6). Finally, in response to increased incomes and a government policy of feeding soldiers wheat products, the diet of the Taiwanese has shifted radically over the past 20 years. Whereas during the 1950s the diet consisted of traditional Chinese foods such as rice, vegetables, fish, chicken, and pork, by the 1980s the diet resembled a Western diet with increased use of wheat and wheat products, dairy, meats, and specialized vegetables and fruits. In the latter category there is a demand for crops grown without the use of chemicals which had become one of the mainstays of food production in Taiwan (Lan, 1987). With the possible exception of specialized vegetables and fruits, neither the space nor the climate of Taipei permits meeting the consumer demands of the new diet.

Some urban agriculture will persist despite these three factors. Environmental constraints will help to preserve agriculture since hilly slope land from which terraces have been carved out is not easily converted to either industrial or other urban uses. In addition some farmers will resist the temptation to sell their land and so pockets of fields in active use will remain. Marginal lands, such as those along rivers and streams, will also remain as small vegetable and rice fields (Figures 3.7, 3.8). But perhaps the most important reason for the persistence of some agricultural activities is

Figure 3.4 The same area as Figure 3.3 once the government rebuilt the road

Figure 3.5 The inclusion of Shihlin and Peitou in Taipei added considerable amounts of agriculturally productive land. Farm houses nestled at the foot of the hills

Figure 3.6 The same area as Figure 3.5 showing the pressure of urbanization on rural areas and the desire for spacious, modern homes

Figure 3.7 In Shihlin during the 1960s river banks were planted with vegetables. The beginning of urban intrusion into the rice fields is seen in the background

Figure 3.8 The same scene as Figure 3.7 in 1991. Although the vegetable gardens remain by the river, rice production has all been abandoned

the entrepreneurial imagination of Taipei farmers. Five examples can be offered of how Taipei farmers are using their skills and land to new advantage in the urban environment. First, despite their association with either major celebrations such as weddings or with death, funerals, and mourning, flowers are now used in a much more Western way – given as gifts or brought to dinners to decorate the table. Farmers are capitalizing on this changed view of the message of flowers, as is readily seen by the presence of women selling flowers outside the central railroad station and other busy transportation nodes, and as a part of the general street commerce one finds in Taipei. Secondly, farmers have taken to growing decorative and annual flowering plants for sale to both house and apartment dwellers. The plants are grown in the farm areas and sold either in adjacent garden stores or in garden stores in the old Taipei City neighborhoods. Thirdly, farmers have begun renting small plots of land to home and apartment dwellers. For a small monthly fee one can rent a plot and grow vegetables or flowers. Commonly rents in the Taipei area are about US$15 a month for a 216 square meter plot (Song, 1990). Fourthly, farmers plant strawberries and then permit people to come in to pick them for a fee (Wang, 1986). Finally, some farmers have used the old fish ponds, or converted old paddy fields to fish ponds and stocked them with fish, thus providing urban people with an opportunity for weekend fishing. This latter use of agricultural land has spawned its own downtown, indoor clone. Clubs and restaurants have built large fish tanks where customers can unwind from a hard day at work with drinks and disco music as they fish for their dinners and then wait as their catch is cooked for them (Quinn, 1991).

In sum, administrative, cultural, geological, and historical reasons account for the past existence of primary economic activities within Taipei City. Changing economic and social conditions have eliminated or reduced some of these activities, whereas other activities such as pottery manufacturing and new agricultural activities remain to take advantage of still exploitable resources and new urban demands.

Manufacturing

Data and the problem of illegal economic activities

Before discussing manufacturing and then services in Taipei, it is necessary to review problems with the data base used in the presentations. For the most part the data from successive industrial and commercial censuses are used in this analysis of Taipei's manufacturing economy. These appear to be more reliable since they measure not only fully registered factories and retail establishments, as the Taipei municipal government data do, but in addition those with incomplete, or no registrations. Factories with improper, incomplete, or no registrations are often referred to as illegal or underground factories; retail vendors lacking proper registration are referred to as informal vendors.

The use of the census data goes beyond some vague notion of the need for accuracy. Rather their use points up five problems involving illegal economic activities. The first issue is the persistence of such activities. Newspaper reports on the presence of, and problems associated with, illegal establishments can be found during the 1950s and continue up to the present. The city council of Taipei is especially bothered by the persistence of illegal economic activities out of fear that the vendors, the public, and foreigners will assume that longevity implies unofficial sanctioning of activities which violate the law. In general in Taiwan there is a great concern to show that the Republic of China fosters a society run according to the rule of law.

Secondly, the magnitude of the illegal establishments is hard to estimate but most likely very large. For example, in 1966 a survey of Taipei City and Sanchung City (just west of Taipei City) found that there were 1080 illegal factories in Taipei City (*Report on the Survey of Illegal Factories in Taipei City and Sanchung City of Taipei Hsien*, 1967). This number

Table 3.2 Estimate of informal sales sector

	1966	1986
Number of registered workers	69 111	260 284
Census employment	53 462	233 616
Estimated informal sales sector	15 649	26 668
Ratio: registered:census	1.29	1.11
Percentage informal	22.6	10.2

compares with a total of 2739 factories reported in the industrial census. If in fact a large number of the illegal factories are included in the census data, then up to 39 percent of all factories could have been illegal. These findings are consistent with later estimates of illegal factories which assume that they occur in a ratio of 1.15 to every legally registered factory (Lee, 1981, 1982). The latest reported estimates of the number of illegal factories suggest that there were some 1794 in 1991 (*China Post*, Jan. 26, 1991). This number shows a slight increase over the 1967 survey data, to 41.1 percent, in the proportion of illegal factories.

In terms of the retail sector there have been no publicly available government reports on the number of illegal shops or vendors. The city government is very reluctant to share its estimates of unlicensed vendors lest the data be interpreted to mean, as with underground factories, that the city condones such activities (Hsia, 1993). However, it is possible to estimate their number, as was done for the Philippines by Alonzo (1991), using a residual method which compares the numbers of retail and wholesale workers registered in the mandatory population register with the same classification of workers in the industrial and commercial censuses. Table 3.2 shows the results of the comparison. These estimates are well within the range of 10 000 to 30 000 unlicensed vendors published by the *China Post* (May 25, 1987). A 1993 survey suggested that there were 4100 *licensed* vendors out of a total of 41 000 vendors actually operating within the city (Huang, 1993). These data suggest that the informal sector of Taipei, while it has grown in size, has shrunk as a proportion of all sales workers and revenues generated. There is a strong possibility, however, that these appraisals underestimate the true size of the informal sector for two reasons: there can be a considerable delay in changing one's address with the population register, and people engaged in informal sales do not necessarily have to live in Taipei City – given the relatively rich mix of public and private transportation, sales people could live not only anywhere in Taipei Basin but even elsewhere, down island. This second reason is very evident from the type of display used when selling the goods. Frequently goods are merely spread out on a large cloth, which in fact is the wrapper for transporting the goods. Often the goods are

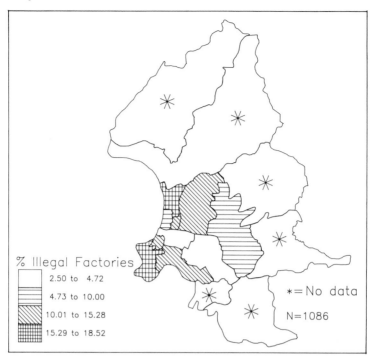

Figure 3.9 Distribution of illegal factories

displayed from a wagon or other type of vehicle which the sales person pushes or drives from place to place. Similarly, when the sales day is ended, it is not uncommon to see goods packed up and put into the back of a taxi cab or reloaded onto a wagon. Such simple packing and transportation arrangements also make it easier to move whenever there is a police sweep or check of registration in an area. As in the case of manufacturing, it seems that a substantial part of retail activity is not legal.

The third problem with illegal economic activities is that their spatial distribution correlates weakly with legal ones, with a rank order correlation of 0.80 (for a 64 percent explanatory power). In 1966 the spatial distribution of illegal factories (Figure 3.9) was heavily concentrated in two *chu*, Tatong with 18.52 percent and Shuangyuan with 15.46 percent of illegal factories respectively. Chiencheng (14.17 percent), Lungshan (11.76 percent), Chungshan (10.46 percent), and Kuting (10.28 percent) were also *chu* with substantial numbers of illegal factories. The residential *chu* of Ta-an and the administrative *chu* Chengchung had the fewest illegal factories. In terms of location quotients comparing the distribution of illegal factories to that of the population (Barber, 1988), Tatong, Chiencheng, Shuangyuan, and Lungshan show the heaviest

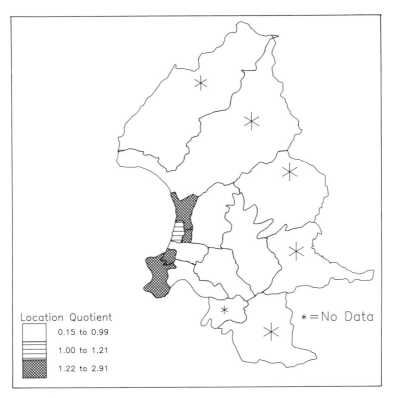

Figure 3.10 Location quotient for illegal factories

concentration of underground factories (Figure 3.10). This pattern of high location quotients is almost identical to the pattern for all factories (see Figures 3.13, 3.14). This pattern of concentration is also found when comparing the ratio of legal to illegal factories in each *chu*.

Structurally four types of industry have had the majority (60.77 percent) of the illegal factories. These are basic metals (24 percent), machinery (12.4 percent), printing (15.2 percent), and wood (9.17 percent). These industries in turn are heavily concentrated in a few *chu*: 60 percent of the illegal basic metal factories are found in Chiencheng, Tatong, and Chungshan *chu*; 58.95 percent of machinery factories are in Chiencheng, Chungshan, and Sungshan; 53.94 percent of underground printing factories are in Shuangyuan and Lungshan; and 54.5 percent of the wood factories are in Shuangyuan, Tatong, and Yenping. There were no illegal factories producing beverages, tobacco products, or petroleum and coal products. The lack of illegal establishments in tobacco and petroleum products was no doubt related to the fact that the government, either through a monopoly or state run corporation, was the only manufacturer of these products.

The spatial distribution of illegal vendors is somewhat more difficult to describe precisely. The informal sector is found anywhere that there is room for the display of merchandise: pedestrian over- and underground passes; under bridges; in front of legitimate retail stores on the spaces between the stores and the street. A confusion of merchants is often created when legitimate store owners move their own racks or displays of merchandise out onto the sidewalk. This approach to sales and marketing reflects a continuation of the longstanding failure to separate both private and public and work and living spaces, as described in Chapter 2. Very often the informal sector sells a product or delivers a service directly related to the formal sector activity it is found near. For example, washing of cars is frequently done by informal operators right outside either car salerooms, body shops or service stations. As with the formal sector, individual informal sellers often specialize in a very specific good, and bargaining is not only possible but expected.

The fourth problem with illegal economic activities is their possible impact on city income. The Taipei City Council is concerned over the lost tax revenues (*Free China Journal*, December 1, 1988). It has been estimated that the income generated by the informal sector was US$8.6 billion for 1981 and US$18 billion for 1988, compared with US$22 billion generated by the formal sector in 1981 and US$89 billion generated in 1986. Obviously substantial tax revenues are being lost due to the presence of the informal sector.

The fifth and final concern over illegal economic activities is the difficulty in eliminating them via official means. Raids on factories do not seem to have been effective. Rather, negative externalities and neighborhood pressure, discussed more fully below, have succeeded in forcing both legal and illegal factories out of Taipei City. In terms of informal vendors, the government continues to try to eliminate them (Huang, 1993). In addition to periodic police sweeps aimed at forcing the vendors off the streets, the city has offered vendors job retraining programs, but most vendors rejected the offer, preferring to stay in a high income occupation. Vendors' incomes have been estimated to be in the US$40–80 000 range after one year of effort. Those who did accept the offer of job retraining also demanded that the city government find them jobs paying at least US$2000 a month! The city has also offered to provide designated areas where the unlicensed vendors could conduct their business legally. This offer was also rejected. The government has tried to eliminate the vendors by appealing to the public to boycott them. Part of the boycott appeal focuses on the two most obvious public negative aspects of the vendors – the additional costs of keeping the city clean and the increases in traffic congestion generated by displays or vendor carts. Thus despite police activities to clear the streets of the vendors, they not only persist, but have become more sophisticated. The vendors are no longer the country

Table 3.3 Manufacturing data, Taipei

| | Number of factories | | Number of employees | |
	Registration data	Census data	Registration data	Census data
1954		4 448		56 147
1961		6 655		70 756
1966		2 739		79 749
1971	2 343	4 135	89 442	139 622
1976	2 920	6 815	109 580	192 966
1981	3 222	9 361	87 100	194 368
1986	3 077	10 842	96 500	211 292

Sources: *Taipei Municipal Statistical Abstract*, various years; *Industrial–Commercial Census, Taiwan-Fukien Area, Republic of China*, cited years.

bumpkins they appeared to be a generation ago, but rather include sophisticated businessmen who conduct their business over cellular phones and drive fancy cars. Many are college graduates who have tired of nine-to-five desk jobs. The government's difficulties in trying to eliminate the informal vendors is complicated by mixed public attitudes towards the vendors. In a survey sponsored by the city council, 80 percent of respondents said that unlicensed vendors should be taken off the streets; unfortunately 60 percent admitted that they habitually buy things from the unlicensed stands (Huang, 1993).

Spatial analysis of manufacturing

Taipei City is the main manufacturing center in Taiwan. This is true whether manufacturing is measured by the number of factories, the number of employees in manufacturing, or the value of total output. However, its dominance over the industrial sector of the Taiwan economy has steadily eroded over time. The exact degree of industrial decline in Taipei depends on which of two data bases is used to measure industrial change (Table 3.3). According to factory registration data collected by the Taipei municipal government, the number of factories grew to a maximum of 3222 in 1981 and declined thereafter. However, data in the successive industrial and commercial censuses conducted by the central government of the Republic of China show that the number of factories in Taipei has continued to increase since 1966, although the rate of increase in all the measures of manufacturing, number of factories, area in manufacturing, number of employees, and value of industrial output has decreased over time and fallen behind national trends.

Two sets of measures demonstrate the declining dominance of the Taipei manufacturing sector relative to all Taiwan manufacturing (Table 3.4).

Table 3.4 Taipei's dominance over Taiwan manufacturing

Year	Percent Taiwan industrial Workers in Taipei	Location quotient
1954	13.66	1.76
1961	15.58	1.67
1966	13.38	1.33
1971	11.77	0.92
1976	10.19	0.80
1981	8.92	0.71
1986	7.74	0.58

Sources: Calculated from data in *Taiwan-Fukien Demographic Fact Book* and *Industrial–Commercial Census, Taiwan-Fukien Area*, years indicated.

First, the percentage shares of Taipei's factories, area in manufacturing, industrial employment, and value of output have declined since 1954. By these measures the erosion of Taipei's position started during the 1950s although there was some recovery for some measures during the 1960s. Nevertheless by the 1970s the decline in Taipei's dominance had begun. A more refined measure of the decline is found in the series of location quotients comparing the percentages of Taiwan factories and population located in Taipei. These measures clearly show the decline in the number of factories, and presumably the decline in all other measures of manufacturing, starting during the 1960s; by 1971 Taipei had already fallen below the number of factories needed even to achieve a one to one ratio with the proportion of population residing in Taipei.

The reasons for Taipei's dominance and subsequent decline are easily enumerated. Early dominance was related to market, political, and transportation factors. As the largest city in Taiwan Taipei had a significant marketing advantage over other places. But beyond being the largest city on Taiwan, Taipei's status as the provisional capital also gave it considerable market advantages. The government itself was a major market; the foreign diplomatic community needed to be served; the American military, both the resident advisers and their families as well as soldiers on rest and recreation from Vietnam, presented a substantial market for furniture, rugs, and handicraft souvenirs.

Politically, Taipei was the location of both government offices and financial institutions. Since permits and loans from these offices and institutions were required to buy land for a factory, import raw materials or plant, properly register a factory, and then ultimately export, there was a perception that location in or at least near Taipei City was a necessary condition for a would be entrepreneur. Such a location would allow for the frequent visits to officials processing all the required applications. Should a problem with an application arise, the entrepreneur could consult directly with the officials concerned and if need be draw on personal relationships with old friends and schoolmates with appropriate contacts in government offices and financial institutions to intervene.

Transportation factors focus on the road and rail links between Taipei and the port city of Keelung some 25 kilometers to the northeast. The road link, the MacArthur Highway, was the first modern limited access highway in Taiwan. Additional transportation factors included an international airport within the city limits (moved, as discussed in Chapter 1, to a new site in Taoyuan *hsien* some 30 kilometers southwest of Taipei in 1979), and road and rail links with the other major cities and *hsien* capitals along the west coast.

The relative decline in Taipei's dominance over Taiwan manufacturing is related to economic, environmental, political, and structural factors. Some of the economic and environmental factors will be analyzed fully in Chapter 6, Coping with world city status. Therefore the material presented here is in abbreviated form.

The main economic constraint on continued rapid growth of Taipei industry is the high cost of land. The cost of land for all purposes in Taipei has been a difficult economic, political, and social issue from at least the 1960s (Lai, n.d.). The most expensive land in Taipei has increased from NT$25 713 per square meter in the late 1960s to some NT$376 000 in 1989, an increase of some 1362 percent; prices for the cheapest land have gone from NT$3 per square meter to NT$200 in the same period, an increase of 6566 percent. The ratio of the most expensive to the cheapest land has actually narrowed from 8571 in 1968 to 1880 in 1989. One of the net results of these land price increases has been to push manufacturing with large or new space needs out of Taipei City.

A second influential economic factor has been a chronic labor shortage. The same low unemployment rates which contributed to the decline of primary activities are also taking their toll on manufacturing. The structural and locational details of the growth of the service sector are described in the next section of this chapter. However, several simple measures can demonstrate here the competition for workers between these two sectors of the economy. Since 1968 the percent of Taipei workers in manufacturing has decreased from 23.37 percent to 21.27, while for service workers there has been an increase from 62.74 percent to 71.26 percent. In terms of the changing number of workers, industrial employment has grown some 104.5 percent over the period 1968 to 1989, while employment in services has grown some 155 percent. Finally, in 1968 for every industrial worker there were 2.68 service workers; by 1989 the ratio had increased to 3.36.

The main factor drawing workers out of manufacturing is wages. In manufacturing wages grew from NT$11 160 in 1966 to NT$62 810 in 1986, while wages in services grew from NT$17 011 to NT$191 544.

What is perhaps most important about the changes is that the net US dollar difference in salaries between the two sectors grew from $146 in 1966 to $4720 in 1986. This lag in wages, combined with a long-standing Chinese cultural preference for office or desk jobs or self-employment in a business, has contributed to the decline in manufacturing. The decline in manufacturing because of wages is systemic throughout the Taiwan economy and has led to chronic labor shortages and illegal migration (Selya, 1992). Taipei City is only perhaps the most glaring example of the problem.

Environmental reasons for the decline in manufacturing include air, water, and noise pollution. Especially hard hit by these problems are food processing, metals, chemicals, and transportation industries. The precise extent of the pollution problem, and the reason for the problem only becaming a factor in the decline in manufacturing in the 1980s, are discussed in Chapter 7.

Structural reasons for the decline in manufacturing in Taipei reflect national changes in the mixture of industry. Taiwan industry is in the painful process of shifting from labor intensive, low technology to capital extensive, high technology manufacturing owing in part to increased world competition and rising wages across the Taiwan economy. In order to compete, Taiwan entrepreneurs are either technically upgrading their plant and employees or, more commonly, transferring their operations overseas. While these attempts to recapture some initial advantages are most common in those industries relying on low technology, low wage processes such as textiles and furniture, manufacturers across the product line are also involved in either upgrading or transferring operations. Regardless of which strategy firms employ to remain viable, the net result is a consolidation and reduction in the number of factories.

The main political factor influencing manufacturing in Taipei was the changing nature of the United States military and political presence. The dissolution of the Military Assistance and Advisory Group of the United States in Taiwan in 1979 was a major loss to the furniture, clothing, and wood industries just as their presence had been a boon. The declining number of foreign embassies in Taipei has a similar depressing effect on the demands for Taipei produced goods.

The rise and fall of Taipei's role in the total industrial economy have been reflected in the changing distribution of industry within the city itself. The changing distribution is analyzed using three measures: number of factories, location quotients and indices of dissimilarity derived from Lorenz curves (Taylor, 1977). Both of these latter measures are derived from comparing the number of factories in a district to the population.

Figures 3.11 and 3.12 show the distribution of manufacturing for 1966 and 1986. In 1966 industry was located in Old Taipei and in particular Tatong, Lungshan, Yenping, and Shuangyuan which accounted for 44.7

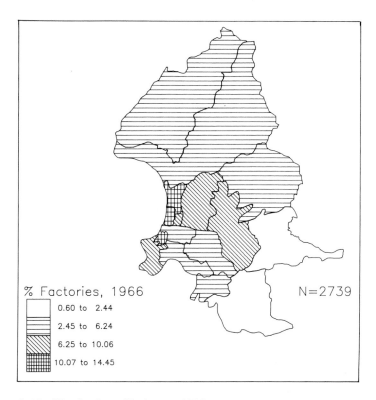

Figure 3.11 Distribution of industry, 1966

percent of the factories. In 1986 most industry was still located in Old Taipei; some shifting within the area had taken place, but Sungshan, Chungshan, and Shuangyuan still accounted for 37.5 percent of all factories. Only one of the new districts, Mucha, was a major industrial area with 10.6 percent of all factories. For both years the old district of Ta-an, and the new districts of Chingmei, Neihu, and Shihlin, do not contain larger percentages of factories. These regional patterns contrast with the differential growth rates for the numbers of factories. Here the new districts have the highest rates and the old districts have the lowest. This in part is a statistical artifact reflecting the initial number of factories in each district: small increments over a small base yield large growth rates, whereas even moderate increases in the number of factories over a large base yield a small increase. However, the shifts to the newer areas are also a reflection of the availability of cheaper land and better accessibility in the areas outside Old Taipei.

One important characteristic of the distribution of factories is the degree of diversity for each district. In 1966 Sungshan and Tatong districts had

Economy

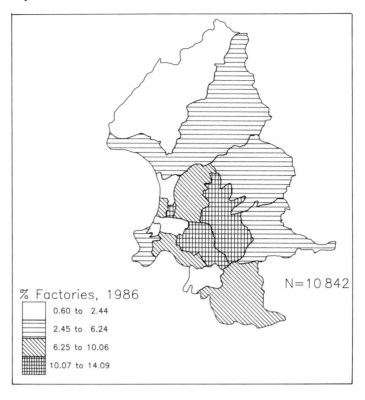

% Factories, 1986

	0.60 to 2.44
	2.45 to 6.24
	6.25 to 10.06
	10.07 to 14.09

N=10 842

Figure 3.12 Distribution of industry, 1986

both the most diverse mixture of factories and the greatest number of factories in each type of manufacturing. By 1986 the greatest diversity was found in Chungshan, Sungshan, and Shihlin districts. The converse of diversity, specialization, also has some interesting geographical patterns within the city (Tables 3.5 and 3.6). In 1966 the Old City districts were the centers of specialization. By 1986 the only new districts which had eroded the specialization hold of the old districts were Shihlin, Peitou, and Nankang.

Figures 3.13 and 3.14 give an alternative perspective on the distribution of industry in Taipei. The location quotients show that the three Old City districts of Tatong, Yenping, and Lungshan have the greatest per capita concentration of industry. Over time the concentration of industry in the old districts is extended by 1986 when Chengchung and Shuangyuan rank high in the location quotients. Of the new districts only Nankang appears to have achieved the status of a major industrial concentration. In terms of specific industries we find a similar pattern: the Old City districts have strong concentrations which only Nankang challenges in 1986.

72

Table 3.5 Industrial mix in Taipei (figures as %)

	F	C	M	P	W	Ch	Ma	T	E	All
1954										
Chengchung	9.6	16.0	8.0	25.7	16.9	13.7	5.7	18.3	28.0	660
Lungshan	12.6	14.4	19.1	33.5	24.0	19.0	11.5	12.5	9.6	753
Yenping	14.5	13.9	8.9	9.6	13.3	10.2	11.5	6.7	11.2	540
Chiencheng	10.7	10.8	17.7	14.6	6.2	6.8	23.1	8.2	22.4	510
Chungshan	8.7	6.8	16.9	2.9	5.8	8.3	19.2	13.2	5.6	406
Kuting	12.3	16.2	3.1	5.8	9.8	10.2	1.3	17.1	8.0	496
Ta-an	7.1	9.3	5.1	2.3	6.0	4.4	0.6	9.6	2.4	288
Ta-tong	8.5	3.4	10.6	2.0	9.6	8.3	16.0	5.5	5.6	301
Shuangyuan	8.1	2.1	6.8	3.2	4.9	16.1	2.6	3.6	5.6	232
Sungshan	7.8	6.8	3.7	0.3	3.5	2.9	8.3	5.3	1.6	262
Totals										
(No.)	719	1 022	350	289	450	235	156	416	125	4 448
(Column %)	100	100	100	100	100	100	100	100	100	
1986										
Sungshan	9.7	11.5	12.4	5.8	11.5	15.6	12.3	9.2	18.4	1 300
Ta-an	10.2	6.8	3.9	4.9	5.6	10.2	4.9	3.2	5.9	702
Kuting	3.9	2.3	3.4	7.9	2.7	3.1	1.2	1.5	2.0	428
Shuangyuan	6.1	4.1	4.8	37.5	4.6	3.3	2.7	0.4	3.3	1 260
Lungshan	3.3	2.3	1.9	6.9	27.4	2.3	1.9	0.0	0.9	334
Chengchung	8.4	4.7	0.8	3.9	2.2	6.4	2.8	1.1	4.5	418
Chiencheng	3.5	2.6	2.0	3.3	1.5	2.5	2.2	2.8	0.4	266
Yenping	5.8	14.2	0.9	2.3	1.7	2.1	0.8	0.6	0.5	348
Tatong	6.9	6.6	6.3	7.9	3.7	5.5	11.2	2.6	3.2	687
Chungshan	15.3	22.1	9.7	6.7	11.6	21.7	11.9	39.3	13.9	1 538
Neihu	4.1	2.9	8.9	0.8	2.4	6.5	10.9	21.2	7.5	611
Nankang	4.4	3.2	11.7	0.9	3.4	8.8	13.8	8.8	16.9	877
Mucha	2.3	0.4	1.9	0.4	0.7	0.6	0.3	0.4	1.7	104
Chingmei	1.9	1.2	2.1	1.7	1.7	1.4	1.9	0.2	2.9	189
Shihlin	7.9	10.0	16.9	7.7	10.9	6.8	18.0	6.6	8.7	1 150
Peitou	9.3	5.4	12.0	1.0	8.2	3.4	3.0	2.1	9.2	630
Totals										
(No.)	430	1 331	223	2 304	305	1 059	594	254	1 321	10 842
(Column %)	100	100	100	100	100	100	100	100	100	

Key: F=food; C=textiles and clothing; M=basic metals; P=printing; W=wood; Ch=chemicals; Ma=machinery; T=transportation; E=electrical

Sources: computed from Chen (1957); *Industrial–Commercial Census of Taiwan-Fukien Area, Republic of China* (1986).

One final means of understanding changing industrial distribution is in the use of indices of dissimilarity derived from Lorenz curves. The indices (Table 3.7) show that from 1954 to 1981 industry within Taipei actually became more concentrated, especially in the Old City districts of Lungshan, Yenping, and Tatong. By 1986 the distribution had become

Table 3.6 District industrial specializations

Product	% factories per type	
	1966	1986
Food	Yenping (18.7)	Chungshan (15.3)
Textiles	Yenping (16.7)	Chungshan (22.1)
	Sungshan (13.3)	Sungshan (11.5)
	Tatong (13.3)	Yenping (14.2)
Wood	Lungshan (15.9)	Lungshan (27.4)
	Chengchung (15.9)	Chungshan (11.6)
	Tatong (13.3)	Sungshan (11.5)
	Sungshan (13.3)	
Printing	Lungshan (37.6)	Shuangyuan (37.5)
	Chiencheng (12.5)	
	Yenping (11.5)	
Chemicals	Shuangyuan (16.7)	Chungshan (21.7)
	Chungshan (12.9)	Sungshan (15.6)
	Tatong (14.5)	Ta-an (10.2)
Non-metallic minerals	Peitou (24.5)	Chungshan (20.8)
	Sungshan (24.5)	Peitou (13.2)
	Chungshan (13.9)	Ta-an (12.0)
Basic metals	Sungshan (35.7)	Chungshan (14.8)
	Tatong (21.4)	Nankang (14.8)
	Shihlin (14.3)	Shihlin (13.0)
		Sungshan (12.6)
		Tatong (9.4)
Metal products	Tatong (25.7)	Shihlin (16.9)
	Shihlin (16.7)	Sungshan (12.4)
	Chungshan (10.1)	Nankang (11.7)
Machinery	Tatong (10.8)	Shihlin (18.0)
	Chiencheng (10.3)	Nankang (13.8)
	Shihlin (14.1)	Sungshan (12.3)
	Sungshan (10.3)	Chungshan (11.9)
Electrical	Shuangyuan (12.9)	Sungshan (18.4)
	Sungshan (11.1)	Chungshan (13.9)
	Shihlin (9.1)	Peitou (9.2)
Transportation	Sungshan (10.3)	Sungshan (16.3)
		Nankang (16.1)
		Chungshan (15.7)

Source: Tabulated from 1966 and 1986 *Industrial–Commercial Census, Taiwan-Fukien Area, Republic of China*.

more equal. Yet as with the location quotients it is only Nankang which is evolving into an industrial concentration to challenge the districts of the Old City.

The consistent pattern of Old City domination of manufacturing stands in contrast to the findings of Lee (1982) who established substantial shifts out of the Old City. Lee attributed the decline of Old City manufacturing

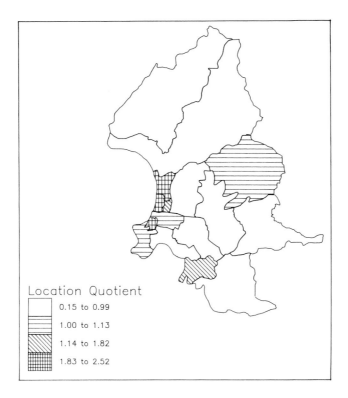

Figure 3.13 Location quotient, industry, 1966

to four main factors: increasing land prices, land use restrictions designed to maintain areas as residential or commercial in nature, increased transportation costs, and difficulties in reducing pollution levels. Several methodological factors may explain the differences between Lee's findings and the analysis presented above. Lee's time period was different, 1969 to 1979; he used employment data based on factory registration rather than data based on more accurate censuses. In addition he did not investigate the relative changes in the New City districts.

Surprisingly however, Lee provides a possible reason which would not only account for the persistence of the Old City industry, but would also be in accord with data from the industrial censuses. Lee points out that Taipei industry is basically small scale. The average area per factory was small even by Taiwan standards (Orru, 1991) (Table 3.8). In 1961 the average factory in Taipei operated in 358 square meters. This increased to 1 140 in 1966 but has since declined to 520 square meters in 1986, as compared to the Taiwan average of 210. The average number of employees shows the same growth patterns. Average output increases from 1961 to 1966, then declines in 1971, and then increases through 1986.

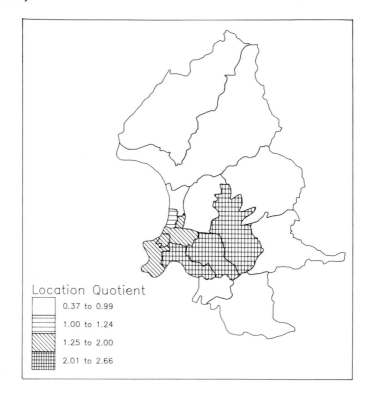

Figure 3.14 Location quotient, industry, 1986

Table 3.7 Indices of dissimilarity

Year	Manufacturing	All services
1954	21.34	28.24
1966	25.21	
1971	25.62	26.51
1981	34.31	
1986	22.81	23.69

Source: Computed from *Industrial–Commercial Census, Taiwan-Fukien Area, Republic of China*.

The increases, however, have not kept up with Taiwan averages. Only in total assets does Taipei industry appear to be operating on a larger scale than the Taiwan average.

The small scale of industry has important locational implications. The Old City locations, with advantages in access to rail and road transportation, availability of water in the Keelung and Tamshui rivers, market,

Table 3.8 Scale of manufacturing: Taipei and Taiwan compared

	Taipei						Taiwan					
	1961	1966	1971	1976	1981	1986	1961	1966	1971	1976	1981	1986
Area	358	1 140	2 241	1 603	865	520	858	2 166	2 040	2290	911	2 210
Wages	8.6	89.5	33.7	28.3	20.7	19.4	8.6	21.2	17.0	26.2	23.0	22.0
Output	.69	16.2	7.9	9.9	15.3	19.5	.73	3.0	3.5	11.1	23.1	30.3
Assets	.4	21.8	9.1	79.1	103.9	126.5	.42	3.2	3.1	15.1	22.4	87.3
Salary	7.8	15.9	28.8	54.9	126.5	211.4	6.9	12.5	21.6	46.8	26.3	171.3

Units: Area – number of square meters
Wages, value of output, assets, and average salary – NT$10 000

Sources: computed from *Industrial–Commercial Census, Taiwan-Fukien Area, Republic of China.*

and employees, and presence of agglomeration forces, still retain these advantages. Those industries which either are public nuisances owing to pollution or require more space have located in areas such as Shihlin and Nankang, or moved out of either the city or Taiwan altogether. Barring competition for space, workers, and access from the service industries, strict enforcement of urban land use regulations, or municipal district planning and renewal, only a major upscaling and upgrading of Taipei industry will diminish the locational advantages of the Old City and its large manufacturing base.

There are attempts to help maintain Taipei as a major industrial center. For example, the Industrial Development Board of the Ministry of Economic Affairs is planning to establish a software industry zone in Nankang district. The planning of this zone comes at the suggestion of the Medium and Small Business Administration of the Ministry of Economic Affairs, in response to pressure from software writers and vendors who want an industrial zone similar to the Science Based Industrial Park in Hsinchu, some 70 kilometers southwest of Taipei. The Nankang zone would accelerate the development of locally produced software which lags behind the development of locally produced hardware. The Nankang site has two advantages: first, it would be built on some 12 hectares of land owned by the government-owned Taiwan Fertilizer Company and thereby help to alleviate the problem of paying high land costs which then translate into high rents; secondly, the site is accessible to other enterprises, banking institutions, and schools. A second site in Neihu has been suggested for light and precision industries (*Central Daily News*, Aug. 18, 1990).

Services

The central role of the service sector to the economy of Taipei has been referred to when discussing both the declining importance of primary activities and the shifts in the manufacturing sector. It will come as no surprise that Taipei's economy is not only dominated by service activities (Table 3.9), but that Taipei also dominates the entire service sector of Taiwan. This latter position is true no matter how services are measured – by number of service establishments, number of service employees, or revenue generated by services. Taipei has about 20 percent of all trade, service, and transportation establishments, between 30 and 40 percent of all service employees, and generates between 63 and 80 percent of all service revenue. There have been some slight shifts of course in the overall dominance of Taipei in the service sector; however, the location quotients for service industries (Table 3.10) contrast sharply with the same measures for manufacturing. Only in the area of construction activities does Taipei

Table 3.9 Service mix by year, type, and location

| District | 1954 | | | 1986 | | |
	Trade	Services	Transport	Trade	Services	Transport
Sungshan	369	128	8	11 655	3 238	1 532
Ta-an	528	201	57	9 017	2 710	567
Kuting	794	272	89	4 781	1 277	571
Shuangyuan	204	56	23	4 904	721	383
Lungshan	1 127	407	84	3 412	704	91
Chengchung	2 073	474	92	6 012	2 021	304
Chienchung	930	220	64	3 452	531	67
Yenping	1 523	259	19	3 412	438	48
Tatong	269	108	12	3 486	556	170
Chungshan	640	191	66	17 356	3 882	1 146
Neihu				1 660	382	482
Nankang				1 818	481	412
Mucha				865	226	247
Chingmei				1 737	514	257
Shihlin				4 679	1 133	609
Peitou				3 468	941	655

Sources: Chen (1957); *Industrial–Commercial Census of Taiwan-Fukien Area, Republic of China* (1986).

Table 3.10 Dominance of Taipei service sector

Year	% Taiwan service workers in Taipei	Location quotient
1966	19.45	1.69
1971	18.47	1.51
1976	19.07	1.51
1981	20.35	1.63
1986	22.64	1.71

appear to be substantially below national figures. In terms of growth, however, Taipei lagged behind the rest of Taiwan except in the growth of the number of total service establishments and the number of commercial/ trade establishments. However, given Taipei's large service base this is no surprise. The lag may also be a function of the unclear status of the informal vendors described above.

The dominance of Taipei persists in two interesting ways beyond mere percentages. First, the dominance remains even as the definitions of services become more refined and include ever more numerous and sophisticated activities. For example, the 1954 *Industrial and Commercial Census* listed some 20 different categories of services including retail food shops (listing rice, vegetables, fruits, confectionery, and fish separately), pawn shops, drug stores, and clothing stores dominated both the Taiwan and Taipei economies. By 1986 3 trade categories (further broken down into 29 more specific groupings for wholesale and retail activities), 13 types of business services, and 7 types of personal services are enumerated. Food related services still dominated but newer services such as electrical appliance sales and service, car sales and service, and beauty and barber shops dominate both the Taiwan and Taipei economies. Secondly, the mix of service activities found in Taipei is remarkably stable: some 74 percent of all establishments and workers are in trade activities, some 20 percent in services, and the remaining 5 to 6 percent in transportation.

This long-term dominance is quite understandable given Taipei's political and economic functions. Governments are both providers and consumers of services. The presence of two governments in Taipei, national and municipal, serves to magnify the role of service provider and consumer. In addition there is growing awareness both in the theoretical literature (Coffey and McRae, 1989; McKee, 1988; Price and Blair, 1989; Riddle, 1986) and in Taiwan (Wieman, 1987; Chi, 1989) that a strong and growing service sector is at least a necessary condition for a strong and growing industrial economy. As such the presence and strength of the Taipei service economy follow from its importance as a manufacturing and exporting sector. After all, products must be attractively packaged, foreign buyers must be located, contracts for exports must be signed, and products must be shipped. All of these service activities have been present and expanded in Taipei.

Furthermore, as the economy of Taipei has grown, demands for two new types of services have developed. The first type, various forms of consulting, engineering, and environmental services, is a reflection of the changes both in the structure of the Taipei economy and in the growing demand by the public to deal with some of the negative consequences of economic growth such as pollution and traffic congestion. The second type of service, consumer services, derives from the increases in both education and income which have accompanied rapid economic development. Greater amounts of discretionary income and more free time have led to the growth of such services as fast food and convenience stores, personal services, and recreational activities.

In terms of the location of services within Taipei the dominant role of the government is quite evident (Figures 3.15 and 3.16). Over time services have located near government offices in Chengchung and adjacent districts. The addition of the six further districts in 1968 did not appreciably change the overall distribution of services. Indices of dissimilarity derived from Lorenz curves decline from 28.24 in 1954 to 23.64 in 1986, indicating a slight shift towards a more equal distribution of services. However, location quotients show (Figures 3.17 and 3.18) a persistence of Old Taipei and the areas near government offices as the

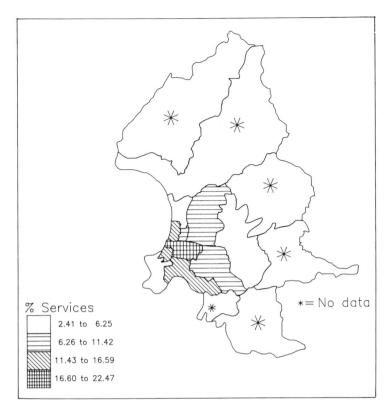

Figure 3.15 Distribution of services, 1954

major centers of services. The new districts are the locations of recreational services such as the Palace Museum (Shihlin), the Taipei Zoo (Mucha), hot springs and mountain climbing (Peitou), and urban farm activities (Shihlin and Peitou). Newer services such as fast food and convenience stores are located throughout Taipei. These commonly cluster together and frequently occupy sites formerly part of market districts.

A microeconomic perspective

The economy of Taipei is vibrant and changing, characterized by long-term labor shortages and low unemployment, and evermore structured around the service sector. How do these general economic characteristics intrude into the daily lives of Taipei residents? In a series of articles Chen and Chen (1983) and Tsai (1977; 1978; 1981; 1985) have attempted to answer this question. What emerges from their research is that there are several rhythms of economic activity found in Taipei which depend on

Economy

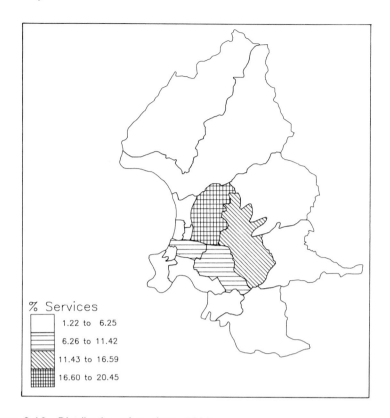

% Services

1.22 to 6.25

6.26 to 11.42

11.43 to 16.59

16.60 to 20.45

Figure 3.16 Distribution of services, 1986

one's occupation and shopping habits. In general peaks of activity occur between the hours of 10 and 11 a.m. and 2 to 4 p.m. One common link between all activity patterns is the long hours caught in traffic. Those involved in wholesale activities start earliest in the commuting day, with those in government, business, and up-scale retailing following in that order. In the evening it is business and government sectors which close first followed by up-scale services. One activity, food stalls, has two separate cycles: a short morning one which supplies commuters with breakfast or a light snack and then a long afternoon and evening one which provides snacks and meals until nearly midnight. These food activities have two general locational orientations: major commuting nodes and the neighborhoods in which the food sellers live.

Specific shopping patterns follow the well recognized notion of differences between convenience and shopping goods (Berry, 1967). For convenience goods shopping is done close to one's home or place of work. But large shifts have taken place in such convenience shopping. For example, during the 1950s and 1960s most food shopping was done once

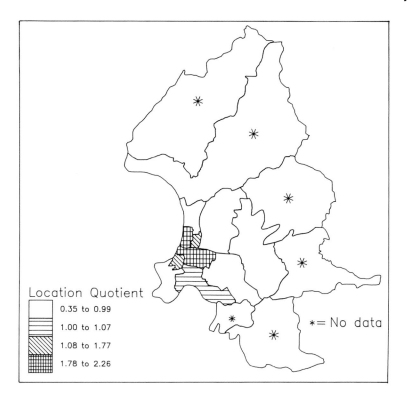

Figure 3.17 Location quotient, services, 1954

a day very early in the morning and focused on the 70 traditional markets maintained by the municipal government (Figure 3.19). Early shopping was necessary to ensure a supply of fresh foods at a period in Taipei's history when home refrigeration was not common; some last-minute shopping might be done just before the evening meal. While food shopping the shopper would find other goods and services offered within close proximity to the public market.

By the 1980s this pattern of early morning shopping had been radically modified. Several factors account for these shifts. First, refrigerators were found in some 98.76 percent of all Taipei households so that shopping did not have to be done on a daily basis. Secondly, the public markets had been challenged by the invasion of all night convenience stores such as the 7-Eleven chain and its Taiwan clones, and modern supermarkets including hypermarkets (Figure 3.20). Even the municipal government has had to respond to this change in shopping patterns by building in 1988 13 modern supermarkets and upgrading the general lighting and cleanliness of the other public markets (Lin, 1992). Furthermore, with more women working daily shopping is not as convenient.

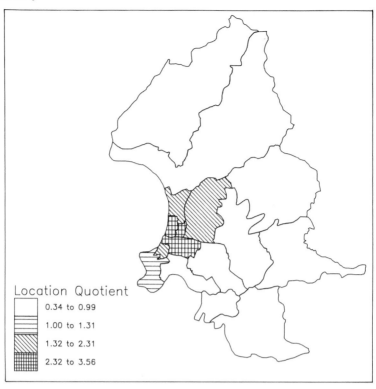

Location Quotient

	0.34 to 0.99
	1.00 to 1.31
	1.32 to 2.31
	2.32 to 3.56

Figure 3.18 Location quotient, services, 1986

A similar dichotomy between the old and new also exists in terms of shopping goods. For low-end products night stalls are still found throughout the city. These supplement more established areas such as the shopping district of Old Taipei, Wanhwa, and Haggler's Alley near the Main Post Office downtown. These night stalls remain very popular. According to Tsai (1981), 71 percent of the people he interviewed at night stalls liked them and saw a role for them in the modern Taipei economy. The government has tried to capitalize on their popularity in two ways. It has established special areas, such as under expressway overpasses, as designated speciality markets. Secondly, it has used the logical extension of night stalls, shopping streets, as the basis for urban renewal, such as the Dihua and Wahsi Special Districts in the western parts of Old Taipei. These two streets are part of the system of over 3000 such speciality shopping streets which were described in Chapter 2. Some of these streets, such as several streets in Chengchung district, specialize in books or medical equipment, and have been serving the public for four or five decades, while others such as Yenping North Road and its dozens of shops specializing in wedding gowns and trousseau items are relatively new.

Figure 3.19 Hsin-yi public market in 1968 was the focus of daily shopping, with vendors setting up carts outside

Figure 3.20 The Hsin-yi market in 1991 is all but abandoned, with vendors having been replaced with a 7-Eleven

At the upper end of the shopping scale there are specialized areas. It is hard to generalize about these areas for several reasons. First, at any one time there are several areas which contend for the title of being most fashionable. As this trophy passes along streets and between neighborhoods, individual stores may quickly see a change in occupant and good or service offered. A good example of this is the shift in perceived desirability in location which occurred during the 1960s and 1980s. During the 1960s Chungshan North Road was *the* place to go shopping, challenged only by the general, modern department stores in the western part of the Chengchung district, the Shimenting area, or Haggler's Alley. No doubt part of Chungshan North Road's attraction was the presence of several first class hotels, several very well designed insurance and bank buildings, and its proximity to the United States Commissary, Officers' Club, and Taipei Zoo at the extreme northern end of the road just before the bridge over the Keelung river. But by the 1980s the best location had shifted to the newer, eastern parts of Nanking East Road and Kuang-fu and Dun-fu North Roads. To be sure, Chungshan North Road still houses stores which offer an ever changing array of fashionable clothes and foods. However, it is the Kuang-fu–Dun-fu North Road area where stores offering Waterford crystal, Mercedes Benz cars, or Pierre Cardin fashions are likely to locate, along with foreign banks, airlines, and domestic and foreign corporate headquarters. Similarly, as fashions in food, clothing, and recreation change, all shopping areas see changes in the goods and services offered for sale. Secondly, each of the six new districts added to Taipei in 1968 had central and specialized shopping districts which have continued to function and to adapt to the overall changing Taipei economy.

There were also changes in the daily patterns of shop owners and providers of services during the period from the 1960s to the 1980s and 1990s. The main change was a separation of place of residence and place of work. During the 1960s and 1970s the two places literally coincided. In Chapter 2 the main architectural design which accommodated working where one lived was described as the shophouse, a two- or three-story building with a frontage of some four meters and an overhanging upper story which provided a sheltered passage for shoppers and pedestrians (Pannell, 1973). Typically a family lived in the back of the shop or directly over it. Shoppers frequently had to awaken a family member or interrupt a meal in order to obtain service. By the 1980s this residence/work link had begun to weaken. Of course, in older neighborhoods the link is still present for both retail sales and business offices. And even new office buildings and apartment complexes include both a first floor devoted to commercial space and the overhanging upper stories. But shop owners do not necessarily live behind their shops. This is especially true for the convenience stores, supermarkets, and bakeries which have no space behind them for living quarters. Fast food chains, which rely heavily on teenagers, also draw their labor supplies from outside their immediate neighborhoods. In addition there is growing concern and resentment toward business offices in residential buildings. All too often offices are in violation of both zoning and safety regulations, which has resulted in fires and accidents. Furthermore, once an office is in place in an apartment complex, the precedent turns into a temptation to allow the opening of additional manufacturing and businesses which further contribute to all forms of pollution and congestion. Despite the changes in work/residence patterns, therefore, the shophouse form has not been abandoned. Modern office buildings and apartment complexes frequently have space at the ground level for shops and the overhanging upper story. The use of the passage thus created has been modified as the change in work/residence patterns has come into effect. Previously the passage was accessible to shoppers and pedestrians, although some entrepreneurs would literally bring their shops into the passage. For example, bakers and tatami mat makers would frequently work out in the open especially in good weather. By the 1980s shop owners were less likely to be producing a good in the passage and more likely to have filled the walkway with racks of goods in order to attract customers or to display special sale items.

Summary

The economy of Taipei is somewhat more diverse than that of many cities owing to the presence of primary economic activities. Despite the fact that both primary and secondary activities are declining in importance, they both continue to have a significant impact on the landscape and to play important roles in employment patterns. The decline in these two sets of activities and the rise in service employment are a reflection of the continued importance of Taipei to the total economic development of the Republic of China. The shifts over time in the location of all economic activities reflect changes in ecological, economic, political, and social values within Taiwanese society, and can be readily understood in terms of location theories. Locational shifts within the city itself demonstrate the continued advantages of the Old City despite problems with pollution, transportation, and competition for space.

References

Alonzo, R. P. (1991) The Informal Sector in the Philippines, pp. 30–70, in A. L. Chickering and M. Salahdine, eds., *The Silent Revolution. The Informal Sector in Five Asian and Near Eastern Countries.* ICS Press, San Francisco.

Barber, G. M. (1988) *Elementary Statistics for Geographers*. Guildford Press, New York.

Berry, B. J. L. (1967) *Geography of Market Centers and Retail Distribution*. Prentice-Hall, Englewood Cliffs.

Central Daily News (1990) Taipei City Plan for Industrial Zone, Aug. 18, 8.*

Chen, C.-S. (1957) *Taipei*. Fu-Min Geographical Institute of Economic Development, Taipei.

Chen, K.-c. and H.-m. Chen (1983) Location of Bookstores and Consumers Shopping Behavior in Taipei, *Geographical Research* 9, 1–19.*

Chi, S. (1989) Restructuring Taiwan's Economy in the 1980's and Beyond, *Economic Review* 252, 8–21.

China Post (1987) Unlicensed Vendors Flourish, May 25, 5.

China Post (1991) Get Rid of Factories in Residential Areas (editorial), Jan. 26, 4.

Coffey, W. J. and J. J. McRae (1989) *Service Industries in Regional Development*. Institute for Research and Public Policy, Halifax, N.S.

Fok, G. (1990) Thirst for Better Life Quenched at Plantation, *Free China Journal* Sept. 3, 3.

Free China Journal (1988) Crime Does Not Pay, Dec. 1, 7.

Ho, C. S. (1988) *An Introduction to the Geology of Taiwan. Explanatory Text of the Geologic Map of Taiwan*. Second edition. Central Geological Survey, Ministry of Economic Affairs, Taipei.

Ho, C. S. and C. N. Lee (1963) *Economic Minerals of Taiwan*. Geological Survey of Taiwan, Taipei.

Hsia, H.-j. (1993) Director, Department of Business Management, Taipei City Government. Personal Correspondence, March 22.

Hsieh, C. M. (1964) *Taiwan-ilha Formosa. A Geography in Perspective*. Butterworths, Washington, D.C.

Huang, H. (1993) Success of Roadside Stalls Makes Crackdown Difficult, *Free China Journal*, 9 March, 6.

Huang, Y. M. (1983) The Business of the People Congregates on Special City Streets, *Free China Review* 33:4, 4–21.

Lai, C. (n.d.) *Research on the Taipei Land Price Problem*. Taiwan Commercial Press, Taipei.*

Lan, S.-c. (1987) Health Foods Phenomenon Takes ROC by Storm, *Free China Review* 37:5, 40–45.

Lee, S. F. (1981) Analysis of Metal Products Industry in Taipei, *Geographical Research* 7, 129–152.*

Lee, S. F. (1982) A Quantitative Analysis of Manufacturing Location in the (*sic*) Old Taipei City, *Geographical Research* 8, 41–77.*

Lin, D. (1992) Taipei Acts to Bring Order to Clutter Caused by Old Street Markets, *Free China Journal* May 22, 5.

McKee, D. L. (1988) *Growth, Development, and the Service Economy in the Third World*. Praeger, New York.

1967 Taiwan Demographic Fact Book, Republic of China (1968) Department of Civil Affairs, Taiwan Provincial Government, Nantou.

1986 Taiwan-Fukien Demographic Fact Book, Republic of China (1987) Ministry of the Interior, Taipei.

Orru, M. (1991) Institutional Logic of Small-firm Economies in Italy and Taiwan, *Studies in Comparative International Development* 26, 3–28.

Pannell, C. W. (1973) *T'ai-chung, Taiwan: Structure and Function*. The University of Chicago, Department of Geography, Research Paper no. 144, Chicago.

Price, D. G. and A. M. Blair (1989) *The Changing Geography of the Service Sector*. Belhaven Press, New York.

Quinn, A. (1991) Dateline Taipei; City Hooked on Indoor Fishing, *South China Morning Post*, Jan. 19.

Report on the Survey of Illegal Factories in Taipei City and Sanchung City of Taipei Hsien (1967) Urban and Housing Development Committee of CIECD, Taipei.

Riddle, D. I. (1986) *Service Led Growth. The Role of the Service Sector in World Development*. Praeger, New York.

Selya, R. M. (1977) Urban Agriculture in Taiwan: Anachronism or Ecological and Nutritional Safety Valve? *China Geographer* 8, 15–28.

Selya, R. M. (1980) Food For the Cities of Taiwan, *China Geographer* 11, 72–88.

Selya, R. M. (1992) Illegal Migration in Taiwan: A Preliminary Overview, *International Migration Review* 26, 787–805.

Song, S. F. (1990) Small Culture, *Free China Journal* Aug. 20.

Taylor, P. J. (1977) *Quantitative Methods in Geography. An Introduction to Spatial Analysis*. Houghton-Mifflin, Boston.

Tsai, W. T. (1977) A Geographical Study on the Daily Rhythm of Functional Activities in Taipei Area, *Geographical Research* 3, 171–214.*

Tsai, W. T. (1978) A Study on the Functional Activities of Major Shopping Streets in Towns and Cities in the Keelung–Taipei–Taoyuan Area, *Geographical Research* 4, 117–150.*

Tsai, W. T. (1981) A Geographical Study on the Functional Activities of Tall Buildings in City Centers – A Case of the Five Largest Cities in Taiwan Area, *Geographical Research* 7, 175–212.*

Tsai, W. T. (1985) A Study on the Night Stalls in Taipei Area, *Geographical Research* 11, 145–172.*

Wang, E. (1986) Suburban Farmers Cultivate Tourists, *Free China Review* 36:2, 28–35.

Wieman, E. (1987) Growth in Services, *Free China Review* 37:1, 40–45.

4
Population

Since 1949 the population of Taiwan has grown from 503 430 to some 2 702 678 in 1989. In this chapter the origins, demographic implications and consequences of this growth are explored. In particular issues relating to growth, spatial distribution and density, structure and dependency, and ethnicity are considered.

Growth

The basic data for tracking population growth are found in Table 4.1. The growth of population in Taipei has averaged 3.48 percent a year. On a cumulative basis this represents an increase of some 363 percent – or about twice the national average. The yearly increases are not uniform, but can be grouped into four periods. From 1949 through 1969, growth averaged some 5.02 percent a year. From 1970 to 1974 growth slowed to an average of 3.47 percent. During the period 1975 to 1988 growth further slowed to 2.28 percent a year. From 1989 onwards growth has averaged 0.70 percent a year. In reality this average distorts the fact that growth rates for Taipei City are approaching negative figures and that demographers are expecting that beginning in 1992 actual growth will be negative and remain so for some time.

Spatially growth has been quite different (Figure 4.1). As might be expected the older districts of Taipei grew more slowly than the districts added during the 1960s. Chengchung, Chiencheng, and Lungshan districts actually experienced a net population loss over the period, while Kuting, Yenping, Tatong, and Shuangyuan hardly grew at all. In contrast Chingmei, Neihu, Nankang, Mucha, Peitou, and Shihlin grew rapidly.

90

Table 4.1 Population growth

Year	Population	% Increase	CBR	CDR	Density	Net migration
1954						15 440
1955	852 670		40.1	5.56	3 137	13 723
1956	907 756	6.46	39.5	5.17	3 335	18 690
1957	943 805	3.98	36.3	5.55	3 468	5 062
1958	990 230	4.91	36.9	4.89	3 638	10 274
1959	1 041 214	5.15	35.7	4.79	3 826	13 830
1960	1 096 891	5.35	33.7	4.72	4 030	18 524
1961	1 131 084	3.12	31.7	4.35	4 155	12 497
1962	1 201 292	6.20	31.2	4.26	4 414	15 819
1963	1 261 422	5.01	30.9	4.18	4 635	21 147
1964	1 332 542	5.64	30.1	3.98	4 896	29 097
1965	1 400 536	5.10	27.8	3.86	5 145	23 182
1966	1 459 261	4.19	27.7	3.90	5 361	11 404
1967	1 525 367	4.54	25.1	3.88	5 604	24 868
1968	1 604 543	5.18	26.8	4.13	5 896	44 524
1969	1 689 732	5.31	25.1	3.84	6 291	72 263
1970	1 740 838	3.02	25.9	3.78	6 502	18 956
1971	1 804 605	3.66	24.1	3.75	6 750	33 300
1972	1 874 354	3.87	22.5	3.66	7 015	34 043
1973	1 933 732	3.17	21.7	3.62	7 156	14 336
1974	2 003 604	3.61	21.8	3.69	7 362	9 407
1975	2 043 318	1.98	20.6	3.62	7 508	5 337
1976	2 089 288	2.25	23.4	3.60	7 677	5 119
1977	2 127 625	1.83	20.5	3.78	7 818	3 085
1978	2 163 605	1.69	20.6	3.68	7 950	−236
1979	2 196 237	1.51	21.1	3.74	8 070	−5 197
1980	2 220 427	1.10	19.9	3.71	8 159	−11 620
1981	2 270 983	2.28	19.6	3.81	8 345	15 085
1982	2 372 641	4.48	18.7	3.76	8 553	22 363
1983	2 388 374	0.66	17.4	3.79	8 775	28 761
1984	2 449 702	2.57	16.6	3.70	9 001	30 143
1985	2 507 620	2.36	15.7	3.71	9 213	28 132
1986	2 575 180	2.69	13.9	3.63	9 475	41 236
1987	2 637 100	2.40	14.1	3.74	9 703	34 861
1988	2 681 857	1.70	15.4	3.87	9 868	14 017
1989	2 702 678	0.78	14.2	3.82	9 944	−7 226

Surprisingly one old district, Sungshan, also grew rapidly. Growth or decline did not occur simultaneously, however. During the 1950s Mucha, Nankang, and Shuangyuan grew most rapidly. Peitou and Shihlin experienced their fastest growth during the mid-1960s. Sungshan experienced a long period of fast growth from the mid-1950s until the mid-1970s. On the decline side Chengchung, Chiencheng, Lungshan, and Yenping first experienced losses during the late 1950s. These losses continued until the early 1970s when Lungshan, Kuting, Shuangyuan, and

Population

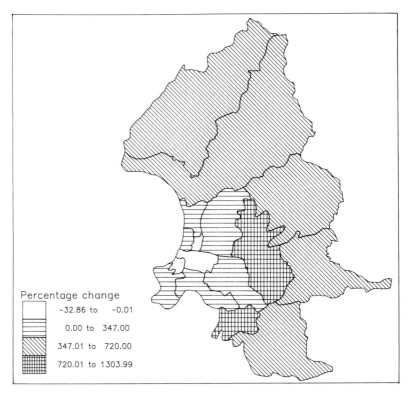

Figure 4.1 Population growth

Tatong began experiencing declines. During the 1980s Chengchung, Chiencheng, Lungshan, Shuangyuan, Tatong, and Yenping continued to lose population.

Sources of growth: migration

There has been considerable interest in determining the sources of population growth and change in Taipei. It has been estimated that during the 1950s and 1960s migration accounted for some 40 percent of all population growth in Taipei (World Bank, 1972). During the 1960s this percentage went up to 43 (World Bank, 1972). For the period 1968–1973 Tsay (1982) has given three estimates. Using data from population registrations, he finds that 45 percent of the growth was due to migration. Since the Taipei City population is estimated to be 8 percent underenumerated, he corrected the registration data to account for people who never changed their residency registrations or who registered late, and finds that immigration accounted for 51 percent of the growth. Finally he corrected the data to account for the probable negative impact of migration on fertility and derives a direct 52 percent migration impact and an indirect immigration impact of 30 percent. Speare and Liu (1977) argue that migration would have been even greater had it not been for the transportation system which permitted commuting.

The early 1970s mark two important changes in the impact of migration on the population of Taipei City. Up to 1973 migrants were from predominantly rural areas. Huang (1984) has estimated that 60 percent of the immigrants came from rural areas. Young women 20–25 years old tended to dominate the migration streams, presumably because their male counterparts were still serving in the military (Speare and Liu, 1977), and since there were job openings for young, educated women in both manufacturing and services. In general migrants were better educated than their Taipei City counterparts (Speare and Liu, 1977), and as such quickly moved into white-collar occupations (Tsay, 1983). After the mid-1970s the net number of migrants has declined and sometimes been negative. So large is this net outmigration that by 1978 100 percent of population growth was due to natural increase alone; by 1989 the percent of growth attributable to natural increase stood at 170 percent!

In addition to the migration streams becoming negative, the sources of new migrants also changed. After 1973 it has been estimated that 17 percent of the migrants came from other major cities in Taiwan (such as Keelung, Taichung, Tainan, and Kaohsiung); an additional 37 percent came from other urban areas, especially those with populations greater than 250 000 (Speare and Liu, 1977). Those migrants from rural areas tended to come from the central mountain areas and the east coast and in general were less educated and more unskilled than the migrants who had come earlier (Liu, 1986). Although this group of migrants had no trouble finding jobs, the jobs they did find tended to be inadequate with respect to both income and educational levels (Liu, 1986).

Sources of growth: fertility and mortality

Given the importance of the rate of natural increase in the growth of Taipei's population, it is of value to analyze how it has changed over time. Figure 4.2 shows the changes in the crude birth rates and crude death rates from 1954 on. The death rate has declined from 5.29 to 1.04, or a decline of 27.79 percent. Although the general trend of the change is decline, there were 12 years when the crude death rate actually went up. The largest of the increases in the death rate occurred during the 1950s and 1960s when outbreaks of cholera were still a problem. In contrast the crude birth rate has declined from 39.64 to 3.82, or a decline of 64.08 percent. Again despite an overall decline, there were some 10 years when the crude birth rate actually increased. The largest of these increases occurred in 1976, when the crude birth rate shot up some 13.39 percent compared to the

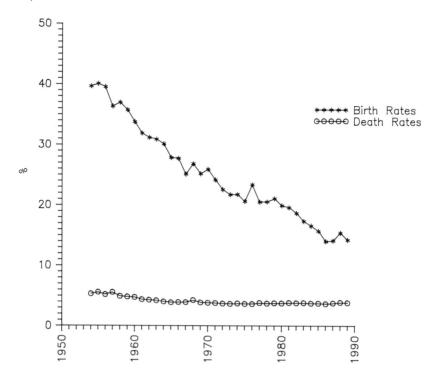

Figure 4.2 Demographic transition

level of 1975. Other years showing large increases were 1968 (with an increase of 6.98 percent), 1970, 1979, 1983, 1987, and 1988 (with increases averaging 3.04 percent). Two alternative explanations for these increases can be constructed. First, some of the years, such as 1976 and 1988, may represent reactions to slowdowns in the growth of the Taiwan economy. It is not uncommon when the economy starts to slow down and layoffs occur for the marriage rate to go up, with the following year showing an increase in the crude birth rate. One major problem with this explanation is that there were other years, such as 1983 and 1985, when aggregate economic growth rates showed marked declines and the marriage rate did not go up, and the crude birth rate continued to decline. Goodkind (1991) has suggested a second possible explanation for increases in crude birth rates. He argues that now that modern birth control devices are available, Chinese populations can make more active use of the traditional 12 year Chinese zodiacal cycles where certain animals (such as the dragon) are seen as especially good years to conceive and bear children. As it would happen, both 1976 and 1988 were years of the dragon. Interestingly, Taipei was not the only Chinese area to display increases; they were also found in Taiwan, Singapore, Peninsular Malaysia

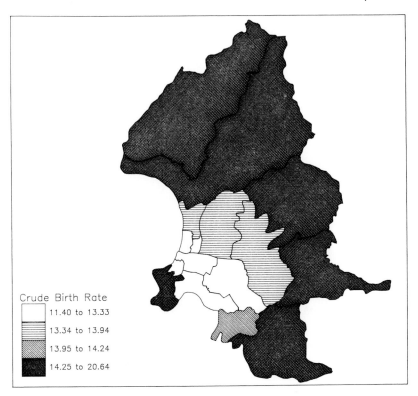

Figure 4.3 Crude birth rate, 1989

(amongst the Chinese), Hong Kong, and the People's Republic of China. Other years associated with other zodiacal signs may have an equally strong influence on the year to year shifts in the crude birth rate, thus leading to deviations from a generally downward trend in fertility.

Despite their overall temporal decline, crude birth rates in Taipei display particularly similar and stable spatial patterns. Since there is a high correlation between measures of fertility (crude birth, general fertility, and the total fertility rates) and year to year spatial patterns of these measures, only the map of birth rates for 1989 is included (Figure 4.3). In general the old district of Shuangyuan and new districts of the city display the highest crude birth rates; the highest crude birth rate is found in the new district of Neihu. Old city core districts, especially Chengchung, Chiencheng, Ta-an, Kuting, and Yenping, consistently have the lowest crude birth rates. All districts have experienced similar declines in the crude birth rate in the order of some 61.89 percent. Interestingly Shuangyuan and Nankang, both high birth rate areas, experienced the largest proportional drop in the crude birth rate, while Neihu, with the highest crude birth rate, lagged behind all the districts in decline. The

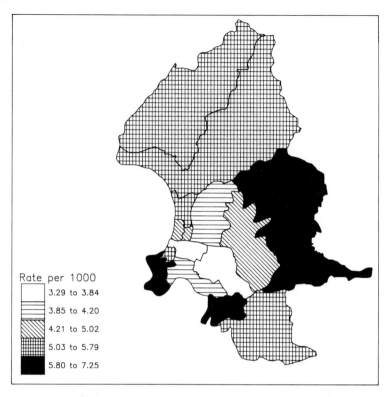

Figure 4.4 Crude death rate, 1961

spatial pattern of fertility is related to patterns of migration and population structure, to be discussed below.

The other component of natural increase, mortality, is somewhat more complicated. As we have seen, the decrease in the crude death rate is smaller than the decline in fertility. At first glance there seems to have been a complete reversal in the spatial patterns of the crude death rates. As seen in Figure 4.4, in 1961 the areas with the highest crude death rates were the new districts and Shuangyuan. In 1989 only the old districts of Ta-an and Yenping have low crude death rates; the rest of the old districts have experienced increases in the crude death rate, especially Sungshan and Kuting, while all the new districts have much lower crude death rates (Figure 4.5). Since crude death rates are sensitive to the sex–age structure of the population (Lilienfeld and Lilienfeld, 1980), the time series data for Taipei as a whole and the district data for 1989 were standardized using the population of 1961 as the standard. The age-adjusted death rates for all of Taipei are all *lower* than the crude death rate, suggesting that a combination of factors has influenced mortality: lower fertility, and inmigration of workers in their twenties who have aged *in situ*. Spatially

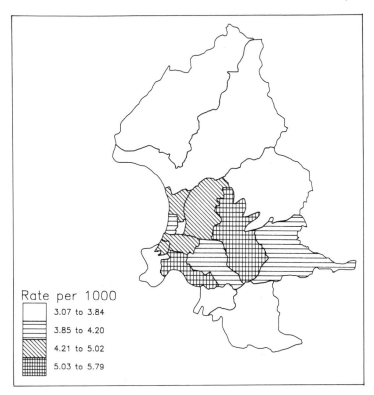

Figure 4.5 Crude death rate, 1989

(Figure 4.6) what we find is that among the older districts Lungshan, Kuting, Sungshan, and Ta-an have experienced a significant increase in the proportion of their populations in the older age groups and thus have higher crude death rates; among the new districts only Shihlin displays any significant difference between the crude and age-adjusted death rates. The reason for the difference is the same as that for the older districts.

Mortality has declined in Taipei for reasons beyond migration and ageing of the population. One main reason for the decline is that Taipei City, as with all of Taiwan, has gone through the epidemiological transition (Omran, 1971). Basically this means that the leading causes of death have shifted from infectious and parasitic diseases to chronic and degenerative diseases. Taipei does not fit this model precisely since vascular lesions of the central nervous system and cancer were the two leading causes of death in 1961 (see Table 4.2). But pneumonia, gastritis, and tuberculosis were significant causes and have declined, as is the case for pneumonia, or disappeared from the list of major killers. (In contrast infectious diseases such as diphtheria, typhoid fever, Japanese encephalitis, malaria, infectious tuberculosis, and hepatitis type B remain public health

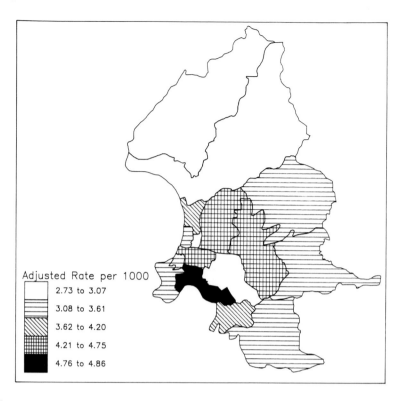

Figure 4.6 Age-adjusted death rate, 1989

problems requiring constant vigilance.) Taipei's low rate of death due to infectious diseases so early in its modern urban history is no doubt related to the effectiveness of the basic public health and environmental sanitation measures, such as access to tap water and either sewerage or septic tanks, first implemented by the Japanese and then extended by the Chinese (Barclay, 1954, 136–38; *Taiwan 2000*, 1989).

The conversion of agricultural land to urban uses also helped to reduce the incidence of intestinal infectious and parasitic diseases, both by paving over areas and cutting down on wind-blown transmission, and by reducing the use of night soil and the resulting exposure to parasitic diseases.

What of the role of improved medical facilities and increases in the number of medical personnel in reducing mortality? To be sure the number of these has increased dramatically (Table 4.3). In addition, from 1970 on the health infrastructure was improved. Not only were new hospitals and clinics built, but older institutions such as the MacKay, Seventh Day Adventist, and National Taiwan University hospitals were all either rebuilt or major new additions constructed (Figures 2.12 and 2.14).

Table 4.2 Major causes of death

Rank	Cause	1961			Rank	Cause	1989		
		No. cases	Rate	% All deaths			No. cases	Rate	% All deaths
1	Vascular lesions CNS	524	55.8	13.11	1	Cancer	2 552	95.96	25.19
2	Cancer	432	46.0	10.81	2	Cerebro-vascular diseases	1 537	57.79	15.17
3	Senility	351	37.38	8.75	3	Accidents	1 053	39.59	10.40
4	Other heart diseases	338	35.99	8.66	4	Heart disease	994	37.38	9.81
5	Pneumonia	259	30.78	7.23	5	Diabetes	448	16.55	4.42
6	Gastritis	253	26.94	6.33	6	Hypertension	286	10.75	2.82
7	Tuberculosis	230	24.49	5.75	7	Chronic cirrhosis	270	10.15	2.67
8	Accidents	224	23.85	5.60	8	Pneumonia	263	9.89	2.60
9	Infancy	114	12.14	2.85	9	Nephritis	212	7.87	2.09
10	Suicide	90	9.58	2.25	10	Bronchitis and emphysema	208	7.82	2.05
	All deaths	5 311	469.55			All deaths	10 398	384.73	

Sources: *Taiwan Provincial Health Administration, Annual Report* (1961); *Health and Vital Statistics. 2, Vital Statistics* (1990).

Table 4.3 Health facilities

	1954	1989
Hospitals and clinics		
Hospitals		
provincial	5	2
municipal	3	9
public	1	9
private	13	82
Clinics		
municipal	9	18
public	2	6
private	883	2 121
Personnel		
Physicians	554	4 825
Dentists	131	1 722
Pharmacists	241	2 771
Midwives	254	157
Nurses	1	8 807
Dispensers	83	1 178
Traditional practitioners	253	817

Beyond these broad improvements, however, there is the question of accessibility and use. These issues can be brought into focus by reviewing the correlations between the crude, infant, and age-adjusted death rates and the ratios between the population and the number of physicians and the number of hospitals (Table 4.4). For 1954 the correlations are *positive* for the crude death rate and both the health facilities measures. For 1989 all the correlations are *negative*, as would be expected. However, the correlations are all very low, and the correlations between the infant mortality rates and the population:physician and population:hospital ratios are not even statistically significant. No doubt the unexpected positive correlations for 1954 reflect the generally underdeveloped state of health care in Taipei. But what accounts for the low correlations in 1989?

The answers lie in the distribution and structure of health facilities in Taipei. Indices of dissimilarity for hospitals compared to population have decreased from 23.26 in 1954 to 18.38 in 1989. This reflects a deliberate government policy of putting one large, comprehensive, hospital in each of the major commercial and residential districts, and locating these along major transport routes (Liu, 1978). However, in terms of location quotients, this policy has had a limited impact on the relative distribution of hospitals. In 1954 four out of the ten districts (Chengchung, Chiencheng, Kuting, and Lungshan) had location quotients above 1.00. In 1989 six of the ten old districts (Chengchung, Chiencheng, Chungshan,

Table 4.4 Health correlations

Variables	1954	1989
CDR & Population/physicians	0.5733	−0.2975
CDR & Population/hospitals	0.4042	−0.3640
IMR & Population/physicians		0.0637*
IMR & Population/hospitals		0.0164*
AADR & Population/physicians		−0.1373
AADR & Population/hospitals		−0.1860

* Not statistically significant
Key: CDR: Crude death rate; IMR: Infant mortality rate; AADR: Age-adjusted death rate

Kuting, Lungshan, and Yenping) had location quotients above 1.00. None of the new districts has location quotients above 1.00.

What has evolved therefore is a three-level system of hospitals (Liu, 1978). Level one includes the national training and research hospitals such as National Taiwan University, Veterans, and Military Hospitals. In terms of location and utilization it is important to realize that some 40 percent of their patients come from outside Taipei City. This group of hospitals is located in the parts of the city with the lowest (i.e. sometimes negative) population growth. Their location in the old, southwest part of the city is a function of history, availability of land, and overall accessibility to their potential patients.

Level two facilities provide general medical treatment and are usually preferred by Taipei residents, in part because many of these facilities are public ones, thus providing free treatment and services. These facilities also tend to be located within Old Taipei. In general 50 percent of their patients live within three kilometers of the hospital.

The level three facilities comprise mostly public clinic type units. In addition to promoting general public health, they also provide a wide range of services such as outpatient services, physical examinations, women and child care, and family health care. In general people travel up to five kilometers from their homes to use these facilities.

In terms of overall distribution, Liu (1978) concludes from the analysis of the three levels of hospital facilities that there are zones of surplus and shortages. Chengchung and Lungshan are areas of surplus, and Nankang and Neihu areas of the most severe shortages.

In terms of the distribution of physicians, the indices of dissimilarity increase from 17.92 in 1954 to 22.82 in 1989. In terms of physician: population ratios in 1954 the highest are in Sungshan, Shuangyuan, and Tatong. In 1989 they are highest in Mucha, Neihu, Shuangyuan, and Sungshan. In terms of location quotients in 1954 half of the Old City districts (Shuangyuan, Sungshan, Ta-an, Tatong, and Yenping) had quotients below 1.00. By 1989 the pattern had shifted and only Chiencheng, Shuangyuan, Sungshan, and Tatong had ratios below 1.00, while only Peitou amongst the new districts had a quotient above 1.00. The apparent inconsistency between the location quotients and indices of dissimilarity on the one hand and the population:physician ratio on the other indicates several things. One is that the areas with high population:physician ratios are all in the fastest growing parts of the city and no doubt reflect physicians' general preferences for this type of demographic environment (Lankford, 1974; Reskin and Capell, 1974). In contrast, physicians also prefer locations with good accessibility to level one and two hospitals.

Distribution and density

The changing location of population in Taipei City can be described using four different measures: distribution (discussed as percent of total Taipei population in each district), location quotients (comparing the percent of total Taipei population in each district with the percent of total Taipei land area in each district), indices of dissimilarity derived from Lorenz curves (which graphically display the summed percent of population and area based on ranked ratios of density), and density of population (number of persons per square kilometer). All four measures show basically the same pattern: the old districts of Taipei are gradually being emptied while the populations of the new districts are increasing.

Before discussing the perspectives which these four measures give on distribution, it is important to remember that regardless of how large the Taipei population was, is, or will be, there are both environmental and legal constraints on distribution. There are two environmental constraints, the first of which is topographic. According to Meng (1982) some 40.25 percent of Taipei is higher than 50 meters above sea level. Although the center of Taipei Basin is virtually flat, as one goes out in all directions hills, slopes, and mountains gradually intrude, especially in the new districts. In order to preserve these areas and avoid problems with slope development, areas over 50 meters have been protected by placing them in forest protection or scenic zones. Planners have generally assumed that this land above 50 meters also involves slopes in excess of 30 percent and as such should not be subject to intensive development. Their argument is that the cost of foundations and retaining walls and the extra cost of road and utilities services would render these areas unfit for development merely from an economic point of view. In addition, modification of the slopes is not recommended since the geology of the hilly areas makes contour modification difficult. Were such modifications to be made the areas would then be subject to slides when saturated with heavy rainfall and vibrated by constant minor earthquakes (*Taipei-Keelung Metropolitan Regional Plan*, 1968).

The second environmental constraint is flooding. Given the heavy precipitation in Taipei Basin, the flat nature of the basin floor, the silting of the Tamshui river, and the disturbance of local drainage patterns by urban building, flooding is a problem along the Tamshui and its tributaries. Thus those areas adjacent to the rivers are not only too environmentally sensitive to permit high density occupation, but flood control walls also consume space which would otherwise be available to urban uses. Historically only the poor occupy this environment (Herr, 1968). Programs to deal with flooding are discussed in Chapter 6.

The legal constraints to settlement include the equalization of land rights, land expropriation, and city land consolidation schemes. These are discussed in more detail in Chapter 5.

Distribution

Given these constraints the distribution and density of population can be more readily understood. During the 1950s Chungshan district had the largest share of Taipei's population followed by Ta-an, Kuting, and Chengchung, in that order. During the 1960s all four districts lost some of their relative shares of population while Shuangyuan, Sungshan, and Tatong grew. By the end of the 1980s Sungshan has regained its place as the major population center of Taipei while Shihlin, Peitou, and Neihu also attracted significantly larger populations. In terms of overall patterns of shift in population distribution over the study period, Sungshan and Chingmei grew the fastest, followed by Peitou, Shihlin, Neihu, Nankang, and Mucha (i.e. the new districts). Chengchung, Chiencheng, and Lungshan actually experienced population declines while the other old districts grew more slowly than even the slowest growing new districts (Figures 4.7 and 4.8).

In other words, it seems that the population distribution of Taipei has become more equal. This is confirmed by the indices of dissimilarity derived from Lorenz curves (Table 4.5). In 1954 and 1955 population stood at its most unequal distribution with an index of dissimilarity of 0.5979. By 1986 it had declined to 0.399 and seemed to be stabilizing.

Location quotients also confirm these trends although different patterns of growth are found. During the 1950s all of the new districts had location quotients below 1.00. The highest quotients, ranging from 11.50 to 21.47, were found in the old districts of Chiencheng, Yenping, and Shuangyuan; Kuting, Chengchung, and Tatong had quotients ranging from 4.96 to 11.49. The remaining old districts were above 1.00 but below 4.96. By the late 1980s all of the old districts and the new district of Chingmei had a

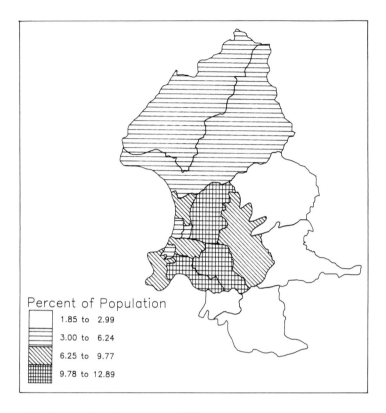

Figure 4.7 Population distribution, 1961

location quotient below 1.00. Nankang, Peitou, and Shihlin had the highest quotients in the range 2.00 to 2.71. Nankang and Neihu had quotients in the range 1.00 to 1.99. The overall shifts in quotients over the study period show Peitou and Shihlin gaining the most, followed by Nankang and Neihu. All the old districts plus Chingmei have negative shifts in location quotients with Chengchung, Chiencheng, Kuting, Lungshan, Tatong, and Yenping experiencing the greatest negative shifts.

Density

In terms of density two patterns have evolved. First, overall density has increased in the city as a whole from 4161 persons per square kilometer in 1954 to 9945 persons per square kilometer in 1989, or an increase of 2.4 times. Yet at the district level there have been both an amelioration and an increase of densities. For example, in 1954 the highest density was 67 262 in Chiencheng; density was quite high also in Lungshan and Yenping with

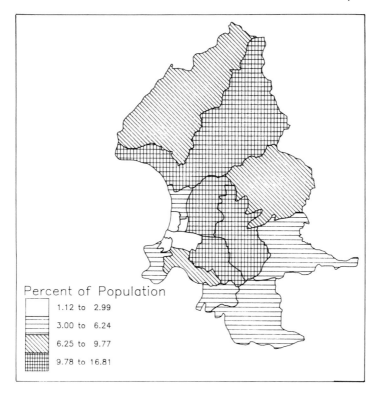

Figure 4.8 Population distribution, 1989

Table 4.5 Indices of dissimilarity for population distribution

Year	Index	Year	Index
1954	0.5979	1966	0.5555
1955	0.5977	1971	0.5300
1957	0.5914	1976	0.4852
1959	0.5869	1981	0.4349
1961	0.5756	1986	0.3990

densities in the range of 35 609 to 55 792. The new districts plus Chungshan and Sungshan had fairly low densities, in the range 500 to 8527. By 1989 the highest densities were in the range of 19 825 to 39 988 (in all of the old districts except Chengchung); the new districts had increased their densities some to the range 3832 to 8527, with Chingmei having a moderately high density of 19 737. In terms of overall shifts in density for the study period, Chiencheng and Yenping experienced overall

105

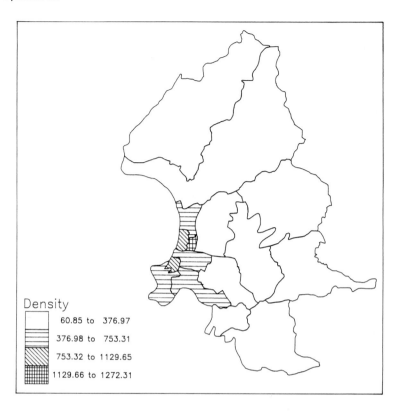

Figure 4.9 Population density, 1961

declines in density, while the rest of the old districts, with the exception of Sungshan, experienced moderate increases. Nankang, Mucha, Peitou, and Shihlin had slightly elevated increases while Chingmei and Sungshan experienced high increases. Neihu had the largest increase in density (Figures 4.9 and 4.10).

All the measures of distribution and density show similar patterns, raising the twin issues of why these shifts occurred and what demographic processes produced them. Meng (1982) argued that the redistribution of population is not the same as that seen in Western cities since the movement out from the center was not as strong. He saw accessibility and transportation as the key influences on redistribution. In contrast Liu (1986) sees redistribution as a response to the modernization of business organization (with increased separation of places of residence and work), increased use of both private and public transportation, and an overall rise in the standard of living. Regardless of which economic or social processes operated to induce people to move, it is internal migration which actually created these new patterns.

106

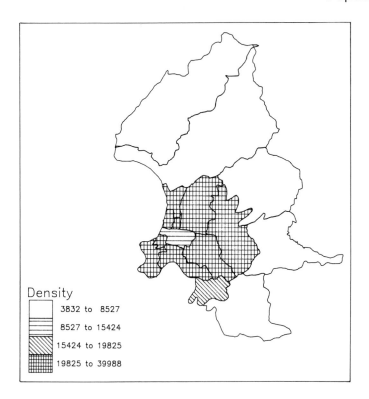

Figure 4.10 Population density, 1989

Two migration patterns must be considered. First, there is inmigration. Although the general outline of where people migrated from was discussed in the above section on growth, here the areas which received the migrants are enumerated. By ranking the number of migrants coming into each district preferred and undesirable areas can be listed. Chungshan, Kuting, Shihlin, Sungshan, and Ta-an fall into the former category, while Chengchung, Chiencheng, Lungshan, Mucha, Nankang, Tatong, and Yenping fall into the latter one. Since both groups contain mixes of both old and new districts, no clear preferences in those terms are discernible. An alternative approach to measuring the importance of migration is to calculate the inmigration rate. On this scale all the new districts were the most desirable places, and all the old districts were the least desirable. This pattern suggests that migrants in general did not become acculturated into the city via the immigrant ladder as was the case for American immigrants (Ward, 1968).

The second migration pattern is that of intra-urban movements. Again two approaches to the phenomenon are possible. First is the pattern of internal movement within districts. Over the years the rate of such movements has gone down. For the period 1969 to 1980 the average rate of internal movements was 63.46 per 1000 residents; from 1981 to 1987 the rate averaged 53.48, while during the last years of the 1980s it fell again to 42.08. Kuting, Peitou, Sungshan, and Ta-an all displayed high rates of internal movement, while Chengchung, Chiencheng, Neihu, and Yenping displayed low rates. In regard to intra-district movements a similar pattern of falling averages is seen: from 1969 to 1980 the average rate of intra-district migration was 77.79; during all the 1980s it averaged 65.66. Preferred areas of such intra-district migration changed over time. Before 1975 Chungshan and Sungshan were the preferred targets; Neihu and Ta-an become fashionable from the late 1970s on. Chengchung has a fairly consistent appeal. The least appealing areas with net inmigration were Peitou and Shuangyuan. In contrast Chengchung, Chienchung, and Yenping were the neighborhoods most likely to lose residents to other districts, while Nankang, Neihu, and Peitou were the least likely to do so.

Structure and dependency

Given the importance of migration into and within Taipei it is no surprise that the demographic structure of the population has shifted dramatically since 1954. Three measures are used to document the changes: sex–age pyramids, sex ratios, and dependency ratios.

Sex–age pyramids

Figures 4.11 and 4.12 show the sex–age structure of Taipei for two years, 1961 and 1990. Several features are clear. During the 1950s and 1960s there were high birth rates. The difficult times of the transition from Japanese to Chinese rule clearly appear with a smaller than expected cohort. For all ages except 70 plus the 1961 pyramid is distorted in favor of males. In contrast the 1989 pyramid shows the effects of declining fertility and heavy inmigration especially of females. Nevertheless, the same unnatural bias in favor of men appears for the age groups 55 and over. If past and current trends continue then the sex–age structure of Taipei will soon evolve into a cartouche shape and then into a narrow based football, indicating at first a no-growth and then a contracting population.

Sex ratios

The unusual bias in favor of men in certain age groups can also be seen in the sex ratios in Taipei (Table 4.6). Assuming that a normal population

Age Group (years)

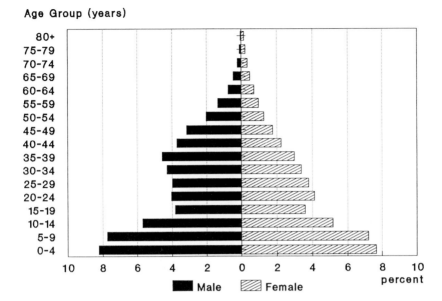

Figure 4.11 Population pyramid, total population, 1961

Age Group (years)

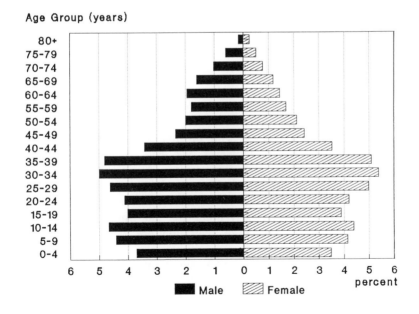

Figure 4.12 Population pyramid, total population, 1990

Population

Table 4.6 Sex and dependency ratios

Year	Sex ratio	Dependency ratio	%<15	%>65
1954	117.85	83.0	78.5	0.5
1962	115.34	76.4	41.4	1.8
1963	116.69	75.5	41.0	2.1
1964	123.45	75.7	40.6	2.1
1965	116.10	75.2	40.6	2.2
1966	114.26	74.9	39.7	2.2
1967	113.79	71.0	39.2	2.2
1968	113.42	64.6	36.9	2.3
1969	118.15	64.6	36.9	2.3
1970	116.66	63.2	36.3	2.4
1971	116.20	61.3	35.4	2.6
1972	114.55	60.1	35.1	2.7
1973	113.24	59.6	34.4	2.8
1974	111.88	58.3	33.7	2.9
1975	110.42	56.8	33.0	3.0
1976	109.76	55.6	32.5	3.2
1977	109.34	55.1	32.0	3.3
1978	108.73	53.4	31.2	3.6
1979	107.92	52.5	30.6	3.8
1980	107.37	51.2	30.0	4.0
1981	106.49	50.9	29.4	4.2
1982	105.98	50.3	29.0	4.4
1983	105.42	50.0	28.7	4.5
1984	104.36	49.8	28.3	4.7
1985	104.36	48.2	27.2	5.0
1986	103.85	48.0	27.0	5.2
1987	103.34	47.4	26.3	5.5
1988	102.98	46.8	25.8	5.7
1989	102.42	46.1	25.5	5.9

has a sex ratio in the range 99 to 101, it is obvious from the data in Table 4.6 that Taipei's population is not normal. What explains this deviation from other populations? One possible source would be a male-dominated migration stream. However, we have seen that females in general have dominated the migration streams. Again the data in Table 4.6 clearly show that males grossly dominated for only four years, and for perhaps nine years during the 1970s there was a near balance in the streams; after 1980 females clearly dominate. But what the data clearly suggest is that factors other than migration are responsible for the distorted overall sex ratios.

Coale (1991) has shown that such situations can result from the interaction of three possible demographic processes: male-dominated migration streams, lower age-specific death rates for males, or biased sex ratios at birth. For the Taipei case, male-dominated migration streams can be discounted. So too can lower age-specific male death rates. It is just the

110

opposite: for any year since 1954 females have had lower age-specific death rates. This leaves only grossly biased sex ratios at birth. In fact Taipei has had excessive sex ratios at birth and the ratios become more distorted with each passing year. On a district by district basis only Chengchung, Kuting, Musha, Nankang, Ta-an, and Yenping have sex ratios at birth within the normal ranges. Since these districts all have widely different inmigration rates, migration alone cannot account for these distorted sex ratios at birth. Neither can migration alone account for the spatial variations in overall sex ratios. Since the problem of grossly distorted sex ratios was only brought to the attention of Taiwan demographers in 1992, no final conclusions regarding the causes of the distortion have been derived. However, the implications of the distortions are clear: marriage patterns will be severely distorted since there are not enough females, and with increasing numbers of elderly men unmarried, new means will have to be found for caring for these men. Both implications suggest a breakdown in traditional Chinese family orientations and values.

Dependency

The final measure of population structure is that of dependency. The dependency ratio in Old Taipei increased during the 1950s and 1960s, reaching a peak of 91 in 1962 and 1963. For all Taipei it peaked in 1954 and since then has declined steadily to 46 in 1989. The decline actually masks two divergent processes. On the one hand, the percent of the population below 15 years of age has declined from a peak of 41.55 percent in 1962 to 25.5 percent in 1989. However, at the same time the percent of population greater than 65 years of age has been increasing from a low of 0.5 percent to 5.9 percent in 1989. Thus while the number under 15 has declined by some 43 percent, the number over 65 has increased by some 213 percent.

Spatially the city can be divided into three zones based on dependency ratios. Chingmei has the lowest ratio. The old districts of Chengchung, Chiencheng, Kuting, Sungshan, and Ta-an plus Musha, have intermediate ratios. The rest of the city has high ratios. However, the old districts have high ratios due to the ageing of their populations, while the new districts derive their high ratios from higher birth rates and overall lower rates of natural increase.

Projections for the percent over 65 for the year 2020 are in the 10 to 12 percent range (Chinese Center for International Training in Family Planning, 1987). This "greying" of the population is also found in the Taiwan population and is subject to considerable government discussion. Since a population with greater than 7 percent in the age group over 65 is considered an elderly population (Tien *et al.*, 1992), concerns have been expressed over whether or not the human resources to maintain the economy will be available, and who will staff and support the new social services needed to take care of the older population. For Taipei the answers to these questions are just as problematic as they are for the entire country. In the past migration might have provided the answer, but as we have seen, rates of migration to Taipei are negative and projected to remain so.

Ethnicity

At first glance a discussion of ethnicity seems either out of place or superfluous. After all, broadly speaking the Chinese constitute one major ethnic group in themselves. Yet for Taipei, the issue is important and involves two different sub-groups of Taipei residents: foreigners and aborigines. Furthermore, within the Chinese community there is a history of residential segregation by origin.

Foreigners

Given the city's history of Japanese rule and United States military protection, and its current status as a world city, the foreign population in Taipei has been and still is important in the cultural, demographic, economic, educational, political, and social life of the city. Over the years some 53 separate foreign nationalities have been registered by the authorities.

The percentage of the foreign population reached its peak in 1944, with some 122 716 persons, or 30.56 percent of the total population (Table 4.7). Of these 99 680, 81 percent, were Japanese. After World War II the percentage of the foreign population declined dramatically to a nadir of 0.07 percent in 1950. Since then the foreign population has gradually increased to 13 460, or some 0.59 percent of the total population. As the numbers and percentage of foreigners have increased their origins have changed. From 1950 until 1969 United States nationals were the single largest foreign group averaging some 36.99 percent of the foreign population. The Japanese were the second largest group with some 20.44 percent. In 1970 there was an abrupt change in the United States presence in Taipei with a drop to only 17.46 percent. Several political events contributed to this decrease. First was the suspension of U.S. aid services. These were terminated as it was felt that the Republic of China had reached a level of economic growth where such assistance was no longer necessary (Jacoby, 1966). Military assistance was also terminated. This was possible not only for economic reasons but because it was felt that the

Table 4.7 Foreign population in Taipei

Year	% foreigners	Sex ratio	Year	% foreigners	Sex ratio
1944	30.56	0.98	1967	0.34	1.62
1946	0.70	0.99	1968	0.42	1.43
1947	0.22	0.68	1969	0.40	1.48
1948	0.11	0.84	1970	0.46	1.60
1949	0.08	0.96	1971	0.40	1.65
1950	0.07	1.21	1972	0.33	1.67
1951	0.09	1.88	1973	0.38	1.49
1952	0.14	1.91	1974	0.40	1.49
1953	0.16	1.23	1975	0.43	1.34
1954	0.17	2.03	1976	0.46	1.20
1955	0.11	2.81	1977	0.48	1.35
1956	0.14	1.39	1978	0.49	1.41
1957	0.15	1.49	1979	0.54	1.40
1958	0.17	1.68	1980	0.61	1.32
1959	0.21	1.69	1981	0.57	1.34
1960	0.24	1.91	1982	0.54	1.25
1961	0.23	1.66	1983	0.51	1.28
1962	0.22	1.69	1984	0.47	1.24
1963	0.20	1.75	1985	0.44	1.21
1964	0.24	1.40	1986	0.43	1.15
1965	0.27	1.48	1987	0.55	1.20
1966	0.30	1.56	1988	0.56	1.22
			1989	0.59	1.25

Republic of China military was able to plan and develop its own defense (Jacoby, 1966). These two suspensions led to a major outflow of United States citizens, since both the aid and military communities included not only government personnel, but also dependents. The end of the Vietnam War also contributed to the decline of United States workers in Taiwan. Taipei had been the center of both logistical support for the Vietnam War and the preferred location of the families of some diplomatic and aid workers. The last contributing event was the suspension of United States diplomatic recognition of the Republic of China in 1979.

Since 1970 a new foreign mix has established itself. The Japanese are the largest group with 24.38 percent, followed by the United States with 22.11 percent. Southeast Asians are the next largest group with Malaysians (18.59 percent), Philippines (3.42 percent), Indonesians (3.01 percent), and Thais (2.09 percent). Koreans account for some 7.08 percent and Indians some 4.12 percent. Collectively Europeans account for 5.6 percent. In terms of occupations foreigners work across the spectrum including construction, industry, and services. Some are entrepreneurs, running factories or services. Others work as consultants to business, government, and industry.

The foreign population displays two interesting demographic features. The first is extremely distorted sex ratios. During the Japanese period (1895–1945) distorted sex ratios among the Japanese on Taiwan reflected Japanese migration policies and preferences, development priorities for Taiwan, and the course of the World War (Barclay, 1954). On average for Taiwan Japanese sex ratios declined from a high of 157.57 in 1907 to a low of 108.75. Koreans had distorted sex ratios in the opposite direction: the average from 1933 to 1943 was 0.5828. For other foreigners the sex ratio (from 1933 to 1943) averaged 134.52. During the transition period (1945–1950) in Taipei the sex ratio averaged 0.8675, but after the retreat to Taiwan the sex ratio jumped, reaching a peak of 2.81 in 1955. Thereafter the sex ratio declined to a level of 1.14 during the late 1980s. As we shall see in the discussion on Taipei as a cultural center, the distorted sex ratios have had an impact on the perception of Taipei as a place to work and visit, and on what type of recreational activities were supported.

The second interesting demographic feature which foreigners display is their distribution. During the Japanese period most foreigners, and especially the Japanese, were concentrated in Ta-an district (Gates, 1981). Detailed data on residential references of foreigners after 1949 are not available but several broad generalizations can be made. United States aid, diplomatic, and military personnel tended to live in Peitou and Shihlin, especially since more modern housing was available there. In addition, for those with children, proximity to the Taipei American School in Shihlin was an advantage. Other United States government personnel tended to locate near their places of work or near those other United States installations which were pick-up stops for government bus routes. Other foreign nationals located either in close proximity to where their work was located (i.e. near business areas, libraries, universities), or where host companies and institutions had housing available.

Aborigines

As mentioned in Chapter 2, Taipei Basin was originally inhabited by Formosan aborigines. According to an analysis of surnames in the 1956 census data there were only 156 aborigines (some 0.02 percent of the total population) in Taipei in 1956 (Chen and Fried, 1968). By 1989 this number had increased to 3800, representing some 0.17 percent of the total population. Since aborigines are not identified as such in the main demographic and statistical sources, the long-term sources and trends of this increase cannot be identified. However, some important demographic and geographic characteristics can be described.

The aborigines can be identified in terms of their spatial and tribal

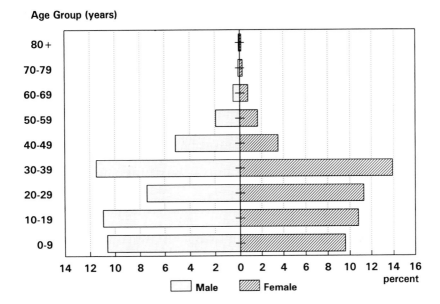

Figure 4.13 Population pyramid, aboriginal population

origins. Overall, the ratio of mountain to plains aborigines is 0.32, showing a clear attraction of Taipei for the plains tribes. By specific tribe, the Ami, from the east coast *hsien* of Hualian, clearly dominate as they constitute some 69.7 percent of the total aboriginal population in Taipei. The next most dominant group are the Tai-ya, from the central mountain area, with 13.9 percent. There is a significant drop in the numbers of aborigines after these two groups, the next largest group, the Paiwan (from the southern mountains), constituting 7 percent. Thereafter the remaining six tribes vary from 3.6 to 0.5 percent of the aboriginal population in Taipei.

Unlike the Chinese population, the sex ratio of the 1989 aboriginal population is closer to "normal." However, for ages 20–39 there is a strong bias in favor of women, an issue which will be further reviewed in Chapter 6. This bias is clearly shown in the sex–age pyramid of the aborigines (Figure 4.13). The pyramid also suggests that the increase in aborigines is relatively recent, and may have been started by males rather than females. The map of sex ratios (Figure 4.14) shows that there is a clear distinction between "normal", and over- and under-represented *chu*. In common with the entire population the highest sex ratios are found in the oldest *chu*. Another similarity with the entire Taipei population is the *chu* of Sungshan, where both groups display a "normal" sex ratio. Although as with the entire population the lowest sex ratios are found in

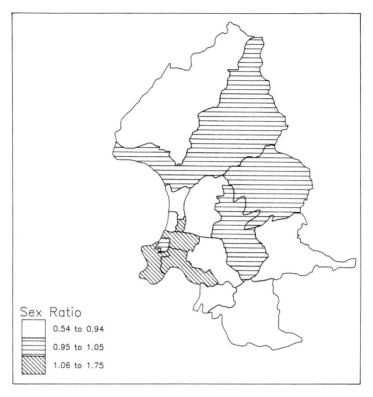

Sex Ratio

	0.54 to 0.94
	0.95 to 1.05
	1.06 to 1.75

Figure 4.14   Sex ratios, aboriginal population

the new six *chu*, plus the old *chu* of Chungshan, Ta-an, Tatong, and Yenping, for the aborigines these areas have ratios below 99.

In terms of distribution the aborigines also show a marked contrast with the Chinese population (Figure 4.15). The aborigines clearly prefer Neihu and Nankang – with 43.7 percent of them living in these two *chu* alone! If the next three preferred *chu* – Shihlin, Sungshan, and Peitou – are included the total comes to 68.9 percent. In contrast the Chinese population prefers Sungshan and Ta-an, but these two *chu* only account for 29.3 percent of the population; the most popular five areas (Chungshan, Shihlin, Sungshan, Peitou, and Ta-an) account for 58.3 per cent of the Chinese population. There are some minor deviations from these aboriginal preference patterns when their origins are considered. The plains aborigines are concentrated much more highly in Nankang and Neihu (with 25.44 and 26.87 percent), while the mountain aborigines are more spread out in Chungshan (11.3 percent), Neihu (12.15 percent), Mucha (10.13 percent), Shihlin (8.96 percent), and Peitou (10.66) percent.

Population

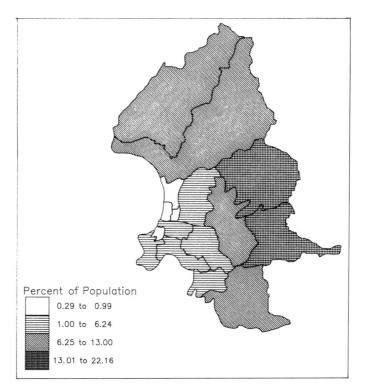

Figure 4.15 Distribution of aborigines

Residential segregation

The third issue is the division between Chinese of mainland and local ancestry. Since all Chinese were migrants from the mainland (Hsieh, 1964), the distinction appears to be without any meaning. The distinction made, however, is based on when the migration took place. Those Chinese who migrated before 1949 are referred to as local, while those who migrated during the 1949 retreat are referred to as mainlanders. The precise demography of the 1949 migrants is not known. It is estimated that some one million military personnel retreated from the mainland and that an additional one million non-military individuals also arrived.

The net result was a rapid increase in the percentage of Taipei residents coming from the mainland. During the Japanese period the percentage was never higher than 6.2 per cent (Liu, 1986). The percentage apparently peaked in 1962 at 38.30 and has been declining to the point where in 1989 some 26.95 percent of the Taipei population are from the mainland. According to Gates (1981) the mainlanders were concentrated in

117

Chengchung, Chungshan, Kuting, Mucha, Sungshan, and Ta-an. These were the areas where the Japanese had been; some of these, such as the Chengchung area, contained old government housing compounds which the mainlanders occupied owing to their government positions. The net impact of the decision to house the mainlanders in this way has tended to emphasize the cultural, political, and social differences and distances not only between mainlanders and Taipei local residents, but between all mainlanders and all Taiwanese (Gates, 1981). The patterns of segregation were then reinforced when the Taiwanese and local Taipei population advanced more quickly than the mainlanders as the Taiwan economic miracle unfolded. This permitted them to move to the more affluent suburbs. By 1973, some 73 percent of those who had moved to the newer neighborhoods of Taipei were Taiwanese (Gates, 1981).

There is some evidence that these patterns of segregation are not as strong or important as they once were. For example, Hsu and Pannell (1982) concluded in their study of Taipei's spatial structure that although residential segregation based on nativity or subculture persists, it has diminished over time and been eroded by rising income levels and land prices. In their list of variables influencing residential choice central and local government allocation of housing is only one factor among five which include changes in car ownership rates, availability of public transportation, limited land supply, inheritance of a dwelling, and traditional work place–residence patterns. They find therefore that there are seven social/residential areas in Taipei: agricultural (Shihlin), rural–low economic status (northern and southern periphery of the city), urban–low economic status (Mengchia, Shuangyuan, and Tatong), mixed, single adults (old business and government core with shophouses and peripheral areas), middle class, and upper class (Ta-tao-chen, Chungshan North Road).

Map analysis of the distribution of mainlanders and location quotients comparing mainlanders and the total population also support the idea that residential segregation based on origins has diminished in importance. During the 1950s and 1960s mainlanders made up the majority of the population in Chengchung (81.61 percent of the population), Kuting and Ta-an (80 percent), and Chungshan (60.13 percent). Chienchung has the smallest percentage of its population coming from the mainland – 29.43. By 1989 Ta-an had the largest percentage of mainland population – 37.99; Kuting had 37 percent followed by Chingmei and Mucha with 35 percent. Tatong had the smallest percentage with 14. The general downward trend in percentage of population masks the fact that four districts, Chengchung, Chiencheng, Lungshan, and Yenping, have absolute losses; only Sungshan, Shuangyuan, and Ta-an actually gained significant numbers of mainlanders. In terms of location quotients in the 1950s and 1960s the range was from 0.55 to 3.31, with only Chiencheng having a value above 2.5. Four old districts have values below 1.00: Chengchung, Chungshan, Kuting, and Ta-an. By 1989 the location quotients displayed a much narrower spread: from 0.55 to 1.41. Only four of the old districts (Chengchung, Kuting, Sungshan, and Ta-an), and three of the new districts (Chingmei, Mucha, and Neihu) had location quotients above 1.00.

Summary and conclusions

The growth of the Taipei population has varied over both space and time. The basic demographic processes which generated growth have also varied over space and time. Although natural increase became the main source of growth by the early 1990s, even it was expected to decline so that the population of Taipei will actually begin to decline. Population growth was accompanied by significant shifts in the distribution of population. In some of the older districts this led to a slight amelioration of population density. In other old districts, such as Sungshan and Ta-an, population numbers and density increased as old style Japanese houses were replaced by large multi-floored, multi-unit apartment houses. Population increases in the new districts were accommodated by the transfer of agricultural land to housing and by the construction of large apartment houses.

The growth of population has presented many challenges to the government and residents of the city. Housing is expensive and in inadequate supply; traffic is highly congested; recreational space is in short supply; pollution levels for air and water are frequently at unhealthy levels. These problems, however, would have to be met regardless of how fast the population grew. Growth has merely exacerbated them. How Taipei has coped with these problems will be discussed in Chapter 7. Meanwhile, Taipei must learn to cope with an ageing population at a time when its pool of human resources is not only diminishing but becoming ever more expensive.

References

Barclay, G. W. (1954) *Colonial Development and Population in Taiwan*. Princeton University Press, Princeton.

Chen, S.-h. and M. H. Fried (1968) *The Distribution of Family Names in Taiwan. Volume I: the Data*. Department of Sociology and College of Law, National Taiwan University, Taipei.

Coale, A. J. (1991) Excess Female Mortality and the Balance of the Sexes in the Population: an Estimate of the Number of "Missing Females", *Population and Development Review* 17, 517–524.

Chinese Center for International Training in Family Planning (1987) *Comparative Study of Fertility Control Experiences in Republic of Korea and Republic of China.*

Gates, H. (1981) Ethnicity and Social Class, pp. 241–281, in *Anthropology of Taiwan Society*, E. M. Ahern and H. Gates, eds., Stanford University Press, Stanford.

General Introduction (1990) The Housing Department of Taipei Municipal Government, Taipei.

Goodkind, D. M. (1991) Creating New Traditions in Chinese Populations: Aiming for Birth in the Year of the Dragon, *Population and Development Review* 17, 663–686.

Health and Vital Statistis. 2, Vital Statistics (1990) Department of Health, The Executive Yuan, Taipei.

Herr, M. (1968) Wicked Cities of the World, Part II, *Holiday* 43, 46–49, 113, 115, 117, 128.

Hsieh, C. M. (1964) *Taiwan-ilha Formosa. A Geography in Perspective.* Butterworths, Washington, D.C.

Hsu, Y.-r. A. and C. W. Pannell (1982) Urbanization and Residential Spatial Structure in Taiwan, *Pacific Viewpoint* 23, 22–52.

Huang, N. C. (1984) The Immigration of Rural Women to Taipei, pp. 247–268, in *Women in the Cities of Asia: Migration and Urban Adaptation*, J. T. Fawcett, S.-e. Khoo and P. C. Smith, eds., Westview Press, Boulder.

Jacoby, N. H. (1966) *U.S. Aid to Taiwan. A Study of Foreign Aid, Self-Help, and Development.* Praeger, New York.

Lankford, P. M. (1974) Physical Location Factors and Public Policy, *Economic Geography* 50, 244–255.

Lilienfeld, A. M. and D. E. Lilienfeld (1980) *Foundations of Epidemiology*, Second Edition. Oxford University Press, New York.

Liu, A.-t. (1978) A Medical Care System Survey in Taipei City from a Spatial Point of View, *Geographical Research* 4, 259–283.*

Liu, P. K. C. (1986) Urbanization and Employment Growth in Taipei Metropolitan Area, *Industry of Free China* 65:5, 1–12; 65:6, 15–24.

Meng, J. (1982) The Spatial Variation of Population Distribution and Growth in Taipei City, *Geographical Research* 8, 219–236.*

Omran, A. (1971) The Epidemiologic Transition: A Theory of the Epidemiology of Population Change, *Milbank Memorial Fund Quarterly* 49, Part i, 509–538.

Reskin, B. and F. L. Capell (1974) Physician Distribution Among Metropolitan Areas, *American Journal of Sociology* 79, 981–998.

Speare, A. and P. K. C. Liu (1977) Migration to Taipei City, *Philippine Economic Journal* 16:1 and 2, 228–246.

Statistical Abstract of Taipei Municipality, 1990 (1990) Bureau of Budget, Accounting, and Statistics, Taipei.

Taipei-Keelung Metropolitan Regional Plan (1968) Council for International Economic Cooperation and Development, Executive Yuan, Taipei.

Taiwan Provincial Health Administration, Annual Report (1961) Taichung, Taiwan.

Taiwan 2000. Balancing Economic Growth and Environmental Protection (1989) Institute of Ethnology, Academia Sinica, Taipei.

Tien, H. Y., T.-h. Zhang, Y. Ping, J.-n. Lui and Z.-t. Liang (1992) China's Demographic Dilemmas, *Population Bulletin* 47, 1–44.

Tsay, C.-l. (1982) Migration and Population Growth in Taipei Municipality, *Industry of Free China* 57, 9–26.

Tsay, C.-l. (1983) Migration and the Urban Labor Market: A Case Study of Taipei, *Academia Economic Papers* 11, 325–358.
Ward, D. (1968) The Emergence of Central Immigrant Ghettos in American Cities, 1840–1920, *Annals, Association of American Geographers* 58, 243–259.
World Bank (1972) *Urbanization. Selected Working Papers.*
World Bank, Washington, D.C.

5
Government and planning

No city, let alone a world city, runs by itself. Rather there is a need to fund and deliver essential services, to enact and administer rules and regulations, to react to new needs, and to give direction to the future development of the city. In this chapter these issues will be explored through an analysis of the form, structure, and functioning of the municipal government. Special attention will be given to the planning process.

Government

Taipei is governed by a mayor/city council form of government. In addition to describing the functions and relations of these two elements, this section will also include materials dealing with the status of Taipei and past and proposed changes in the number of its administrative districts (*chu*) and subdistricts.

The status of Taipei City

Taipei occupies a distinctive position in the hierarchy of Taiwan settlements. Not only is it the provisional seat of the capital of the Republic of China, in addition it holds the status of special municipality of the Republic as well. This special designation, granted on 1 July 1967, effectively placed Taipei under the direct administration and supervision of the central government. One of the main features of such an administration is the process by which the mayor of Taipei is selected. A mayoral candidate is recommended by the Premier and approved by the President of the Republic of China.

There is considerable discussion in the literature as to the rationale and timing for elevating Taipei to this status. According to official government sources, the elevation was the result of repeated requests, starting in 1956, by the Taipei city council for such status. Additional weight was given to the city council's requests when at the 1954, 1960, and 1966 sessions of the Plenary Meetings of the National Assembly the same suggestion was discussed (*China Yearbook*, 1968). Finally in 1966, then President Chiang Kai-shek advocated the elevation of Taipei as the first special municipality in the Republic of China (*New Image of Taipei*, 1988). Such a designation was possible because Taipei had attained the necessary minimum number of characteristics specified in article 3 of the City Organization Code. This article specifies that when a city meets one or more of the following criteria it is eligible for elevation: national capital, a population greater than one million, or has acquired a special political, economic, or cultural significance (Wang, n.d.). (There is an analogous status possible in the People's Republic of China. As such Beijing, Tienjin, and Shanghai are special municipalities (Shabad, 1972).) Although Taipei had been designated the provisional national capital in 1949, this ambiguous political status was apparently not sufficient to warrant elevation. However, by mid-1963 the 10 districts of Old Taipei had a population of the necessary one million. Since in general the administrative system in Taiwan appears to be based on the organization of population, not territory, as populations change, the political status of places changes too (Wang, n.d.). Therefore the delay in awarding special status to Taipei is understandable.

There were several reported benefits of the new status: it would help modernize Taipei more rapidly, and it would permit Taipei better to fulfill its responsibilities as a wartime capital. Special status was also seen as offering the city better methods of, and opportunities for, raising revenues, since as a special municipality it would have the power to issue revenue bonds and levy special taxes (Pannell, 1973). In addition, Chiang Kai-shek was reported to have seen urban land equalization, to be discussed below in the context of the planning process, as one of the most pressing problems he wished to deal with (*China Yearbook*, 1971/1972).

There is an alternative to this official explanation of the elevation of Taipei. The alternative view argues that the elevation was a deliberate attempt on the part of the Kuomintang (Nationalist Party) to deny, inhibit, or restrict the political power of the city's Taiwanese-speaking majority, and weaken the power bases of popular Taiwanese politicians (Butterfield, 1984; Copper, 1990; Pannell, 1973). These goals would be achieved by the appointment of the mayor by the Prime Minister. A slightly different interpretation of the motivation for elevating Taipei emphasizes the dilemma faced by the Kuomintang (Nationalist Party). It was not clear to party leaders which of two models of rule should be adopted. On the one hand they could manage local political systems with outsiders who are above local conflicts but lack local support. Alternatively they could manage local affairs with local politicians but at the risk of dragging the party into local conflicts (Winckler, 1981). As a result of opting for the first model of rule the Kuomintang leadership has had to live with continued clamor to permit the popular, direct election of the mayor. In 1990 the Kuomintang proposed a constitutional amendment to permit direct popular election of the mayor; by 1992 the draft bills were completed by the Ministry of the Interior for consideration by the Legislative Yuan. The final bill, along with specifying four-year terms for the mayor, does permit direct elections of the mayors of both Taipei and Kaohsiung. Although the Kuomingtang attempted to delay them, the first direct elections are scheduled to take place on 3 December 1994; candidates have been nominated by the Kuomingtang, the Democratic Progressive, and the New (a Kuomingtang splinter) parties (Yu, 1994).

It is somewhat difficult to evaluate these alternative explanations. On the one hand, the second, more cynical view is undermined by the fact that the first appointed mayor was Kao Yu-shu. Kao had been elected mayor in 1954 but was defeated in a re-election bid in 1957 amid allegations of miscounting of votes. In 1960 he withdrew from the mayoral contest when the Kuomintang refused his request to station observers at polling places (Winckler, 1981). If the Kuomintang in fact sought to undermine local politicians, why appoint the popular Kao?

On the other hand Kao appears to be the last popularly approved mayor and a list of his successors reads like a virtual *Who's Who* in Kuomintang politics. What has apparently developed is best described as an interlocking of appointments and exchange of personnel among provincial and local party organizations (Winckler, 1981). In particular the mayoral appointment appears to have been a necessary stepping-stone along the path from local and provincial appointments to higher political offices (Table 5.1). No doubt the best example of this is Lee Tung-hui, who after his tenure as mayor in 1978–1981 ultimately became President at the time of Chiang Chingkuo's death in 1988, having served after the expiration of his mayoral term as Governor of Taiwan province and then Vice-President. Even Kao appears to have been co-opted into the Kuomintang hierarchy, ultimately achieving the rank of Minister of State.

Administrative districts

The politicized atmosphere surrounding the office of the mayor contrasts with a more reasoned approach to configuring and dividing the city for administrative purposes. There are three levels of subdivision: *chu* (districts), *li*, and *lin*. As noted above, the main variable used as the basis for the system of subdivisions is population. The number of districts has changed twice since 1968 (Table 5.2). First 6 townships were added to the original 10 districts; in 1990 the 16 districts were consolidated into 12. No

Table 5.1 Mayors of Taipei

Dates in office	Name	Subsequent government positions
1964–72	Kao Yu-shu	Minister of State
1972–76	Chang Feng-shu	Minister of Interior, of State
1976–78	Lin Yang-kang	Minister of Interior, Vice-Premier
1978–81	Lee Tung-hui	Governor, Taiwan Province; Vice-President; President
1981–82	Shao En-hsin	
1982–85	Yang Ching-tsun	
1985–87	Hsu Shui-teh	Minister of Interior, ROC Representative to Japan, Secretary-General of KMT
1988–90	Wu Poh-hsiung	Minister of State Minister of Interior
1990–	Huang Ta-chou	

sooner had this change occurred than Mayor Wu Poh-hsiung proposed a further consolidation to 10. Under the mayor's plan the population range for a district is to be from 150 000 to 450 000. Districts larger than 450 000 are to be subdivided. In addition to these major changes in the *chu*, minor additions and adjustments were made in 1983 when four small villages along the Takang river were incorporated into Nankang. Under the mayor's proposed plan, *chu* (districts) are to be subdivided as they have been historically into *li*, which in turn are subdivided into *lin*. Each *li* is made up of from 700 to 1400 households; *lin* are made up of between 20 and 35 households. As a general rule once a *lin* has grown to 50 households, registrations are capped and new population growth in the area is assigned to a new *lin*. Adjustments to both *li* and *lin* reflecting population change were made in 1972, 1974, and 1975 (*New Image of Taipei*, 1988).

Although configured on the basis of population, the *chu*, *li*, and *lin* all have political, administrative, and even religious functions. For example, the *chu* is the level at which household population registers are maintained and school attendance theoretically determined (see the discussion in Chapter 7 for actual practices involved in selecting a school). At the *li* level there are people's meetings. Originally started in 1949 as monthly meetings, these annual gatherings afford the residents of Taipei an opportunity to express their concerns and needs to their elected representatives, and to hear directly from city officials about the status of projects having a direct impact on their neighborhoods (*New Image of Taipei*, 1988). At the *lin* level there is the popular election of heads whose responsibilities include transmittal of government directives and draft notices, and delivery of welfare payments. The *lin* heads are also a part of local ceremonies in the worship of the earth god (Rohsenow, 1972).

Table 5.2 Changes in the *chu* (administrative districts) of Taipei City

Date	Districts
pre-1968	Original City (Old Taipei): Sungshan Ta-an Kuting Shuangyuan Lungshan Chengchung Chienchung Yenping Tatong Chungshan
1968	Original City Areas from Yangmingshan administrative district: Shihlin Peitou Areas from Taipei *hsien* (county) Neihu Nankang Chingmei Mucha
1983	1968 districts plus small additions to Nankang
1990	Realignment of sixteen *chu*: Sungshan: parts of Sungshan and Chungshan Hsin-i: southern part of Sungshan, southeast part of Ta-an Ta-an: core of Ta-an Chungshan: Chungshan Chungcheng: Chungcheng and parts of Kuting Tatong: Tatong, Chiencheng, and Yenping Wanhwa: Lungshan, Shuangyuan, and parts of Kuting Wenshan: Chingmei, Mucha Nankang: Nankang Neihu: Neihu Shihlin: Shihlin Peitou: Peitou Mayor's 1989 proposal: Sungbei: northern parts of Sungshan; parts of Chungshan Sungnan: southern parts of Sungshan; parts of Ta-an Ta-an: parts of Ta-an, Sungshan, and Kuting Tingyuan: parts of Kuting, Shuangyuan, and Lungshan Chungcheng: Chengchung, Chiencheng, Yenping, Tatong and parts of Lungshan, Ta-an, and Shuangyuan Chungshan: parts of Chungshan and Sungshan Kanghu: Neihu, Nankang Wenshan: Chingmei, Mucha Shihlin: parts of Shihlin and Chungshan Peitou: Peitou and part of Shihlin

Since the population of Taipei is both growing and relocating, it is reasonable to expect that the internal divisions of Taipei will continue to be changed. However, it is likely that the actual area administered by the municipal government will grow as well. Since 1985 the Ministry of the Interior has been exploring various alternative administrative groupings of the townships of Taipei county (*hsien*), which completely surrounds Taipei City. The planning for such a change is part of a larger scheme known as the *Three Cities, One Province Plan*. The rationale for further enlarging Taipei City is straightforward: Taipei is an underbounded city and the solutions to many of its problems – environmental pollution, garbage disposal, transportation and traffic congestion, housing, recreation – can only be developed at a metropolitan scale (*Central Daily News*, May 19, 1987). As it stands now there are municipal, *hsien* (county), *hseng* (provincial) and national agencies and departments working to solve or ameliorate these problems. Their success is limited due to the overlap in jurisdiction and mission, difficulties in coordination, and lack of technical staff. By enlarging Taipei at least the overlap issue could be eliminated or reduced, and mechanisms for coordinating planning more readily enacted and enforced. No doubt the completion of the Taipei Mass Rapid Transit System (discussed in Chapter 6) will act as an important catalyst for incorporating more townships into Taipei City.

The office of the mayor

Although the mechanism for choosing a mayor is subject to intense political debate, the functions which the mayor must fulfill are not directly political in nature. There are three main functions of the mayor: when the city council is in session the mayor must periodically submit an oral or written report on the city government's administrative policies, and on other significant city government activities; he must report on the progress of implementing city council resolutions and specifically explain any delays in implementation; and he must submit a detailed budget for the next fiscal year to the city council for approval. In his work the mayor is supported by a secretariat, and 23 departments (Table 5.3). The mayor's office also supervises the City Bus Administration, the City Bank, public pawnshops, and municipal hospitals.

Given the highly political nature of the mayoral appointment process, it may come as a surprise that individual mayors have seemingly non-political goals and agendas for the city. Sometimes these goals have a direct and dramatic impact on the landscape of Taipei. For example, Mayor Kao will be well remembered for his program of paving the sidewalks of Taipei during the 1960s. Although there was some controversy involving nepotism and favoritism in regard to the selection of the supplier of the red tiles used for the project, there is no question but that

Table 5.3 Departments and organizations under the direct supervision of the Taipei Mayor's Office

---

Secretariat
Bureau of Civil Affairs
Bureau of Finance
Bureau of Education
Bureau of Reconstruction
Bureau of Public Works
Bureau of Social Affairs
Taipei City Police Headquarters
Bureau of Health
Department of Environmental Protection
Department of Land Administration
Department of Public Housing
Department of Rapid Transit Systems
Department of Information
Department of Military Service
Bureau of Budget, Accounting, and Statistics
Department of Personnel
Civilian Employee Training Center
Taipei Water Department
City Bank of Taipei
Research, Development, and Evaluation Commission
Urban Planning Commission
Commission on Elections
Rules and Regulations Commission
Commission for Examining Petitions and Appeals
Feitsui Reservoir Administration
Bureau of Labor Affairs
Administrative District Offices (one for each *chu*)

---

the new sidewalks improved the quality of life for Taipei citizens as well as improving the city's image. There was also an improvement in the aesthetics and recreational space of the city, for when tiles were put down open sewers were covered and wide sidewalks created. Thus walking became more than an exercise in avoiding mud holes, street ruts, traffic, and refuse. In addition open spaces where children could play without being directly exposed to traffic were created. As with any improvement, the paving created new problems. Often drainage outlets were not provided so that streets frequently flooded during rainstorms; there was also inadequate attention paid to flushing the storm drains so that it became necessary to uncover the sewers and clean them out. Frequently the residue from the cleaning was left for prolonged periods on the sidewalks. The new sidewalks also made ideal areas for parking bicycles and motorcycles. Such informal parking lots create their own congestion and safety hazards.

Similarly Mayor Lin will be remembered for resolving a major dispute during his first week in office. The dispute involved the city government and managers of a private park, part of which was on city land. Closure of the Rong Shing gardens would have deprived the city of one of its most beautiful open spaces.

Several mayors have gone so far as to record their goals for the city. For example, Mayor Lin recognized that as per capita income rose in Taipei five substantial problems were either created or exacerbated – traffic congestion, pollution, housing shortages, water supply, and drainage. Thus he set out to create the mechanisms for solving the problems, even though the completion of many of the projects would extend beyond his tenure in office (Ambruster, 1976). Mayor Hsu sought to develop Taipei has a vibrant, orderly, and hospitable model city based on Sun Yat-sen's Three Principles of the People (*Welcome to the 21st Century*, 1987). Mayor Huang wanted to build Taipei into an orderly, energetic, and charming city. He proposed turning Taipei into a modern, international city. He was quite concerned with correcting its chaotic traffic conditions. He was convinced that successful solutions to its problems involved making citizens realize that their cooperation was vital as construction projects proceeded. Mayor Wu's goals were no less than establishing "a first-rate city with first-rate citizens." He foresaw a city which was vibrant, orderly, and modern yet also characterized by the combination of Chinese traditions and technological development (*Introduction to Taipei City Administration*, 1988).

One mayor, Lee Tung-hui, went beyond these general, programmatic types of goals and enunciated a complete set of time-specific objectives (Lee, 1980). In developing his goals for the city Lee assumed that in many ways the problems confronting Taipei were the same as those requiring attention in all modern cities. However, since Taipei was and would remain the political nerve center and cultural hub of the Republic of China, there were also special objectives to be attained. In general Lee sought to establish guidelines for development projects which would make Taipei into a modern city combining dynamism with good order and courtesy. Plans were to be developed which preserved China's cultural past while also providing Taipei citizens with a peaceful environment, comfortable and clean housing, economical and convenient transportation, sufficient employment and a reasonable income. Lee recognized that if he was to be successful he would have to coordinate city, regional, and national needs. He enunciated a set of goals and strategies for meeting these goals over a 10-year period (1984–1994). Further, Lee's approach separated the goals into basic construction and service goals, thereby permitting ready identification of bureaucratic responsibility for the implementation and evaluation of proposals. In fact, most of the substantial infrastructure projects and changes in the delivery of government services coming to fruition in the 1990s and beyond were due to Lee's approach to city administration.

Municipal bureaucracy

Regardless of the origins of reforms and development goals and plans, the mayor does not directly implement changes. Rather he is assisted by a bureaucracy. The bureaucracy for all municipal departments and units has grown from some 20 000 in the 1960s to 51 980 in 1990. Historically this bureaucracy has been one of the largest employers in Taiwan (Ambruster, 1976). The data from the 1986 *Industrial and Commercial Census* indicate that this is still the case. For example, the average number of employees in all of Taiwan's enterprises is 8.45; the average workforce in government-owned corporations is 2044. The average number of employees for the 746 companies with more than 500 workers is only 1515.

Yet it can be argued that for all its size Taipei residents on a per capita basis are not served by a particularly large bureaucracy. For example, in 1968 there were 59.23 residents per municipal employee; by 1990 there was one government employee for every 52.32 residents of Taipei. In contrast, in cities in the United States with populations between one and three million people there was one municipal government employee for every 23.26 residents (*Local Government Employment in Major County Areas*, 1985); for Hong Kong there were 30.48 residents per government employee (*Hong Kong*, 1992). Furthermore the growth of the bureaucracy not only reflects a growth in the population of Taipei but an expansion in the number and complexity of services provided. For example, the enforcement of environmental protection measures required an increase in both technical and managerial staff; when the Mass Rapid Transit System was initiated, a new staff was required to plan and implement the construction of the system; the expansion of the public water supply involved the creation of a separate office to construct and manage the Feitsui reservoir. In short virtually every new endeavor of the city has required either the expansion of an existing office or the creation of a new one.

Despite the growth in responsibilities of the municipal government it has retained a strong commitment to education. Since the 1960s, on average every year 50 percent of Taipei's government workers have been teachers! This is virtually the same as the major cities in the United States during the same period.

As the bureaucracy has grown the government has sought to improve the delivery and quality of services to residents. Four measures were adopted to these ends. First, a municipal civil service training center was established to improve the attitudes, skills, and work habits of city workers (*Introduction to Taipei City Administration*, 1988). Secondly, district (*chu*) offices were established in 1976 to supplement the central headquarters of the civil, social, military, economic, and construction

Figure 5.1 Government service centers, with public markets on the bottom floors and offices on the upper floors, have been built to provide better public access and improve the delivery of government services

departments (*Introduction to Taipei City Administration*, 1988). Frequently the offices for these units are housed in multi-purpose government centers, with the bottom floor occupied by modern and clean markets for fresh produce, and the upper stories devoted to individual government departments (Figure 5.1). Thirdly, in March 1987 the government adopted a policy of flexible hours so that citizens could have more convenient access to services (*Welcome to the 21st Century*, 1987). Finally, the government has adopted more modern data management practices, including the computerizing of records, and maintenance of a professional library of books and journals on effective data management for the use of staff members (*New Image of Taipei*, 1988).

City council

In contrast to the mayor, members of the city council are directly elected (Long, 1969). Elections are supervised by the Minister of the National Department of Civil Affairs. Supervision involves informing electors and officials of the date of voting, the division of the city into constituencies, setting the dates for registration of candidates and for the establishment of a local election office, and setting limits on campaign funds for each candidate. The Minister is also responsible for punishing those who violate election laws during the campaign period, choosing and inviting election supervisors, disqualifying candidates who violate the law, and presenting certificates of election to the successful candidates.

The city, however, must actually administer elections through an *ad hoc* election office. Five people are appointed by the Minister of Civil Affairs to run the office. If a mayor is not running for election, he will be appointed as one of the five. Frequently the remaining members are drawn from college and university faculty or presidents and city council members. The chief judge of the Taipei local court is never appointed lest a disputed election come before him for adjudication; similarly party cadres are not appointed to avoid any possible conflicts of interest. The five-person committee is assisted by a staff which includes a secretary-general, clerks, accountants, and other personnel as necessary. Since the election office is not permanent its staff is commonly made up of members of the existing city bureaucracy; in particular the secretary-general is the director of the Taipei City Bureau of Civil Affairs. The election office is charged with all preparations for actually holding the election. Thus it arranges for the registration of candidates, reviews candidates' qualifications, publishes the list of final candidates, sets and staffs polling stations, schedules meetings for candidates to meet with the public, and publishes the final election results.

Maintenance of voters' lists is the responsibility of district offices. In order to vote in a local Taipei election, one must be a Chinese citizen, be at least 20 years of age, and have established residency in the voting district at least six months before the election. In order to run for office one must be at least 23 years old, have at least a high school diploma, and meet the citizenship and residency requirements necessary for voting in Taipei (*Republic of China, A Reference Book*, 1988).

The size of the city council is determined by a strict formula specified in the organic regulations of the Taipei City Council (*Republic of China, A Reference Book*, 1988). For every one million residents there are 40 seats on the council; one additional seat is added for every additional 100 000 residents. Hence the number of council members has increased from 55 in 1968 to 66 in 1990. For election purposes, the city is divided into five precincts (Table 5.4). The precincts are made up of adjacent *chu* and seem

Table 5.4 City council election precincts

Precinct no.	Districts within precinct
1	Shihlin, Peitou, Tatong
2	Sungshan, Neihu, Nankang
3	Chungshan, Yenping, Chiencheng
4	Ta-an, Lungshan, Chengchung
5	Kuting, Shuangyuan, Mucha, Chingmei

to be free of any attempt at gerrymandering. Within each precinct one female must be elected for every seven council members; if there are fewer than seven councillors, then the ratio is one in five.

Between 1949 and 1967 there were six city council elections. The first, in 1950, replaced a provincially appointed city council of April 1949 (*Republic of China, A Reference Book*, 1988). Since the elevation of Taipei to the status of special municipality in 1967 there have been six elections, in 1968, 1973, 1977, 1981, 1985, and 1989. It has been suggested that a detailed analysis of the returns from these elections is not illuminating (Winckler, 1981). The reason for this conclusion is that elections within Taipei City display what are termed "locality effects", which implies that political cooperation is more likely among people living near each other than amongst those living far apart. Candidates from historically defined communities within Taipei then tend to carry their own communities even against very popular opponents. Furthermore, the balance between the Kuomintang and various opposition parties in the city council is thought also to reflect two additional factors well beyond the control of the political parties themselves (Goldstein, 1985). First, Taipei voters are increasingly better educated and more politically aware. The first characteristic is easier to document than the second. For example, the percentage of the population considered illiterate fell from 15.17 to 2.09 between 1961 and 1990. Conversely, the percentage with a higher level of education rose from 7 to 20.31. The gains have been especially dramatic for women. Their percentage illiteracy fell from 27.1 to 3.94 between 1961 and 1990 while the percentage with a college education or more went from 3.67 to 18.34. Viewed another way, the ratio for college-educated males to women fell from 3.63 to 1.23 from 1961 to 1990, while the same ratio for illiterates increased from 0.27 to 0.488. Secondly, voters have tended to vote for opposition parties when scandals break out such as the Cathay financial crisis in 1985, in which there were banking irregularities involving businesses owned by Kuomintang legislators; or the 1984 Chinese underworld organization murder of Henry Liu in California – after the publication of his less than flattering biography of Chiang Ching-kuo his murder was apparently ordered by members of the Taiwan military intelligence (Butterfield, 1984); or after a series of bad industrial accidents and food safety scandals (Goldstein, 1985).

What are of interest, however, are the changes in age and gender mix, and educational levels of council members. In terms of age the median age group for male councillors has been 40 to 44 for three of the six elections. For the second and fourth election it was 45 to 49. In the last, 1989, election there was a drop in median age to 30 to 34. For female councillors the median age has been consistently younger for each election with the exception of the last one. So for the first and second elections the median age was 35–39; for the third and fifth elections the median age was 40–44; for the fourth election the median age was 30–34; for the last election it was 35–39 again. In terms of gender mix there are four trends. First, the percentage of candidates who are women has increased from 10.39 to 24, although for the second through fifth elections the percentage was stagnant at around 13.25 percent. In contrast, the percentage of female candidates winning seats has been quite volatile. For the first two elections 87.5 percent of the women won seats; for the third election all women running were elected. The percentage dropped to 63.64 for the fourth election and rose to 90 for the fifth, only to drop again to 41.67 percent in the last election. A third trend involves the difference between the minimum number of female seats as allocated by law and the number of women actually elected. If we assume 6.86 women must hold seats in each of the city council assemblies, then only in the third, fifth and sixth elections were more women than mandated actually elected with 8, 9, and 10 women victorious. In all the other elections seven women won and since this is as close as one can get to 6.86 women, the fractional addition is not meaningful. The last trend in the gender of councillors is that districts one, three, and five more often send women to represent them than the legal minimum.

In terms of education it appears that city councillors are increasingly better educated. For example, the percentage of councillors with a higher education (i.e. university degree) increased from 47.92 in the first assembly to 90.2 in the sixth. This was accompanied by a decline in the percentage having a secondary education (from 27.08 percent to 9.8), a military education (from 16.67 percent to zero), and for unspecified, "other" educational backgrounds (from 8.33 percent to zero). All three of these trends, age, gender, and education, mirror similar trends in provincial and national elections, where increasingly more women are being elected on their own personal strengths, and all representatives are generally younger and better educated than their predecessors (Pun, 1992).

Once elected, the city councillors participate in semi-annual assembly sessions. Each session lasts for 60 days during which time the council is expected to fulfill eight basic functions (*Republic of China, A Reference Book*, 1988): adopt bylaws and regulations which govern the rights and obligations of the citizens of Taipei; approve budgets and audit disbursement reports submitted by the city government; approve of the disposal of municipal property; approve bylaws and regulations of city government-controlled enterprises; examine proposals proposed by the city government; examine proposals made by the councillors; hear petitions from citizens; and carry out other functions according to the law. Council business is carried out under the direction of a speaker and deputy, both of whom are elected by the council. Three individuals have dominated these leadership positions since 1968: Lin Ting-sheng, Chang Chien-pang, and Ch'en Chien-chih. Lin, a member of the Kuomintang Central Standing Committee, was also chairman of the Tatong Company, one of Taiwan's premier electric appliance and electronics firms; Chang, before serving as deputy and then speaker of the city council was president and then chairman of the board of Tamkang University, and chairman of the YMCA in Taiwan. Ch'en does not appear to have had any similar posts before his election to the city council.

In terms of work perhaps the best measure of city council activities has been the increase in the number of bills it has handled. Since 1967 the average number of bills debated has increased from several hundred to 519 in 1991. For the most part, legislative action emphasizes public security, traffic, pollution and the environment, education, and social issues (*Republic of China, A Reference Book*, 1991/92). Bills are carried on the vote of a simple majority.

Budget and finance

By law the budget of Taipei must be balanced (*New Image of Taipei*, 1988). As such there may be years when there is a disparity between allocated and expended funds resulting in short-term or apparent shortfalls. It is also possible that genuine surpluses can be recorded, as was the case in the period 1974–1976. What is most common, however, is the adoption of an initial budget plan by the city council and then a series of revisions as revenue streams become more established and predictable. In addition, special projects can be allocated funds from designated taxes, subsidies, trust management, or payment of public debts. Given the legal framework of the budget there are three basic questions which must be answered: how has the budget changed over time, what are the changing sources of revenues, and what are the patterns of allocations?

Between 1968 and 1990 the budget of Taipei City grew from NT$2.3 billion (US$57.9 million) to NT$61.5 billion (US$2.2 billion). These funds were derived from varying combinations of some thirteen different sources (Table 5.5). By far the single most important source is taxes. However the mix of taxes has shifted over time (Table 5.6). This mix is the result of agreements between the central and city governments (*New Image of*

Table 5.5 Sources of revenues (percent)

Source	1968	1990
Taxes	61.25	71.14
Public construction	0.37	0.36
Fines, indemnities	0.65	1.98
Fees	2.22	2.10
Property	1.40	2.13
Public businesses	3.98	1.65
Subsidies	13.62	0.09
Public debt	10.34	8.67
Vehicle fuel tax	1.30	2.64
Lottery tickets	1.42	0.00
Surplus/carry over	0.00	6.60
Trust management	0.00	0.72
Bridge tolls	0.00	0.56

Table 5.6 Percent of revenues from various taxes

Year	Tax type														
	1	2	3	4	5	6	7	8	9	10	11	12	13	14	15
1968	7.9	12.9	11.6	34.7	3.9	10.9	7.7	7.7	0.0	3.6	0.4	3.21	0.0	2.9	xx
1990	0.0	6.9	24.3	53.1	3.2	6.7	0.0	0.1	1.8	0.0	2.2	0.0	1.2	0.6	0.1

Key: Tax types:
1. Field
2. Land
3. Increase in value of land
4. Business
5. Vehicle
6. House
7. Butchery
8. Amusement
9. Stamp
10. Feast
11. Deeds
12. Household
13. School
14. Fees
15. Inheritance
xx No data

Taipei, 1988). Two features of the mix are notable: the lack of revenues from income tax, which are entirely allocated for use by the central government, and the heavy reliance on both business and land taxes. The 1990 mix actually represents an improvement in the ability to control revenues. Before 1967, when Taipei was under the jurisdiction of the Taiwan provincial government, few if any taxes collected in Taipei were actually returned since the provincial government had its own budgeting priorities which did not include Taipei City (Glenn, 1968). After 1967 not only could Taipei receive back some of the tax revenues it collected for the central government, but in addition it was empowered to levy its own taxes (*New Image of Taipei*, 1988). This has been attempted on two occasions. In 1988 the city council debated curbing tax evasion in five major "underground" (i.e. unlicensed) economic activities: sex, vendors, jewelry stores, investment houses, and illegal lotteries and number games. It was estimated that the city could raise twice its current business tax revenues by collecting taxes on these activities (*Free China Journal*, December 1, 1988). It is not clear whether collections from these sources have met expectations. Secondly, on the recommendation of the mayor, the city council in 1990 authorized a new lottery. After 40 years of existence lotteries had been terminated in January 1988 by the provincial government after efforts to curtail illegal gambling and lottery-related crimes, such as kidnapping and fraud, failed. Another socially negative result of the lotteries was that on the days the winning numbers were announced people quite literally deserted their workplaces. The city council authorized the lottery to help satisfy the hunger for gambling which pervades Taipei society (and was satisfied by gamblers illegally turning to the Hong Kong government's twice weekly Mark Six lottery), and to provide new revenues to fund social welfare programs. Under the lottery, named *aishin* (charity), 25 percent of revenues were to be allocated to programs for the handicapped and senior citizens. Some US$5.45 million in profits were available from the first month of sales alone! Projected revenues for the first year, 1990–91, totaled US$54.5 million. Of this some US$27 million were to be spent on the construction of care centers for the handicapped and apartments for the ageing. Funds were also to be used for medical assistance and job training. Unfortunately, these projections and targeted uses came to nothing, since Premier Hau Pei-tsun rescinded the scratch and win lottery as part of a campaign to calm the public's frenzy for speculating in money games. Although the lottery was only run three times in 50 days, altogether some US$48 million were generated for the city, of which US$36 million were allocated for social welfare projects (Lee, 1993).

Specific spending patterns are somewhat hard to describe since the accounting categories for disbursements have changed considerably over the years. Table 5.7 shows the percentages of city expenditures for 1968 and 1990. One obvious difference is that the *number* of activities and functions funded by the city has increased from 10 to 19. Education remains the single largest budget item. The sheer cost of running the city has increased. New initiatives and functions have taken large portions of the budget. Surprisingly the health budget has not maintained its share of the budget. Given the concern for public order (Chapter 7), the increase in

Table 5.7 Budget categories for Taipei City, by percent of total expenditures

Government function	1968	1990
City council	0.59	0.33
City government	1.81	7.22
Civil affairs	1.47	0.46
Finance	2.62	11.64
Education	35.33	25.10
Reconstruction	0.00	1.40
Economic	9.86	0.00
Communications, transportation	16.77	0.00
Public works	0.00	29.53
Social affairs	1.50	2.87
Police	6.23	6.78
Health	6.66	3.68
Environmental sanitation	0.00	3.72
Land administration	0.00	0.68
Public housing	0.00	0.71
Rapid Transit System	0.00	0.11
Military	0.50	0.19
Feitsui reservoir	0.00	1.24
Labor	0.00	1.31
Reserve fund	0.00	3.03
Water	0.00	0.01

the police budget is small. Some functions have either disappeared entirely, such as the Economic and Commerce Bureaux, or been drastically reduced, such as the Bureaux of Civil and Military Affairs. Some functions, such as elections, do not appear, as they are intermittent.

Planning

One new responsibility which the municipal government had to assume in 1967 was that of planning. Some of the specific problems requiring city planning initiatives will be discussed in Chapter 6, Coping with world city status. At this point, however, it is important to review the legal basis for planning, the history of Taipei City planning, and the current approach to implementing city plans.

The legal basis of planning

The legal basis for planning in Taipei rests on three national statutes: the Urban Planning Law, first enacted in 1939 and revised in 1964; the Land Law, enacted in 1936 and revised in 1946; and the Statute for the

Enforcement of the Equalization of Urban Land Rights, promulgated and enforced in 1954, and amended in 1958 and 1964, with special bylaws promulgated by the Taiwan provincial government in 1956. These special bylaws were further amended and approved by the Executive Yuan in 1964.

The Urban Planning Law seeks to ensure that planning promotes the orderly development of all types of settlements in the Republic of China, not just cities. Thus it defines four categories of places subject to planning: cities, rural districts, special districts, and regions. The law outlines the procedures for drafting city plans which must contain or define nine distinct parts or issues: a survey and analysis of local, national, social, and economic conditions; the borders of the planning area; population projections; zoning of land uses; a description of the main roads and drainage system; land reserved for public facilities; specify scenic spots, historic remains or buildings which could become tourist attractions; a schedule and budget for development; presentation of the complete plan in map and tabular form where possible. Once a plan has been assembled public hearings for local leaders are held and the plan is to be "posted" in appropriate places for 30 days for citizens' comments. Once public comments have been incorporated into the plan it is submitted to appropriate higher authorities for approval. In the case of Taipei this involves submitting the plan to the second section of the municipal Bureau of Public Works, which again holds public hearings and arranges an additional 30-day citizen viewing period. The plan is then submitted to the City Planning Committee for the Ministry of the Interior for final review and approval (*Introduction to Urban Planning of Taipei City*, 1990).

In addition to the above nine issues to be covered, a city plan must be further divided into two sections – a master plan and a series of detailed plans. These detailed plans may focus on commercial, administrative, scenic, or residential districts, or on public facility or special project needs covering either parts of or the entire city (*Introduction to Urban Planning of Taipei City*, 1990). In fact the detailed plans have become the essential substance of all urban planning in Taiwan (Pannell, 1973). Maps of the master plan are typically drafted at a scale of 1:10 000 and feature 10 variables; maps of the detailed plans are drafted at a scale of 1:1200 and include six variables (*A Brief Introduction to the City Planning of Taipei*, 1981). One of the most important elements of the detailed plans is the five-year mandatory review. This review is necessary since the other key elements of the detailed plans – zoning classifications, the type of review required before any given class of land can be developed, density limits, and height and building ratios – are really only ideals not genuine constraints and thus subject to market pressures (Pannell, 1973).

The Land Law contains the main definitions of land types, specifies who can own land, describes how to survey and register land, permits limits to be placed on land uses, provides for the building of public housing, establishes the principle of land requisition for public use, and requires land consolidation. By far one of the most important provisions of the Land Law deals with taxation. Three types are permitted – land value, land value increment, and vacant land taxes. The latter two taxes are direct derivatives of the economic theories of Sun Yat-sen, the founder of the Republic of China. Sun felt very strongly that speculation in land should be discouraged and that any increments to the value of land which resulted from spiraling land costs should be recaptured by the government for the public good. This concept was translated into law under the provisions of the Equalization of Urban Land Rights Statute.

This statute constitutes a form of urban land reform. The 60 articles of the law specify that land owners are to declare the value of their holdings and that the government is to compare these to prevailing values of land of similar class, location, and use. The owner and the government are then to agree on the value of the property. Taxes are levied against this value. When the property is transferred to a new owner, a tax is levied against the difference between the sales price and the taxable value. In the event of transfer owing to inheritance these provisions do not apply. The law also provides for requisition of land with compensation. Replotting (resurveying) of land is also mandated under two conditions: if the land is required for public purposes or if more than half of the private land owners request replotting.

History of urban planning in Taipei

Although the legal framework for planning appears to be rather straightforward and unambiguous, the fate of planning in Taipei has been rather mixed. All attempts to evaluate the apparent lack of universal success in planning Taipei have one thing in common: ambiguity about the history of planning in Taipei.

As with many issues regarding Taipei, the elevation to a special municipality in 1967 has clouded the understanding of pre-1967 plans, and their relationships to newer plans. There is agreement that the *modern* planning of Taipei started under the Japanese. There is disagreement over when the Japanese started to plan, however. According to Ku (1971) and the Taipei Planning Commission (*Introduction to Urban Planning of Taipei City*, 1990) the Japanese began systematically to plan Taipei in 1905; according to this chronology a second plan was developed in 1932 when the size of the city was increased from 1809 to 6698 hectares. In contrast, Chen (1956) dates the first attempts of the Japanese at planning Taipei to August 1911, when a disastrous typhoon destroyed much of the native housing, thus providing the opportunity to plan and build a modern

Table 5.8 Special planning projects as of 1990

Lower downtown redevelopment
Taipei Railroad Station and Changhua Road pedestrian mall
Taipei Railroad Station special land use district
Hsinyi sub-center special land use district
Kuantu Plain development
Shedz Peninsula development
Shihlin community development and urban design study
Keelung river, Shihlin section, reclamation project
Dihua Street special district
Keelung river shortening program
Wanhwa Station development
Urban renewal
Urban survey

city. Although there is disagreement over the dates of the Japanese phase of planning, there is agreement that World War II prevented the implementation of the plan much beyond setting the general grid system of Taipei land use and the development of Ta-an *chu*, where the majority of the Japanese resided.

Taipei City planning documents are somewhat vague about what planning occurred between the Japanese and the post-1967 periods. There were, however, two plans prepared in 1968 by the Urban and Housing Development Committee of the Council for International Economic Cooperation and Development. One plan, *Taipei-Keelung Metropolitan Regional Plan*, was part of a series of regional plans prepared for the major urban areas of Taiwan. The second plan was simply entitled *Preliminary (Sketch) Plan for the City of Taipei*. In terms of the planning laws of the Republic of China both documents are master plans. They are descriptive, and include the nine key elements required of all master plans as described above. Furthermore they are well documented and illustrated with numerous tables, maps, and graphs. Both documents suggest possible changes in land use and propose the building of necessary infrastructure projects such as roads and sewerage treatment plants. Although the two plans should differ only in scale, the second one contains significant amounts of materials found in the first plan. Since the second plan deals only with Taipei there are several maps suggesting detailed intra-urban development opportunities.

Since 1967 two sets of plans for Taipei have been developed. The city planning commission presented one master plan, which was revised in 1989, and is preparing a second to be issued by the mid-1990s. In addition, detailed plans were issued in 1981 and revised in 1988. The detailed plans focus on a series of 13 specific areas or problems. These are summarized in Table 5.8. Many of these projects appear designed to correct the anomalies and discontinuities derived because of the historical land use patterns described in Chapter 2. In this regard the intention to create three distinct central business district like nodes, and the attempt to separate work and living areas, stand out as significant. In addition to these city-based plans Taipei is also included in the 1980 Taiwan North Regional Development Plan (*A Brief Introduction to the City Planning of Taipei*, 1981). The 1980 plan differs in several respects from the 1968 regional plan. First, the geographical scope has increased to include Taipei and Taoyuan *hsien* (counties). Secondly, in contrast to the 1968 plan which defined a series of 10 problems requiring solutions, the 1980 plan sets seven specific planning goals to be achieved by the end of the implementation period. These goals are: reasonable redistribution of the population to stimulate a balance between urban and rural areas; efficient land use; coordination of development; improved accessibility through a regional transportation system; development of a hierarchy of cities to minimize the disparities in standards of living; improvement and preservation of the physical environment; utilization and preservation of natural resources. (*New Image of Taipei* (1988) catalogues the goals somewhat differently: the plan seeks to avoid uncontrolled growth of cities, waste of financial resources on piecemeal additions of public facilities, and irrational use of land. In this version of the goals recreational facilities are included with the development of communications.) The third difference is that a timetable for expanding the geographical scope and implementing the plans is included: the target date was set at 1996. Finally, the master plan includes specific detailed plans for flood control, rebuilding of transportation infrastructure beyond roads, preserving 92 000 to 95 000 hectares of prime agricultural land, protection of slopelands, and calls for the establishment of tolerance studies for public hazards.

Implementation of plans

Beyond the confusion over pre-1967 planning and the slow pace of updating the master and detailed plans from the 1980s, therefore, a series of five explanations have been offered to account for the lack of success in transforming Taipei via the planning process. These explanations include a lack of a current comprehensive plan, lack of adequate numbers of planning professionals, misguided planning principles, general administrative problems, and lack of land resources.

Despite the publication of all the plans it has been claimed that Taipei suffers from a lack of planning (Ambruster, 1976; Glenn, 1968; Ku, 1971). A closer reading of the negative evaluations of the progress of city planning suggests that the real issues are not whether or not a plan physically exists. Rather the true concern focuses on the lack of enforcement once a plan is approved. If a legal framework for planning exists why should the issue of enforcement ever emerge?

The answer to this question is found in the other three explanations mentioned above. Ambruster (1976) and Lui (1978) claim that there are not enough trained professional planners available, although Lin (1991) claims that this is no longer the case. On the one hand this lack has led to an overemphasis on physical planning and inadequate attention to social issues (Ambruster, 1976). On the other hand, reliance on a limited number of planners to prepare plans for all areas in Taiwan has led to impractical recommendations based on lack of familiarity with actual field conditions (Lui, 1978). The lack of trained personnel is no doubt exacerbated by what can best be described as outmoded and inefficient data collection and mapping techniques. Despite the fact that Taiwan is a significant exporter of personal computers, supplying 10 percent of the world market in 1989 (Baum, 1990), as late as 1989 planners working in the city planning department were collecting, collating, and plotting data by hand! This condition existed despite the fact that nine government agencies in Taiwan had operating geographical information systems, and plans were made for sharing the technology and data bases for planning purposes (Sun, 1990). The net result of this administrative situation is that maps are frequently out of date, difficult to revise, and data used to plan are often inaccurate.

In terms of misguided planning principles, it is not clear whose basic interests are being served in the planning process. For example, if planning is designed to enhance the quality of urban life by separating incompatible land uses, then the public perception that "it is folly, if not downright wickedness, to waste building space for wholly residential use" (Glenn, 1968) will lead to conflicts over how best to plan new housing areas. These conflicts are most likely to occur given the actual lack of public participation in the planning and review process (Lui, 1978). Most public reaction to plans is not from individual citizens but from land owners or developers seeking to modify plans for their own private good. Thus it becomes very difficult to balance public needs and interests with private rights. But even when public opinion is voiced, there is no guarantee that it will be heeded. A typical example of this is found in the decision to implement the Chung Hwa shopping complex renewal in the Fall of 1992.

The complex, known to visitors to Taipei as Haggler's Alley, was built between 1959 and 1961 to replace a combination of rundown and squatter housing. For its time the complex was one of the most modern edifices on Taiwan (Lin, 1992) (Figure 5.2). Some shops included both living and working space for shopkeepers; public rest rooms, a rarity at the time, were part of the complex. Many of the 60 restaurants which operated in the complex were famous for their inexpensive cuisine. As the general economy of Taipei and Taiwan changed so too did the goods

Figure 5.2 Chunghwa Road, known as Haggler's Alley, served for almost 30 years as home to numerous small retail shops and famous restaurants

offered for sale in the complex, although there was always a "core" of shops offering antiques, suitcases, clothing, and souvenirs. However, over the years the complex began to deteriorate physically, and the variety of shops declined especially as the east side of Taipei became more fashionable. This decline was a part of the general decline of the west end of Taipei. Thus in October 1992, the government decided to implement existing plans for the general area, to raze the complex and in its place build a 70 meter wide boulevard; the shopping complex itself is to be replaced by 1999 by an underground shopping emporium with some 862 modern shops. Implementation of this project was intended to supplement redevelopment plans for the Shihmenting entertainment district and the Central Railroad Station business district which had already been started by private developers. All three projects are part of a more general plan to revitalize the west end of Taipei.

Public, i.e. shop owner, reaction to these plans was, not unexpectedly, negative. On the one hand protesters among the 1700 shop owners argued that over the years some US$2 million had been invested in the buildings by the shopkeepers. Indeed many of the shops, especially those selling clothing, were as modern and well kept as any found along Chungshan North Road or in parts of the east end. As such they felt the buildings should be seen as their property. On the other hand shop owners also felt that the US$34 000 per household offered for relocation compensation was inadequate; they also felt that priority consideration toward applying for mall retail space and public housing was not strong enough to guarantee their future security. Furthermore, what were they to do during the construction period to earn a livelihood? Despite these protests, the government proceeded with the plan, forcing the shopkeepers to liquidate their goods and then vacate the complex.

In general once a plan has been scheduled for implementation a series of administrative problems may prevent completion of the plan. By far the most serious administrative problem is the lack of adequate financing for implementing plans (Ames and Ames, 1972; Lui, 1978). Financing is achieved via two mechanisms: replotting, to be described below under land problems, and private development. Either way once a plan is prepared the municipal government virtually loses control over planning since developers are free to build what they think is locally marketable (Wang, 1978). In particular developers are able to determine the type and specifications of buildings to be constructed, their distance from roads, and the landscape design (Lin, 1991). Thus the impression develops that either planning does not exist, or that planning and zoning laws may be freely disregarded (Ambruster, 1976; Glenn, 1968).

To say that lack of land resources is the cause of planning failures (Ku, 1971) seems at first glance to be a tautology: one of the goals of the planning process is to compensate for inadequate land by better planning. Given the importance of the land issue in general, this explanation for the overall inadequacies of planning must be carefully analyzed. Such an analysis is especially important since it has been argued that assuring reasonably priced and accessible land can only be achieved in Taipei the way it was in Taichung, Kaohsiung, Chiayi, and Keelung cities, via implementation of the land equalization law and subsequent replotting (Pannell, 1973).

In a planning context there is no question but that land is a constraint. The basic assumption in all Taipei municipal planning documents is that some 60 percent of all the land in Taipei is "inadequate" for urban development. In short much of Taipei consists of slopelands, foothills, farm land, or flood plains of rivers and thus should not be used for urban purposes (*A Brief Introduction to the City Planning of Taipei*, 1981). Of the remaining land, starting in 1956 it was subject to the urban land equalization law. By 1990 the municipal government claimed that the urban land equalization law had been fully implemented in 90.98 percent of the city (*New Image of Taipei*, 1988). A closer inspection of the data shows, however, that only some 3229 hectares of land, or 11.86 percent of the total, had been subject to the true intent of the land equalization law, i.e. reevaluated and replotted with surplus value being taxed. The remaining land had either not been subject to review of land prices, or had been part of a more general review designed to align prices with inflationary pressures. No wonder then that there has been a surge in land prices in Taipei.

Since the late 1960s land prices have increased in terms of NT$ per square meter by 2175 percent for the most expensive land fronting prime streets. This increase is "modest" compared with the 49 900 percent increase in the lowest priced piece of inaccessible land off a prime street, with the 7160 percent increase for the least expensive land on a prime street, or the 4197 percent increase in the highest priced piece of inaccessible land. The major surges in prices occurred during two periods: 1977–1981, and since 1989. Although all parts of Taipei have experienced increases in the price of land, some districts have been harder hit than others. As a consequence, Sungshan, Ta-an, and Chengchung have the most expensive land, while Nankang, Mucha, Chingmei, Neihu, and Shuangyuan have the cheapest land.

The government's reaction to the land price surge was most telling. First the municipal government announced that it would investigate the source of the surge by looking into who had invested funds for land speculation. This led to an immediate 20 percent drop in land prices (Tanzer, 1981). Secondly, the Ministry of Interior announced that it would impose a "vacant land" tax at a rate of 10 to 25 times the value of the land, if empty lots were not used by July 1981. As a result of these two actions it came to light that Cathay Trust and Investment and Asia Trust and Investment held some 55 percent of all vacant lots in Taipei, and that all such investment and trust companies held 81 pieces of land in Taiwan totalling the equivalent of the entire area of Taipei City (Tanzer, 1981). Despite the bad publicity over land speculation and the threats of vacant land taxes, this at best helped to moderate land price increases. At worst real estate projects of questionable long-term viability may have been started. However, the reality is that land is in short supply in Taipei, and such administrative fixes cannot be anything more than short-term palliatives. The best way to demonstrate the land crisis is to describe the fate of one sizeable planning initiative, the Min Sheng New Community (Brandt, 1981; Lin, 1991; Tanzer, 1981).

At first glance, Min Sheng New Community should have been a model of successful implementation. The plan for development had been reviewed and approved by the appropriate municipal and national offices. Replotting had been carried out with the agreement of the owners of land in the area, and it was expected that once the entire area had been resurveyed accurate property lines would create new land which the government would buy or offer for sale both to cover the costs of the survey and blueprints, and to ensure adequate land for public services such as parks. In fact replotting had created an area of some 118 surplus hectares for the project. The area had public sewerage and was generally residential, although some small-scale storage and manufacturing were present. Thus it was possible to envision more public services and facilities than generally available elsewhere in Taipei. The building density and size had been set in accordance with government regulations where the maximum height of a building is determined by the width of the street times 1.5; seven stories were seen as the ideal height. Should higher buildings be constructed the land savings would have been eliminated by the need for deeper excavations, greater wall supports, and elevators.

Despite all these factors in its favor, Min Sheng New Community did not turn out as planners had hoped. Once the project began planners soon saw developers increase the population projected to live there from 45 000 to 95 000. The cause of the increase was simple to find: the cost of land prices escalated so developers tried to compensate by building higher structures. As the actual numbers of people living in the area increased beyond what planners had expected, there was an increase in the demand for services, which were either by then inadequate or non-existent. The best example of this was water: the new water pipes had been laid assuming the ultimate population would be 45 000, so that water pressure was inadequate in many parts of the community; the same holds true for sewerage services. Meanwhile, the general livability of the community declined as parks, seen as a major benefit of the plan, were never built. Noise pollution grew, and light levels in the community declined as building heights increased. A feeling of crowding developed and there were fears that the density would reach the point, 1200 persons per hectare, where stress would be induced. The development of negative externalities was all the more painful since some 14 percent of the land was not developed. No apparent reasons were given for the delay in developing the vacant land, although it does not appear that in this case the replotting of the area resulted in sizes or shapes of land which were incompatible with pre-existing *li* and *lin* divisions, as sometimes happens. What does appear to be the case is that Min Sheng New Community shows the inadequacies of the planning process which removes from planners control over such basic administrative decisions as setback requirements, sidewalks, parking spaces, and parks, and permits these amenities to be sacrificed to the personal financial needs of the developers. Other examples of the problems involved in the use of planning to solve delivery of basic services and to improve the quality of life in Taipei are included in Chapter 6.

Summary

Although the government of Taipei is subject to stresses resulting from Taipei's special status, it has grown as the political culture has matured and new demands for services have evolved. In some cases delivery of government services has been modernized. Two cases stand out as examples of this: the flexible office hours for social services available in district centers, and the new city council chambers and office complex built as a part of the Hsin-yi redevelopment project. In other cases, such as planning, effective delivery of services has been impeded by a legal framework which is both overly ambitious and ambiguous in regard to what is ultimately the public interest, and by inadequate use of up-to-date technologies. The prospect of direct election of the mayor should permit implementation of programs which are ever more sensitive to the needs of the citizens of Taipei. As such Taipei remains a microcosm of the economic and political developments occurring in the Republic of China in general.

References

A Brief Introduction to The City Planning of Taipei (1981) Bureau of Public Works, Taipei City Government, Taipei.

Ambruster, W. (1976) Letter from Taipei, *Far Eastern Economic Review* 93, Nov. 19, 70.

Ames, E. and M. Ames (1972) Taiwan's Development Typhoon, *Nation* Mar. 20, 370–372.

Baum, J. (1990) Chips are Down, *Far Eastern Economic Review* 150, Dec. 13, 63.

Brandt, D. P. (1981) Optimum Residential Building Heights: The Case of the Min Sheng New Community, Taipei, Taiwan, *Third World Planning Review* 3, 432–438.

Butterfield, F. (1984) Slaying Was Ordered from Taiwan, Lawyer Says, *New York Times*, Dec. 12, 18.

Central Daily News (1987) Taipei City Administrative District Transfer Reform, May 19, 2.*

Chen, C.-h. (1956) *City of Taipei*, Fu-Min Geographical Institute of Economic Development, Report no. 71, Taipei.

China Yearbook (1968, 1971/72) China Publishing Co., Taipei.

Copper, J. F. (1990) *Taiwan: Nation-State or Province?* Westview Press, Boulder.

Free China Journal (1988) Crime Does Not Pay Tax, Dec. 1, 7.

Glenn, W. (1968) Growing Like Topsy, *Far Eastern Economic Review* 61, Aug. 8, 280–289.

Goldstein, C. (1985) Chipping Away at the KMT, *Far Eastern Economic Review* 135, Nov. 28, 13–14.

Hong Kong, 1992 (1992) Hong Kong Government Information Services, Hong Kong.

Introduction to Taipei City Administration (1988) Department of Information, Taipei City Government, Taipei.

Introduction to Urban Planning of Taipei City (1990) City Planning Department, Bureau of Public Works, Taipei City Government, Taipei.

Ku, T. C. (1971) Problems Arising from the Rapid Development of Taipei City, pp. 372–400, in A. M. Woodruff and J. R. Brown, eds., *Land for the Cities of China*, John C. Lincoln Institute, University of Hartford, Hartford.

Lee, R. F. F. (1993) State-run Lotteries Reconsidered, *Free China Journal* Feb. 16, 4.

Lee, T.-h. (1980) Goals and Strategies for Taipei City, *Sino-American Relations* 6, 3–7.

Lin, D. (1992) Aged Buildings Yield to Boulevard, *Free China Journal* Oct. 20, 4.

Lin, Y.-y. (1991) Steps to Remodel Cities, *Free China Review* 41, 20–25.

Local Government Employment in Major County Areas (1985) (1985) US Superintendent of Documents, Washington.

Long, Y.-h. (1969) The Administration of Local Elections in Taipei, *Chinese Journal of Administration* 12, 20–27.

Lui, F.-l. (1978) Introduction to Institutional Format and Current Practices in Taiwan, ROC, pp. 299–318, in *Sino-American Workshop on Land Use Planning*, Academia Sinica, Taipei.

New Image of Taipei (1988) Department of Information, Taipei City Government, Taipei.

Pannell, C. W. (1973) *T'ai-Chung, T'ai-wan: Structure and Function*, University of Chicago, Department of Geography Research Paper no. 144, Chicago.

Preliminary (Sketch) Plan for the City of Taipei (1968) Urban and Housing Development Committee, Council for International Economic Cooperation and Development, Taipei.

Pun, A. (1992) Fat Cats Deflated in Election Bids; Voters Reward Enemies of Graft, *Free China Journal*, Dec. 22, 7.

Republic of China, 1988, A Reference Book (1988) Highlight International, New York.

Republic of China. A Reference Book 1991/92 (1991) Kwang hwa Publishing Co., Taipei.

Rohsenow, H. G. (1972) Traditional Taipei Neighborhoods. Some Consequences for Urbanization. Paper presented at the Annual Meeting of the Association for Asian Studies.

Shabad, T. (1972) *China's Changing Map. National and Regional Development, 1949–71*, Completely revised edition. Praeger, New York.

Sun, C.-h. (1990) Development of the National Geographic Information System in Taiwan, *Journal of Geographical Science* 14, 101–108.

Taipei-Keelung Metropolitan Regional Plan (1968) Urban and Housing Development Committee, Council for International Economic Cooperation and Development, Taipei.

Tanzer, A. (1981) End of a Taipei Rents Bargain, *Far Eastern Economic Review* 111, Feb. 27, 79–81.

Wang, H.-k. (1978) On Conceptual and Institutional Problems of Urban Land Use Planning in Republic of China, pp. 319–349 in *Sino-American Workshop on Land Use Planning*, Academia Sinica, Taipei.

Wang, I.-s. (n.d.) Taiwan's Administrative Hierarchy and its Geographical Implications, mimeo.

Welcome to the 21st Century (1987) Department of Information, Taipei City Government, Taipei.

Winckler, E. A. (1981) Roles Linking State and Society, pp. 50–88, in E. M. Ahern and H. Gates, eds., *The Anthropology of Taiwanese Society*, Stanford University Press, Stanford.

Yu, S. (1994) Three Taipei Mayoral Rivals Spar in Lively TV Debate, *Free China Journal*, Oct. 7, 2.

6
Coping with world city status

In virtually every subject area which has been discussed so far evidence of some type of problem or dislocation has been either presented or alluded to. In this chapter the details of the problems which Taipei residents must deal with are described and the programs implemented to deal with them evaluated. For convenience the problems are grouped into three categories: environmental, infrastructure, and social problems. All three categories share three main characteristics: longevity, complexity, and negative consequences. The description of the problems will show that many of the problems predate Taipei's growth; growth only exacerbated them and made their solutions all the more crucial. The evaluation of programs will show on the one hand the difficulties involved in reconciling conflicting economic, public, and social needs and goals. On the other hand the programs also show the extremes to which the government is willing to go in order to solve the problems. For example, in January 1991, Mayor Huang Ta-chou, at the direction of then Premier Hau Pei-tsun, visited Singapore in order to discover how that city-state has successfully coped with problems similar to Taipei's. Since there was no guarantee that such a fact-finding mission would in fact lead to any quick solutions to any problem, the city council balked at paying the travel expenses for Huang and the five city department heads who accompanied him. Nevertheless, the trip was made (*Central Daily News*, Jan. 8, 1991, 7; *China Post*, Jan. 29, 1991, 12).

While some of the negative consequences such as environmental pollution are quite obvious and unequivocal, the negative impacts of other problems are not always readily apparent. For example, there is now an increase in the incidence of panic disorder attributed to traffic jams, population density, and other environmental stresses (Lin, 1992).

In reviewing the three categories of problems it must be remembered that few Western cities could pretend to be able to cope with the magnitude of growth and change which Taipei has experienced (Ames and Ames, 1972). Furthermore, solving even a small part of any one of these problems may in the short run exacerbate others. In fact, in 1989 Mayor Wu Poh-hsiung issued a plea to Taipei residents to be patient during the construction of public projects, such as the building of the Mass Rapid Transit System. Wu centered his plea in part on the necessity of completing the project, lest life in Taipei become unbearable over the next decade (*Free China Journal*, Oct. 30, 1989, 3).

Environmental problems

Schinz (1989) has stated that the site of Taipei is one of the most beautiful urban settings in the world. Yet residents and visitors to Taipei would be more inclined to offer a contradictory hypothesis: that Taipei could not have been located in a worse location. Glenn (1968), for example, has argued that the hills are too far away to be seen even on a clear day. In 1969 Chang (1975) lamented that the blue sky was less visible, and that the city was noisy, dirty, and had fewer trees. Although Schinz's evaluation may rest on abstract aesthetic considerations, the more negative view is firmly grounded on daily experiences and empirical data that Taipei has a set of severe environmental problems. These include ground subsidence, water (in the form of drainage, flooding, supply, pollution, and sewerage problems), air and noise pollution, garbage disposal, slopeland development, and wildlife preservation.

Ground subsidence

Evidence that Taipei City and Basin were experiencing a subsidence problem first emerged in 1950 during a geological survey of the area (Yang, 1982). At that time land was sinking at the rate of 10 centimeters a year. Surveys during the 1970s showed that the rate of sinking had declined to between 2 and 3 centimeters a year. There was concern, however, that the cumulative effects of subsidence would reach dangerous proportions. Later surveys proved this concern to be true: for example, it was discovered that between 1969 and 1989 the site of the Taipei railroad station had sunk some 2.2 meters. In order to correct the problem of subsidence, in 1971 the national government imposed a ban on the pumping of ground water. This ban seems to have had an ameliorative effect since the water levels below New Park in Taipei rose from 40 meters below the surface to 15 meters (*Free China Journal*, Sept. 11, 1989, 3). In the late 1980s, however, the situation appears to have worsened again. In 1986 19 out of 194 monitoring stations showed some subsidence; by 1988 the number of stations with subsidence increased to 107 (*Free China Journal*, May 11, 1989, 3).

There is no one obvious cause of subsidence. Part of the explanation is found in the fact that the Taipei Basin was a salt lake during the late Pleistocene, with drying and uplift occurring much later (Yang, 1982). The Tamshui river was formed as the result of an earthquake said to have occurred during the Kang hsi Era (1662–1722). As such Taipei is located on top of sediments which may still not have reached any equilibrium. Pumping of ground water for industrial purposes and to permit construction of housing is the most obvious proximate cause of subsidence (*Free China Journal*, May 11, 1989, 3). Continued illegal pumping of water for industrial purposes is a most likely cause of the most recent findings of subsidence.

Since subsidence occurs so slowly the impact of the process is not always obvious. In Taipei Basin there has been some permanent loss of both agricultural lands and some plant and animal species, and the quality of ground water has declined due to increased salinity (Yang, 1982). In addition there are now areas that are permanently below sea level (Yang, 1982). The integrity of the foundations of some roads and bridges have been put in danger. Within Taipei City there is now a series of concentric rings of subsidence zones starting at the railroad station (Wester, 1988). In a five kilometer wide zone around the railroad station land has subsided about two meters. Land in a second ring extending out some three kilometers has experienced subsidence of about 1.5 meters. About six kilometers from the station the ground has sunk about a meter, and at seven kilometers there has been sinking of about half a meter. Beyond eight kilometers there does not seem to have been any subsidence at all. Some of this pattern is clearly related to geological features: in some directions as one leaves the railroad station one soon comes to hilly and mountainous areas where subsidence is not geologically possible. Problems arise as to how to deal with the railroad crossings near the Taipei railroad station (discussed below under transportation problems). At one point serious consideration was given to elevating the tracks since ground water was fluctuating at a level too close to the ideal below-ground track level. However, the most dramatic impact of subsidence is the occasional tilting of buildings, such as on 2 March 1993 (*Central Daily News*, Mar. 2, 1993, 7). Most often this occurs when the foundation for another building is being dug. The contractor is usually blamed for the accident and must compensate the owners of the buildings damaged. But ground subsidence is a more likely cause of the problem. Apart from strict enforcement of ordinances against the pumping of ground water, there appears to be little that the government can do to arrest the ground subsidence problem. Other suggested remedies such as improving drainage and dikes do not appear to have been effective (*Free China Journal*, May 11, 1989, 3).

Water

Just as water can appear in three forms, so water problems in Taipei appear in three categories – too much water, not enough water, and dirty water. The problem of surplus water derives from two sources. First, the average yearly rainfall for Taipei is some 2101 cm, with a recorded maximum of 3173 cm (Chen, 1957). The temporal distribution of rainfall is not uniform (Figure 3.1). Three types of regular and predictably recurring heavy rain contribute to the seasonal distribution of rainfall: winter cold fronts, the spring *Mei-yu* or Plum rains, and summer thundershowers (Hsu *et al.*, 1988). Flooding hazards from the winter and summer storms are greater in the southeastern parts of the city, while the hazard from the *Mei-yu* rains is greater in the northwestern parts (Hsu *et al.*, 1988). In addition, Taipei is occasionally hit by typhoons. All of this water ultimately seeks to flow to the center of the Taipei Basin, where the silted, sluggish rivers then carry the water to the China Sea some 200 miles to the northwest (Ames and Ames, 1972). This drainage is not only impeded by the degraded hydrological conditions of the streams, but by two confounding factors. First, the Tamshui river is tidal so that the river itself rises and falls in response to tidal action. When this takes place brackish waters are pushed into the Basin, sometimes at levels well above sea level. Since parts of the Taipei Basin are now below sea level, as discussed above, some form of flood protection is necessary (Ames and Ames, 1972). Secondly, the very walls designed to protect the Basin from flood damage contribute to drainage problems. What occurs is that flood waters are literally impounded behind the dikes and levees and then back up into sewers and into streets. This is what occurred, for example, in 1963, when Typhoon Gloria hit Taipei and waters rose 12 feet in parts of the city (Ames and Ames, 1972).

The need for some form of flood control was first recognized in 1958. However, the area covered by the plan was too small, and the protection it offered was too limited (*New Image of Taipei*, 1988). After Taipei was elevated to a special municipality plans were redesigned based on the standard of accommodating a major flood every five years. Special emphasis was placed on the role of pumping stations to help drain away water after typhoons. By 1969 planning for 350 kilometers of storm drains in Old Taipei was complete, and by 1971 plans for building some 180 kilometers of drains in the new districts were ready. In addition, more comprehensive, multi-stage plans for Taipei Basin and the building of a dike system were included in successive multi-year development plans written by the central government. However, the initial estimates of the total construction costs, NT$15.3 billion in 1975 terms, led to delays in both planning and construction of the dike system (Wong, 1987). In addition to dikes, levees and anti-flood gates were to be constructed and bridges either reinforced or reconstructed (Wong, 1987).

Despite delays some progress has been made in constructing drains and dikes. By 1989 some 319 kilometers of storm drains had been built in the old city area, and some 130 kilometers completed in the new districts (*New Image of Taipei*, 1988). In terms of dikes by 1989 some 76 003 meters of earthen dikes and 19 876 meters of concrete dikes had been constructed; in addition some 25 233 meters of embankments had been built. Along the Tamshui river about 70 percent of the dikes are concrete, whereas along other streams the dikes are most often earthen works. Despite major construction projects, during torrential rainfalls, streets and pedestrian underpasses still become impassable.

In addition to dikes, levees, and drainage systems, restrictions on development on the flood plain were suggested as a means of reducing the danger from flooding. In particular, conversion of paddy fields to industrial sites was to be curtailed, since the paddy land acted as a very effective sponge during floods (Ames and Ames, 1972). Relocation of some economic activities was also tried. Although the combination of restricted development and relocation would have offered the greatest long-term protection against flooding (Fan, 1977), these alternative programs did not succeed. Restrictions on land use transfers were apparently too difficult to enforce, and relocation often led to conflicts. In particular it appears that planners did not adequately take farmers' perceptions of floods or their socioeconomic backgrounds into consideration when targeting activities for relocation and areas for restrictions. The low indemnity the government was willing to pay farmers to relocate was also seen by farmers as a disadvantage (Wong, 1987).

Water shortages refer to the problem of providing the citizens of Taipei with potable water. The public water system was first established in 1908. By 1942 the system had a daily capacity of some 50 000 cubic meters of water. Since retrocession the system has been expanded in a series of four stages such that by 1989 some 250 000 cubic meters of water could be delivered daily (*Water Supply in Taipei*, 1990). The system was expanded by building a series of two dams, the Chingtan and Feitsui, along the headwaters of the Hsintien river. Some 95 percent of the water delivered by the Taipei water department comes from these facilities. Water from these dams is purified at three separate purification plants for delivery to the original city *chu* (districts) and the new *chu* of Nankang, Neihu, Chingmei, and Mucha. Spring and creek waters in the Yangmingshan area are the sources for the purification plants delivering water to Shihlin and Peitou *chu*. Water is delivered to individual homes and buildings through a distribution pipeline which is some 2501 kilometers in length. As with drainage and storm water abatement, development plans for the water system have been included as part of the national government's multi-year economic development plans. With the completion of the Feitsui dam in 1991, planners hope that water demand for the city can be met through to the year 2030. Such hopes were dashed by a 100 day drought in the summer of 1993 which resulted in dangerously low levels behind the dam. Although rainfall increased in the Fall, 1993, and Winter, 1994, precipitation averaged only 43 percent of normal and the entire reservoir system serving Taipei did not refill until late summer, 1994, when several typhoons passed by.

Although most Taipei residents appreciate the increase in the quantity of available water, the question of quality of water remains a vexing problem. Officially all water leaving the purification plants is potable with a zero bacteria and coliform count. However, longstanding tradition leads both residents and visitors alike to avoid drinking raw tap water. Hotels commonly supply guests with boiled water on request, or, increasingly, supply a small water heating appliance in each room. Residents routinely boil water, or drink soft drinks, fruit juices, or bottled water. If in fact the water leaves the purification system pure, where is the problem?

Up until the 1980s the problem was thought to originate in the pipes which delivered water. Many of them were old, rusted, or broken, since they were originally put down by the Japanese. Pathogens in the soil, derived from the use of nightsoil in agriculture or from the leaching of septic tanks, thus contaminated the water. A World Health Organization survey during the 1970s calculated that life expectancy in Taipei was reduced by one year due to the high incidence of gastroenteritic diseases. The per capita cost for treating these diseases was put at $4.00 per year (Ames and Ames, 1972). Although much of the water pipeline has been replaced there is still widespread fear that the water is compromised before it reaches the tap. No doubt much of this fear relates to two telling statistics: only 17 percent of the household waste in Taipei is treated (*Republic of China Yearbook*, 1993); and the entire 103 kilometers of the Tamshui river is polluted with dissolved oxygen levels at zero (*Sewerage Development in Taipei City*, 1991). River water typically has a bacteria count of 360 to 34 000 per milliliter and a coliform count of 35–10 800. The municipal government's position is that pollution of Taipei's rivers is mainly due to domestic sewerage (*Guide to the Department of Environmental Protection*, 1984). If this position is indeed true, it is a relatively new development since the concentration of industry in Taipei was a major source of river pollution during the 1960s and 1970s (Selya, 1975). For the late 1970s industry's relative share of water pollution was put at between 28 and 35 percent (Chang and Tang, 1978). Significantly, one of the main assumptions of the supporting documents for the design of the Taipei Basin sewerage program was that industry was and would remain a substantial contributor to water pollution (*Industrial Wastes Survey*, 1971, V/3). Furthermore, this somewhat restricted view is not necessarily supported by data on the findings of mine and factory investigations by the Taipei Department of Environmental Protection (DEP). On average the

DEP investigates some 1400 cases of suspected industrial pollution a year and finds some 513 of these to be serious enough to warrant fines or threat of prosecution. In some 39 per cent of its return investigations the DEP finds that industrial waste treatment facilities or procedures have not been improved (*Guide to the Department of Environmental Protection*, 1984). Shih *et al.* (1989) were able to identify 79 significant industrial contributors to water pollution.

Regardless of the origins of water pollution, however, the main issue is finding a solution. In terms of industrial pollutants, the focus has been on requiring industries to treat their waste on site. When companies cannot meet this requirement, they either go out of business or move to a new location. In terms of domestic sewerage the solution has taken on the form of building a separate sewerage treatment system. As with other large environmentally related improvements in Taipei, grandiose plans were designed, included in the multi-year national development plans, and then had to be scaled back (*Sewerage Development in Taipei City*, 1978, 1991). A 1972 master plan for the entire Taipei Basin called for three trunk sewers with numerous secondary branches to be operating by 2020. This system was designed so that all effluent would be piped to a sewerage treatment plant at Pa li at the mouth of the Tamshui river. Treated waste would then be disposed of via an outfall in the Straits of Formosa. Although work was begun on this system by 1985 the plan was revised to include only Taipei City, with just one trunk line. Two treatment plants, the Dihua and Minsheng, were built within the city limits. As the length of secondary and service lines was expanded the Dihua plant was upgraded to include secondary treatment. By 1991 the two treatment plants had been completed, as had a nightsoil dumping station. Although some 60 percent of the length of both the main trunk and secondary sewers had been built, only 13 percent of the area, and 22 percent of the households, had been fully connected to the system. Completion of the Taipei-only part of the system is still targeted for 2020, with development of the full Taipei Basin system the responsibility of a joint Taipei City and Taiwan provincial government endeavor, albeit with an indeterminate future date. Although building of the trunk and service lines has been very disruptive of traffic and personal lives, once completed they have served to significantly upgrade the environmental quality of the affected neighborhoods.

Air and noise pollution

In order to evaluate the extent of air pollution and the effectiveness of policies designed to curb it, the history of the administrative framework for dealing with air pollution, especially data collection, must first be reviewed. It was not until 1968 that the Environmental Sanitation

Department (ESD) was established with air pollution as one of its designated responsibilities (*Air Pollution Control in Taipei City*, 1972). The actual collection of data on the quality of air was not started until April 1970, when the first monitoring station was put in place. Over the years a series of 22 air sampling stations, 15 air pollution monitoring stations, and two mobile inspection vehicles, have been added to the monitoring network (*New Image of Taipei*, 1988). The number of monitoring facilities is in excess either of what would be the United States EPA standards for a city with the area and population of Taipei, or for optimal monitoring (Modak and Lohani, 1985).

There was an attempt before 1968 to control one of the main sources of air pollution, the use of soft coal. Although a ban was put into place in 1955 it was basically unenforceable for four reasons (*Air Pollution Control in Taipei City*, 1972). First, it was extremely difficult to control the flow of coal into the city. Secondly, penalties were too light. Thirdly, there was no substitute for burning coal. Fourthly, one of the main users of soft coal, steam locomotive engines of the Taiwan Railroad Administration, were exempt from the ban.

After 1968 the ESD, reorganized and renamed the Environmental Protection Agency (EPA) in 1982, began enforcing the ban. As such it was able to force the closing of coking plants and black tile plants in Nankang. The ESD was indirectly assisted in its efforts to reduce the use of soft coal by the widespread adoption of piped gas for home heating and cooking. In 1968 the four companies supplying gas, the Great Taipei Gas Company, the Yangmingshan Gas Corporation, the Sinsin Gas Corporation, and the Sinhu Gas Corporation, supplied only 4.7 million cubic meters of gas to some 9115 customers. By 1989 they were supplying some 276 million cubic meters of gas to 405 164 customers. There were four reasons for actively pursuing the soft coal ban. First, it was an obvious source of pollution. Secondly, the haze which hung over Taipei as a result of its use was unfavorably compared with levels of pollution in Tokyo during the 1950s and in Manchester, England, during its worst bout of air pollution in the period 1933–44 (Chang and Tang, 1978). Thirdly, technology, in the form of improved furnaces or alternative fuels, could play only a limited role in reducing pollution since entrepreneurs either did not use the new technology properly, or switched to high sulfur oil fuels which only further aggravated pollution. Fourthly, meteorological impacts on pollution in the Taipei Basin cannot be overcome. Given the distribution of hills and mountains around Taipei, three unfortunate consequences follow. First, inversions are common, especially in the summer (*Air Pollution Control in Taipei City*, 1972). Secondly, recirculation of air, and pollutants, is weak (Bierma, 1985). Thirdly, the prevailing winds, from the northeast, frequently do move pollutants from industrial to residential areas (Chang, and Tang, 1978; Chen, 1957).

In addition to enforcing the soft coal ban the ESD strongly advocated the adoption of additional administrative palliatives with the potential of reducing air pollution, including strict enforcement of zoning codes, restricting inmigration to Taipei, expanding green spaces in the city, paving streets and lanes, the drafting of strict national laws on pollution since the ESD could not enforce municipal standards in the rest of Taipei Basin, research on how to improve the combustion efficiency of existing and new coal and oil burning equipment for commercial and home use, and the training of more pollution technicians to serve in the expanded monitoring network (*Air Pollution Control in Taipei City*, 1972).

Starting in 1978, using a combination of fines and government incentives to move, the ESD was able further to curb industrial pollution with the removal of seven out of eight steel mills operating in the city (*Guide to the Department of Environmental Protection*, 1984). According to the EPA, the removal of the main industrial polluters resulted in the removal of 90 percent of the air pollutants in the heavily industrialized parts of Taipei. As such the EPA now holds that apart from dust associated with construction, the greatest source of air pollution in Taipei is motor vehicles (*Guide to the Department of Environmental Protection*, 1984). This view is also supported by the work of Modak and Lohani (1985).

There are several reasons why it is difficult to evaluate the claim that pollution levels, especially for particulate matter, are down and that motor vehicles are now the main source of pollution. First, Taipei always seems to be grimy. Even after a heavy rainfall everything looks and feels dirty. Street washing by city maintenance vehicles or by shop owners rarely improves the appearance of streets or sidewalks. Secondly, the network of monitoring stations is still in the process of being established. As such equipment is often moved from one site to another, so there are numerous sites with either short or terminated data series available. Thirdly, it appears that in terms of particulate matter the EPA has adopted a rather lax standard. It only measures particulate matter which is less than 10 microns, apparently assuming that it is particles of this size which pose the greatest public health hazard (Bierma, 1985). One effect of this do-it-yourself standard is that it reduces the measured particulate matter by one quarter to one half compared to a stricter US EPA standard. Fourthly, Shih *et al.* (1989) found no significant improvement in the quality of the air over Taipei.

Despite the difficulty of assessing the government's claims about the extent and origins of pollution, it is possible to describe some broad temporal and spatial patterns of pollution and review ongoing government programs to reduce pollution. In terms of dust fall annual averages for the entire city have declined from 22.5 tons per square kilometer per month in 1970 to a low of 13.7 in 1985; since then, however, there has been a fluctuating pattern of between 15.1 and 20.6 tons per square kilometer per month. When dustfall by *chu* is the unit of interest it appears that the places which had the dirtiest air in the early 1970s, Shuangyuan, Sungshan, and Nankang, are still the dirtiest. One *chu*, Kuting, has had a significant decline in dust fall, while Chingmei and Neihu have joined the other three dirty air *chu* as problem areas. In contrast, sulfur dioxide concentrations are highest in the southwestern parts of the city and decline as one goes in a northeasterly direction (Yau, 1985). Over the entire city sulfur dioxide levels have fallen from 0.041 ppm in 1973 to 0.0157 in 1989. Concentrations of ozone and carbon monoxide have similarly declined. In contrast, ambient concentrations of nitrogen oxides have increased. Sulfur dioxide concentrations appear to have a distinct diurnal distribution with high levels occurring at dawn and in the early afternoon (Chang and Tang, 1978). Carbon monoxide and ozone concentrations show similar patterns (Modak and Lohani, 1985; *Free China Journal*, Sept. 22, 1988, 3), and are three to fifteen times the annual averages. All these temporal and diurnal patterns are thought to be related to changes in traffic patterns and the mix of transportation types (DeVries, 1989; Modak and Lohani, 1985).

Given the consensus that the main cause of air pollution is motor vehicles, the EPA's emphasis on emissions testing is a reasonable policy. Tests are conducted under four separate programs. First, there are random site inspections, where drivers are subject to sight monitoring and particularly polluting vehicles are ticketed and the drivers fined. Secondly, emissions tests are an integral part of the motor vehicle registration and re-registration process. Thirdly, random roadside emissions tests are conducted periodically. Fourthly, special testing programs for specific types of vehicles, sometimes for specific time periods, are conducted (*Guide to the Department of Environmental Protection*, 1984). An example of this fourth type of program would be the random checking of motorcycles at 30 major intersections which started on 3 July 1989, with the goal of checking 60 000 motorcycles a month (*China Post*, Jul. 3, 1989, 12). This program was an extension of a four-week free emissions testing program from mid-November to mid-December 1988. Two types of vehicles which are especially subject to the first and fourth programs are motorcycles and buses. Restrictions on imports of cars and large motorcycles during the 1960s and 1970s led people to purchase small, two-cycle motorbikes and motorcycles (Bierma, 1985). These are notorious polluters as it is often very difficult to get the oil and gasoline mixtures exactly right. It has been claimed that some 95 percent of all exhaust emissions are from two-cycle motor vehicles (*Free China Journal*, Sept. 22, 1988, 3). Commonly a quarter of both intra-city and inter-city buses operating on the streets of Taipei fail emissions inspections (*Free China Journal*, Nov. 28, 1988, 3).

Given the large number of construction sites open in Taipei for housing and infrastructure development, both described below, the EPA has also targeted contractors for inspection. Long-term improvement in the quality of the air will occur once the major projects are finished and once the vehicle mix on the streets of Taipei includes fewer units which are more fuel efficient (DeVries, 1989).

Before improvements evolve, however, the research agenda of the EPA should be broadened. Little work has been done on the climatological, hydrological, and health impacts of air pollution. Although long-term studies on the climate of Taipei have been conducted for the periods 1898 to 1963 and 1898 to 1965 (Peng, 1967; 1968), only one study on more current data has been published (Wong, 1986). This study suggests that compared with earlier weather patterns in Taipei and Tamshui, precipitation and the incidence of foggy days have increased in Taipei as a result of what Wong terms the "urban climate effect". Bierma (1985) has noted that development of acid rain in Taipei is to be expected given the levels of sulfur dioxide. DeVries has suggested (1989) that the EPA's assumption that winds carry most pollutants out to sea must be more fully tested, since basic knowledge on atmospheric dispersion processes operating in Taiwan is lacking. The considerably higher pollution levels shown on maps in newspapers for Sanchung, due west of Taipei, suggest that such studies of atmospheric circulation would help not only in understanding pollution dispersion but in formulating regional approaches to pollution. Chang and Tang (1978) have postulated that the increase in the incidence of lung cancer in Taipei is related to the increase in air pollution. This hypothesis should be rigorously tested to see whether the lack of safety measures for all types of workers constitutes good public policy. Such questions should be conducted for their own sake. However, given the public awareness of the causes of air pollution and unwillingness to modify behavior to decrease pollution levels (Wu, 1987), unequivocal results from research may be the only way to impose on the citizens of Taipei strong anti-pollution measures.

Just as Taipei always seems dirty, so too it always seems to be noisy. During the pre-1970s period the noise appeared to come mostly from the itinerant merchants who announced their arrival in an area with a distinct noise maker, call or song. After the 1970s noise seems to come from traffic, construction activities, and businessmen using mini-public address systems to play music and announce their not-to-be-missed bargains. The EPA has responded to the din on the streets in four ways. First, it erected a large electronic monitoring station with visual display of the decibel level in front of the Taipei railroad station. During the rebuilding of the old station, described below, this station was moved to a site in the Hsimenting commercial area. Drivers and pedestrians seem to ignore this station. Secondly, the EPA conducts on-the-spot checks of noise levels at industrial, commercial, construction, recreational and religious sites.

Frequently these checks are made in response to complaints by neighbors (*Guide to the Department of Environmental Protection*, 1984). Thirdly, it instituted a ban on loud noises between 8 p. m. and 7 a.m. The ban is supposed to apply equally to residential, scenic, cultural, and educational areas. Religious activities such as temple chanting and use of fire crackers are also prohibited. However, activities related to national holidays – such as Chinese Lunar New Year, Dragon Boat Festival, Mid-Autumn Festival, Double Ten Day (10 October, the day that a revolt against the Ching dynasty started, ushering in revolutionary activities throughout China), and Taiwan Retrocession Day – are exempt from the ban (*Free China Journal*, May 4, 1993, 4). Finally, the EPA advocates the enactment and enforcement of more stringent national anti-noise regulations for vehicles and traffic. Completion of major transportation infrastructure projects should help reduce some noise as noise barriers are constructed, but better driving habits by Taipei drivers and a reduction in the number of vehicles appear to be the only significant changes which will make Taipei quieter.

Garbage disposal

A walk down any street is all that it takes to show that Taipei has a garbage disposal problem. Piles of plastic garbage bags frequently block the way. Makeshift garbage dumps appear anytime a building is being built or renovated. Sidewalk garbage cans are frequently overflowing with refuse. The problem can be readily demonstrated with data from the municipal department of public works. In 1968 Taipei residents generated 440 pounds of garbage per capita each year; by 1989 the per capita production had risen to 925 pounds. On a daily basis the city had to collect 852 metric tons a day; by 1989 this had increased to 3138 metric tons. The growth of garbage exceeded the growth of population by a factor of 3.9 for the period 1968 to 1989. At 1989 rates of garbage production, the waste stream from households alone is expected to grow 10 percent a year. However, it was not the daily chore of avoiding garbage in the streets nor the statistics which finally awakened the government and residents of Taipei to the seriousness of their garbage problem. Rather, it took a two-week fire in 1984 at the city's main garbage dump in Neihu, notoriously known as "garbage mountain." What started as a spontaneous, heat-induced methane fire soon spread over a wide area, feeding on the abundant plastic materials on the dump (Bierma, 1985). The hazard from the fire was worsened by the dense smoke given off as the plastic materials burned.

As a result of the fire the city decided to shut down the dump. In its place a modern sanitary fill was created in 1985 at another site, in Mucha. However, since this new facility had only a six-year use lifespan, and neither the city nor the provincial government could find another area willing to take garbage, the city began building three incinerators. The first, adjacent to the Neihu dump, went on line in January 1991, with a capacity of some 900 metric tons a day. Two others, with 1500 and 1800 ton capacity, are under construction in Mucha and Shihlin.

As with other problems, this one seems to have caught government planners and officials unawares. Some have argued that this is because before 1980 recycling was rather common. Scavengers roamed the streets picking over garbage. However, this system seems to have broken down. Three basic reasons have been cited for the breakdown (Underwood, 1993). First, the world market in raw materials collapsed so that it was actually cheaper to import new raw materials than to recycle. Secondly, with per capita income up, there was less interest in recycling. Rather people wanted the latest in fashions, in entertainment. Thirdly, the arrival of the international fast food chains led to widespread replacement of recyclable food-serving equipment with disposable dishes. Local food vendors soon adopted similar serving containers. Although this step has the potential for breaking the chain of transmission of hepatitis, it has also increased the waste stream.

By law, recycling should play a more important role in disposing of garbage. 1988 amendments to the Solid Waste Disposal Act mandate that industries must properly recycle or dispose of waste they generate. This requirement means that industry must either shift waste to approved landfills or incinerate their waste on site in their own incinerators. Furthermore, everyone is required to recycle PET (polyethylene), glass, tires, cans, and batteries. Unfortunately the law was not enforced until 1990. In order to get PET recycled, consumers are offered a NT$2 refund on bottles they return to stores. Some recycling experts in Taiwan feel that the emphasis on PET is misplaced, since PET is just 1 percent of the garbage stream. In contrast paper constitutes 40 percent (Underwood, 1993). In order to encourage recycling the government permitted in 1989 the import of some 1500 "igloo" recycling bins from the Netherlands. These colored coded (yellow for metal, red for PET bottles, green for glass, and blue for paper) bins were put in Taipei and Kaohsiung City for a three-year trial period. Unfortunately this attempt at recycling seems to have failed, since the bins were removed from the sidewalks after the test period. Environmental groups felt that the bins were too big for Taipei's sidewalks, too expensive to buy and maintain, and inefficient. Part of their displeasure with the bins stems from the monopoly on recycling the collected materials which the government granted to a beverage manu-facturing association (Underwood, 1993). Glass and PET manufacturers also opposed the program as they felt it would destroy their industry. Several programs have developed in place of the bins. Many schools have recycling centers. The city government started a pilot recycling project in

1992 in Neihu with regularly scheduled pick-up places and times. This project was apparently so successful that the city plans to extend it to all the city *chu* by the year 2000 (Underwood, 1993). Garbage collection fees have also been increased in the hope of encouraging more recycling. In addition thought has been given to legalizing the scavengers instead of the city government hiring its own recycling workers. Although not directly related to recycling the city has also sponsored city "clean-up" days, such as the one on 10 September 1989, when residents collected so much trash the event wound up in the *Guinness Book of Records*! In order to make the city more attractive the government in December 1985, began a program of night-time garbage collection. What is obvious to all concerned is that with disposal sites in short supply, residents of Taipei must recycle more or drown in their own garbage. Barring recycling the only alternatives involve heightened levels of environmental pollution and an increasingly unattractive urban and rural landscape.

Slopeland development

Urban development in Taipei is limited by land in two ways. First, some 60 percent of the area is not suitable for urban development due to its slope. Second, land scarcity has led to increases in the value of land. Existing land law does not seem able to deal adequately with the need to curb speculation and ensure land owners a realistic and fair return on their land when they sell it. These two themes permeate all discussions of historical development, economy, government planning, and social and environmental problems in Taipei. Given the inability of the political process to deal with land issues, both the government and developers have sought a less divisive solution – use of slopelands for urban development (Figure 6.1).

Government and developers have started to use slopelands despite the explicit warning against doing so in the first modern attempt at planning (*Taipei-Keelung Metropolitan Regional Plan*, 1968). Physical planners in particular have cited the need to preserve hills to ensure an adequate water supply, to prevent erosion, and to arrest further silting of the river systems in Taipei Basin as a check against flooding. A study by Shih *et al.* (1990) clearly shows, however, that between 1964 and 1984 slopelands in Taipei City and Basin have been increasingly used for urban purposes such as housing, factories, schools, and even golf courses, at the expense of rice fields, orchards, and forests. In particular in areas of northern Taipei with slopes between 15 and 30 degrees and 30 to 55 degrees are being used. Even areas with slopes greater than 55 degrees have had houses built on them. From the perspective of a home buyer slopeland has two attractions: it is cheaper than land closer to the center of Taipei, and since it is elevated

Figure 6.1 The shortage of land has led to the use of hills and slopes for urban uses in place of older and ecologically more appropriate agricultural activities

the presumption is that the air is not as polluted as the air on lower elevations (Wang, 1989). Fan (1985) has argued that there are few really suitable sites for large-scale urban development in the hill areas, and that in deciding to use slopeland for anything but agricultural or conservation purposes a full calculation of all the social, economic, and ecological costs and benefits must be made. What in fact has happened is that local contractors with little professional knowledge or experience with slope-lands go in, clear cut all the vegetation cover, build and pave (Wang, 1989). The resulting landscape looks scarred and unstable. But as was the case in restricting development on the Tamshui flood plain, economic expediency seems to be winning over common sense. Since such behavior increasingly receives official sanction (*Republic of China*, 1988), it will be left to a new generation of politicians and planners to correct the mistakes of developing slopeland.

Wildlife preservation

Perhaps no other single issue better symbolizes the difficulties in resolving the conflicts between genuine environmental concerns and urban develop-ment than wildlife preservation. On paper the conflict has been resolved in favor of the wildlife: in September 1983, 116 hectares of the Kuantu Plain were designated by the national government as one of eight national nature preserves. This set-aside was immediately seconded by the city government (*Welcome to the 21st Century*, 1987). Management of the Kuantu preserve was delegated to the Taipei Department of Reconstruction. On two separate occasions this designation was reinforced by actions taken by the mayor of Taipei. In 1990 a Wild Geese Park was designated in the vicinity of the Huachiang Bridge, at the confluence of the Tamshui river and Hsintien Creek. This 70.8 hectare tract of land was specifically set aside to supplement the area already reserved in the Kuantu Plain (Lee, 1992a). With the cooperation of the Republic of China Wild Bird Society a 520 meter long tile path was built at the Wild Geese Park site to permit better observation of the birds. At each of six stations along the path members of the Wild Bird Society are available to answer questions about the park. In 1991, the Wild Bird Society petitioned Mayor Huang to set up a nature park in Kuantu Plain, and this seemingly duplicative project was immediately granted (Lee, 1991).

Kuantu Plain is a 1300 hectare tract of land bounded by the tracks of the Taipei–Tamshui railroad to the north, and the Keelung river to the south (Figure 2.7). The area is protected by a 3.4 meter dike, designed to prevent a "five-year" flood. The height of this dike is to be increased to accommodate a 200-year flood (Huang, 1989). Since this tract is considered to be the last remaining undeveloped area in Taipei City, concerns have been voiced as to whether or not the refuge designation can be sustained. There are strong fears that no Taipei mayor will be able to withstand the pressures to open the entire area for urban development (*Free China Review*, 1991, 18), despite the desire of the city to keep the area in its natural state and to limit development. There are good reasons for such fears. Property owners with land holdings on the plain have openly expressed an interest in seeing high density development (Welch, 1991), since this will maximize their return on the sale of their holdings. A major east–west road, Taduh Road, already cuts across the plain and a station for the Mass Rapid Transit System (MRTS) has also been planned for the plain (Heikkila, 1988). One final cause for fear was the request from the municipal Research, Development, and Evaluation Commission to the Graduate Institute of Urban Planning of National Chung-hsing University to carry out a feasibility study for development of the plain (Huang, 1989). Although the contents of the final report were not publicized, in 1988 Mayor Wu announced a development plan for the entire plain. The plan called for a nature preserve, a nature park, an academic and cultural center, a man-made lake, a sports stadium (in anticipation of a successful bid to host the 2002 Asian Games), and a mixture of public and private housing. Originally housing was set at a level to accommodate some 210 000 people, although this number was later revised down to 120 000 (Welch, 1991).

Opposition to the development plan came from many quarters. City council members did not understand assumptions which were behind the land allocations in the plan. They wondered how the facilities for the Asian Games could be kept useful once the games were over. One suggestion was that the facilities be converted to a city college of physical education. They also wondered who would be able to afford the low density housing planned for large parts of the plain (Welch, 1991). Conservationists and environmentalists had a wide range of objections. First, they pointed out that the area was seen as a significant ecological area and an ideal location for a wildlife refuge by a recognized authority on mangrove vegetation (Wester, 1988). They wondered why his recommendation that a nature park be established, in what was termed the best bird-watching site in northern Taiwan, was ignored (Wester, 1988). Secondly, they resented the fact that they had not been consulted at any point in the planning process. Thirdly, they felt that the ecological values of the plain had not been properly assessed. For example, the potential role of the flora and fauna on the plain in assessing the environmental quality of the Tamshui river seems to have been ignored in the feasibility study (Lee, 1991). A fourth environmental issue is that development will also require significant expenditure on drainage projects (Huang, 1989). There are several reasons for the need for drainage works. First, the dike walls prevent some rainwater from readily draining into the river. Second, the relatively flat topography is crossed by three creeks (the Kuantu, Sui-mo-kung, and Kwei-tze-kung), which are fed in part from rainwater coming off the nearby Tatun mountains which rise up to more than 1000 meters. Third, the fact that the plain is covered by layers of unconsolidated sedimentary deposits (30 meters deep in the north, and 250 meters deep in the south) also complicates drainage patterns, since the silty clay loam does not drain well. The most logical solution to the drainage problem is a series of artificial lakes, which could be integrated into a housing landscape, and from which storm water could be pumped out on a regular basis (Huang, 1989). Finally, there was concern that since past planning of Taipei had ignored the importance of open spaces, planners still had not taken a long-term view of the potential of Kuantu (Welch, 1991).

City planning officials defend the plan on several grounds. For example, Lee Fan-yen, deputy director of the municipal office of urban development, points out that something must be done to open up Taipei's periphery in order to dampen the frenetic development of the core area, and that Kuantu Plain is located in an area which will permit an opening to the peripheral areas in Taipei county (Welch, 1991). Planning officials also point out that regardless of the details of a plan, someone or some group always objects, that planners are bound by external forces which inhibit their ability to plan freely, and that the public is not interested in integrated development with long-term future advantages (Welch, 1991).

In the debate over how to use the plain properly, two interesting observations seem to have been ignored. First, for all the insistence that Kuantu Plain is the last remaining virgin area, it turns out that until 1965 most of the area was used for rice production. Air photographs from the 1960s and 1970s show the land in active agricultural use, and man-made landscape relics, such as paths, irrigation canals, and even some farm buildings are still present. Large-scale production of rice was abandoned for various reasons. The soils apparently have been degraded by improper use of pesticides. Changes in the hydrology of the area also reduced the ability of the land to produce a large rice crop. Hydrological changes occurred because of dam construction along the head waters of the Tamshui river, the construction of flood control projects including the channelization of the river and dike construction, and ground subsidence owing to over-pumping of ground water (Wester, 1988). Although by 1988 subsidence had stabilized, salinization of the soils had progressed to the point where rice could no longer be grown. Since the abandonment of rice production began natural vegetation has gone through a significant change. Herbaceous phragmites and cyperus have been displaced by mangroves (kandelia) (Wester, 1988). What is present on the Kuantu Plain therefore is a series of mixed vegetation/land use types: some new, "wild" plant communities, some farm land, unvegetated mud flats, and open water. Some of the conditions, such as the bare mud flats considered so ideal for a wild bird refuge, appear then to be rather late developments and may represent part of an ongoing cycle of plant diffusion and succession. In short, the physical conditions of the plain may represent just a temporary ecological phase.

The second observation deals with the planned station for the MRTS. It has been pointed out that the location of this station is not in the center of the plain, where the proposed economic center of development would be. If the peripheral location is retained then the MRTS will not be useful in reducing traffic congestion in the Kuantu area as residents will have to use cars just to get to the MRTS station. If this is the case, it is not clear that cars will be abandoned once the daily commute has started in them (Heikkila, 1988).

Resolving the conflicting desires for long-term use of Kuantu Plain will not be easy. But the resolution will unquestionably revolve around the land issue. For many players in the debate the low, "official" price the government can pay owners for land, even when augmented with a 40 percent supplement, is the main stumbling block to ensuring that even a diminished wildlife refuge remains viable. Since the government is reluctant to take large areas over using its powers of eminent domain, the only realistic alternative is to let market forces dictate development. If this is the case, then high density development will occur at the expense of ecological sense and aesthetic considerations.

Social problems

Given the overall impression of prosperity in Taipei it is possible to assume that few if any social problems exist. Yet from the perspective of the citizens of Taipei at least five social problems – crime, prostitution, the aborigines, the elderly, and poverty – need to be solved.

Crime

Whether or not Taipei has a crime problem depends very much on the perspective of the person who is answering the question. Foreigners have consistently tended to see the relatively low crime rate as a great attraction for visitors (Chang, 1983; Smith, 1981). The Population Crisis Committee (1990) gave Taipei a moderate rating on public safety based on the number and rate of murders. Yet an observant visitor to the city could not help but notice that on top of the walls surrounding older houses it is common to find anti-burglar precautions in the form of sharp glass shards buried in cement and a few strings of barbed wire. Iron bars are also quite common; 70 per cent of all homes and apartments have them according to one poll on crime (*Free China Journal*, Oct. 18, 1990, 3). Those traveling late at night during the 1960s can also remember seeing armed guards in more upscale neighborhoods. Public fist fights, with no attempt at intervention by onlookers or passers-by, have become more common. Rapes and robberies are said to be carried out by one out of every ten cabdrivers (WuDunn, 1990).

When a more precise statistical answer to the extent of the crime problem is sought, the results are just as ambiguous (Table 6.1). It is true that in the period from 1968 to 1989 the number of crimes increased at a rate almost twice that of population growth. It is also true that crime rates in Taipei have ranged from two to three times those of the province of Taiwan (Meng, 1984). And the percentage of the broad categories of crime committed in Taipei is also out of proportion to Taipei's proportion of Taiwan's population (Table 6.2). Furthermore, the crime data published by the municipal government cover three types of crimes each with subcategories: criminal charges (23 subcategories), economic security (5 subcategories), and offenses (4 subcategories). Yet nowhere in these data is there any information about the incidence of rape or traffic violations, suggesting that either these crimes are under-reported, or that they are not counted as crimes, or that their extent is hidden by the classification system used to record and report crimes.

Whichever interpretation ultimately holds, it must be remembered that the data base on which Taipei's problem is judged is at best flawed. So flawed in fact that even officials in Taipei need to conduct special surveys

Table 6.1 Types of crimes in Taipei, 1968 and 1989 (percent)

Type of crime	1968	1989
Burglary	76.03	60.96
Robbery	0.69	5.33
Murder	2.64	1.44
Injury	3.46	6.22
Narcotics	3.41	1.59
Infringement	0.57	1.68
Fraud	2.29	1.54
Threats	1.52	2.25
Corruption	0.06	0.02
Receiving stolen goods	3.16	1.38
Forgery	0.68	1.80
Destruction of property	0.24	1.29
Obscenities	1.33	2.31
Personal freedom violations	0.50	1.42
Gambling	0.40	5.26
Counterfeiting currency	0.01	0.02
Public safety violations	0.49	0.13
Family disputes	0.59	0.82
Public order violations	0.05	0.33
Official duties violations	0.35	0.32
Registration violations	0.11	0.62
False accusations	0.03	0.73
All other crimes	1.27	12.54
Total number of crimes	7 955	18 084

Source: Calculated from Statistical Abstract of Taipei Municipality, 1990 (1990).

to estimate the extent of some problems. For example, a special survey of public schools in 1991 was necessary to establish that only 5.48 percent of the 3850 *Taiwanese* students who use amphetamines are found in the Taipei school system (*China Post*, Jan 12, 1991, 12). Another sign that the data system is flawed is found in the major gain in the "other" crimes category (Table 6.1). In addition it may be that public concern over crime is an over-reaction to the unprecedented rise in bank robberies and murders which took place in 1983 (Chang, 1983). A final complicating factor is the conversion of illegal organizations into legal ones such as real estate, stock brokers, or investment corporations to mask their illegal activities. Some members of organized crime groups have reportedly become city councilmen (Sheu, 1990).

With these caveats in mind, it is possible to describe the temporal shifts in reported crimes and sketch a basic geography of crime. Over the long term two contradictory trends appear. On the one hand there has been a steep increase in the overall crime rate. On the other hand there has been a

Table 6.2 Rates of criminal activities per 100 000 population

Type of activity	1968	1989	% Change 1968–1989
All crime	495.5	669.1	127.3
Burglary	376.9	345.1	54.2
Robbery	3.4	40.3	1 883.0
Murder	13.0	10.4	34.3
Injury	17.0	34.3	237.5
Narcotics	16.0	10.1	73.8
Infringement	2.8	13.9	74.0
Fraud	11.3	9.4	39.0
Threats	7.5	11.8	164.4
Corruption	3.0	0.1	−80.0
Receiving stolen goods	15.6	8.2	−11.5
Public safety violations	24.0	0.4	−71.8
Forgery	3.4	6.8	238.9
Destruction of property	1.2	13.9	1 047.0
Obscenities	6.6	9.2	254.0
Personal freedom violations	2.5	41.3	522.0
Gambling	3.0	1.1	3 390.6
Counterfeiting	0.1	5.4	3 000.0
Family disputes	2.9	3.1	208.0
Public order violations	0.2	2.4	1 975.0
Official duties violations	1.7	3.5	128.5
Registration violations	0.6	3.2	955.6
False accusations	0.1	7.6	6 850.1
Economic crimes	132.4	60.4	−23.1
Offense crimes (vice)	12 170.1	376.3	−94.9
Juvenile delinquency	122.2	152.9	109.4
Population growth			68.4
Teenage population growth			26.1

Source: Calculated from *Statistical Abstract of Taipei Municipality, 1990* (1990).

significant shift in the types of crimes committed: burglary has declined while robbery, injuries, and gambling have all increased. This suggests that there is a shift away from so-called property crimes and towards violent ones. Some types of crimes – corruption, receiving stolen goods, and violation of public safety – have actually diminished, while others – murder and fraud – have grown at a rate far below that of population growth. In terms of annual cycles of crime, August, November, April, and January are the months with highest rates of reported crime, while February and December have the lowest. Over an average week crimes are more often committed on weekdays than weekends. Over a 24 hour period, 65 percent of crimes take place between 6 p.m. and 6 a.m., with the exception of residential burglary (Meng, 1984).

In terms of the geography of crime, two perspectives are possible: where

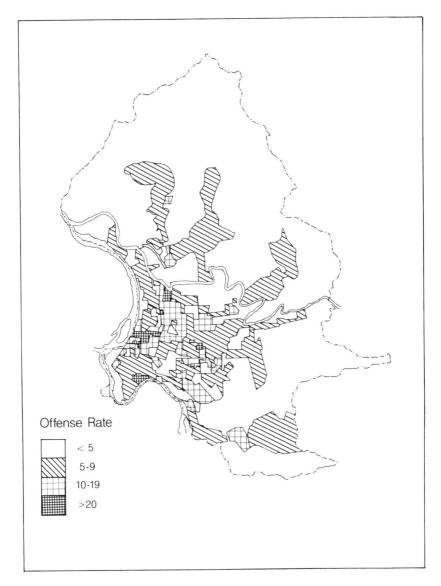

Figure 6.2 Crime (after Meng, 1984, 99)

crimes are committed and where the criminals live. Using disaggregated data Meng (1984) was able to plot reported crime using the 629 Taipei census tracts. He was then able to generate a four-class map of crime zones (Figure 6.2). The highest crime zone, with more than 20 offenses per 1000 persons, is concentrated in the older sections of the city, where there are complicated land use patterns and a declining population. Zone two,

171

with between 10 and 19 offenses per 1000, is located along the main business streets and in a transition zone where reported offences of property crimes are conspicuous. Zone three, with between 5 and 9 offenses per 1000, consists of those areas which are predominantly residential in nature, with low population density but rapid population growth. The last zone, with less than four offenses per 1000, is found at the outskirts of the city, in areas which are less developed due to topographic constraints.

In terms of types of crimes committed violent crimes are found in the central business area (around the Central Railroad Station), and the older adjacent areas, but especially in Chengchung. These crimes tend to be committed in places that suffer from physical deterioration, complicated land use patterns, crowded housing conditions, a mobile population, and social disorganization (Meng, 1984). Property crimes, which at the time of Meng's study constituted 70 percent of all crimes, show two patterns. Residential burglary was concentrated in Chengchung, Chungshan, and Ta-an, that is, the most affluent areas. The new housing developments in Shihlin appear to be becoming the next, obvious targets of this type of crime. Non-residential burglary, the most frequent crime, was concentrated in the western halves of Chungshan and Chengchung *chu*. Meng (1984) argues that in contrast to Western patterns of non-residential burglary, Taipei shows a more dispersed pattern due to the high degree of mixed residential and commercial land use. As it turns out the main target of non-residential burglary was motorcycles. These were an especially inviting target since they were frequently left unattended all day. The same holds true for automobiles. They were most frequently stolen in Chungshan and Ta-an *chu*, areas that were affluent, had a high rate of automobile ownership, and a complicated mix of commercial and residential land use. With the exception of robbery and rape, Meng (1984) found that a strong distance decay function existed from the city center outward to the north, east, and south.

In terms of the distribution of criminals, Meng (1984) discovered the familiar "journey to work" pattern found in crime studies elsewhere. He found that 70 percent of crimes are committed within three kilometers of the criminal's home. The journey to violent crimes is shorter than the journey to property crimes. He also discovered that several of the satellite cities around Taipei, such as Sanchung, Banchiao, Yungho, and Chungho, are where many criminals actually reside. He attributes the short journey to crime to the use of the motorcycle as the preferred means of transportation. His findings compare well with those of Sheu (1990), who found that organized crime was very local in nature and that groups did not extend their activities to other parts of the city or to areas outside the city. Members of non-syndicated organized crime groups in Taipei appear to be naturally formed social congregations of low self-control persons with geographic proximity or knowledge of each other from childhood. This peer link to crime was also discovered by Hsien (1981). Given this organization principle it is not surprising that these groups have codes of honor. The codes stress no intra-group theft and robbery and a ban on the use of drugs. Members pledge to protect their turf and group interest from external insults or invasions. They must also follow the group's master's orders and not betray the master or the group. In addition they are required to be filial to their parents, make friends with only those who are honest and fair, and not to fight each other or rape any women. These latter stipulations are to ensure that their behavior is acceptable to society.

Although organized crime groups seek and apparently receive acceptance from society in general, one group which is of growing concern to all is juvenile delinquents. The rate of delinquency, defined as the number of youths arrested for crimes divided by the total number of youths times 1000, has increased from 122.22 in 1968 to 151.92 in 1989. The increase in the number of delinquents is about four times larger than the increase in the number of teenagers in the Taipei population. However, buried in this long-term trend there are several cycles of delinquency. From 1968 to 1972 there was a sharp decline in delinquency rates, but in 1973 and 1974 there was a sharp upturn followed by a six-year decline. From 1979 to 1981 there was a steady increase followed by a four-year stagnation in the rate. Since 1986 the rate has increased each year. In terms of the crimes they commit, the juveniles mirror very closely the patterns of adult criminals. In 1968 burglary was the most common juvenile crime; by 1989 it had declined with robbery, threats, and injury being the most frequent types of crimes. Hsien (1981) argued that for the most part none of these crimes is committed for financial need. Rather they are committed to satisfy immediate personal gratification. Hsien (1981) also discovered that most predatory crimes were committed by juveniles from disorganized families, while most non-predatory crimes were committed by individuals from non-disorganized families. There are, however, two especially disturbing trends in juvenile crime. First is the increase in female participation in criminal activities. The sex ratio of juvenile offenders went from 1822.5 in 1968 to 1575.1 in 1989; by 1991 it had declined to 917.7. The second trend is in the age and educational background of juvenile criminals. In 1968 15 years of age was the median age for juvenile delinquents, and the educational background was heavily weighted towards either elementary school students or illiterates. By 1989 the median age was 17 and the educational background had advanced to junior middle school and senior high school.

Meng (1984) indicates that most juvenile delinquents lived in Lungshan, Yenping, and Ta-an *chu*, a group suggesting both the stress of poverty and the boredom of middle class life. Hsien (1981), using a sample of 494 juvenile delinquents, discovered that five variables accounted for delinquent behavior: broken homes, criminality of other family members, physical and mental illnesses among family members, poverty, and pathological attitudes and behavior of other family members. Although rapid population growth and modernization complicated family life, Hsien (1981) argued that all five explanatory variables were found within the "traditional" Chinese family setting. What is apparently new about the variables is that if family life breaks down in modern Taipei then children are not adequately supported in acquiring modern social values, which results in delinquency (Hsien, 1981).

What accounts for the overall increase in crime and what is being done about it? Among the Kuomintang elite there is a sense that the increase is just one consequence of the political liberalization which has taken place in Taiwan over the past two decades. In particular there is a feeling that the lifting of martial law in 1987 contributed to a lax attitude towards civic responsibilities. It is also felt that economic development has led to an overall decline in values and morals (Chang, 1983). A set of demographic variables – urban mobility, population growth, and a higher proportion of transients – has been seen as contributing to an attitude of lawlessness and weakened respect for the police (Chang, 1983; *Free China Journal*, Jan. 9, 1989, 3). An increase in smuggled hand guns is also a contributing factor. Finally, the police have been criticized for being inefficient (Chang, 1983).

For their part, the police point out that as Taipei has grown so too has the list of their responsibilities. For example, basic law enforcement has been expanded to include such activities as inspecting buildings for code violations, removing unlicensed vendors from streets, issuing parking citations, administering drunk driver tests, and enforcing air pollution regulations (Chang, 1983), as well as periodic raids on new activities of dubious legality such as MTV studios, KTVs (see Chapter Seven), barber shops, and massage parlors (*China Post*, Jan. 12, 1991, 12).

Thus one solution to dealing with increased crime is to increase the resources of the police. This has been done in several ways. During the early 1990s some 260 additional cars were added to the police fleet. Additional policemen have been added to the force. For example, the number of sergeants on the force has increased from 5798 in 1980 to 7682 in 1991. One problem in recruiting more officers, however, is the low pay and high risk associated with police work (Chang, 1983). In addition to recruiting new personnel, the police have undertaken programs to increase their efficiency and professionalism. Such programs include in-service seminars on law enforcement, systematic reviews of unsolved major cases, and the establishment of a police computer center where the application of modern, scientific investigation equipment is featured (Chang, 1983). A new, quick response unit was added as well, in the hope of providing a highly visible crime deterrent (Chang, 1983). The police also feel that renewed public cooperation is necessary if crime is to be successfully fought. There are three areas of public cooperation the police hope to enlist. First, police hope to instill in the public mind the idea that fighting crime is everyone's business. Secondly, the public must reject the old Confucian attitude that it is sufficient to conduct oneself virtuously, regardless of what is going on around you. Finally, the police urge neighborhoods and communities to initiate self-help crime prevention programs (Chang, 1983). No doubt the greatest boost to crime fighting was the denunciation of crime by Hau Pei-tsun when he assumed the position of Prime Minister in May 1990. Although Hau's appointment was initially seen as a potential threat to the democratization process underway in Taiwan, since he was a former general and military chief of staff, he quickly won public confidence with his concern for a renewed emphasis on social order. To help combat crime the Prime Minister met every Monday afternoon with police chiefs and staff members to review problems and crime-fighting strategies, including a greater military role in crime fighting. In the short term, at least, Hau has been given credit for reducing crime since the arrest of five out of the ten most wanted criminals and the crack-down on criminal gangs took place soon after he came to office (WuDunn, 1990).

Prostitution

Two approaches have been taken to deal with prostitution. The first is a rather traditional "regulationist" method of control (Reanda, 1991). This approach – apparently grounded on a traditional Chinese acceptance of the role and need for prostitutes (Bullough, 1976; Buruma, 1985; Senftleben, 1986; Truong, 1990; Yang, 1945), a positive Buddhist attitude towards sexual matters (Bullough, 1976), and a recognition that prostitution is an integral part of the economic opportunities for development offered by tourism (Enloe, 1989) stresses the regulation of prostitution by a licensing mechanism. As such police would conduct sporadic raids on areas or buildings where unregistered prostitutes were working. Given the ambiguous crime categories used for published police activities, it is not clear how extensive or effective such raids have been. Assuming that these raids fall under the general classification of anti-vice activities, then on average for the period 1968 to 1989 the police each year were involved in some 8286 cases involving some 21 517 individuals. The trend in vice cases, however, is downward, with only some 1737 vice cases and 5408 individuals reported for 1989. The late 1960s and mid-1970s represent peaks in this type of police activity.

In contrast to this rather legalistic approach to prostitution, a second, "abolitionist" approach has appeared. This approach apparently draws on the traditional Chinese prudish attitude towards sex (Bullough, 1976;

Senftleben, 1986), and on that part of feminist theory (Hobson, 1987; Overall, 1992; Reynolds, 1986; Rubin, 1984; Shrage, 1989) and human rights theory (Reanda, 1991) which sees prostitution as demeaning, exploitative, and undesirable. Another, administrative rationale driving this approach is the concern that the need for frequent raids over-extends the already under-staffed police force so that other crime problems get less attention than required (Huang, 1993a). It is interesting that the advocates of this approach have not emphasized the dangerous link found elsewhere between AIDS and prostitution (Lintner and Lintner, 1992) as a rationale for their work, although deaths due to AIDS have occurred in Taipei. From 1984 to 1990 some 66 cases and five deaths due to AIDS were reported. Reportedly all the victims fall into discrete high risk groups: gay men, intravenous drug users, and haemophiliacs (Chiu, 1992); only one Taiwanese prostitute, from Kaohsiung City, has tested positive for HIV (Chen, 1988). Given this grounding, the abolitionist approach seeks to rehabilitate the women engaged in prostitution. One main vehicle for this work is the private Taipei Women's Rescue Association which was founded in August 1987. The overall aim of the Association, and its provincial counterpart which was founded a year earlier, is to rescue and help teenage prostitutes.

Many of these teenage prostitutes have been sold or contracted out by their families. Early reports of this practice estimated that a 14- or 15-year-old girl could be bought for US$5000, or her services contracted out for two years for US$2500 (Goldstein, 1986). Later reports show that young prostitutes are purchased for between US$10 000 and 20 000 (Liu, 1992). All reports of this practice point out that a disproportionate number of the girls sold are aborigines (Senftleben, 1986). One estimate indicated that 60 percent of all Taipei teenage prostitutes were aborigines and that 40 percent of the entire Taipei prostitute population were aborigines (Liu, 1992). Aboriginal teenagers are apparently especially vulnerable to this practice for two reasons. First, with the outmigration of young aboriginal males from their villages, the local economies are impoverished. Sale or rental of teenage girls is a ready source of income for many families. Secondly, many of the aborigines have relatively low levels of educational achievement and skills and therefore there are not numerous employment opportunities in either the village or city for them.

The Association actively intervenes where teenage prostitution and the sale of adolescent girls is taking place. In addition it seeks to promote concern about prostitution and abuse of women, and advocates new legislation that effectively deals with women's problems. It also plans to conduct empirical studies of prostitution. In the first four years of its existence the Association has rescued some 400 teenage prostitutes, 20 percent of whom were tribal girls (Liu, 1992). For the most part rescue involves placing the girls in half-way houses where they can receive clothing, food, shelter, medical attention, psychological and career counseling, and help in completing their education. Until 1990 the Association referred girls to one of the four half-way houses maintained by the Taipei municipal government's Bureau of Social Welfare. In 1990 the Association established its own half-way house. The work of the Association parallels the efforts of not only the Bureau of Social Welfare but also that of the City's Teenage Prostitute Intervention Task Force, administered by the municipal police and the private Taipei Lifeline Association, which offers 24-hour hot line assistance to youths in need. Although all of these programs are too new to evaluate fully, their mere existence suggests that Taipei and its residents have matured economically, politically, and socially to the point where the acceptance of the *status quo* is no longer the only option available for dealing with social problems.

Aborigines

In themselves the aborigines are not and should not be problems. In addition to the problem of teenage prostitution, aborigines in Taipei and Taiwan, as elsewhere around the world, do find themselves subject to the twin dangers of discrimination and assimilation.

In general, the large-scale outmigration of aborigines from their rural townships started during the 1960s (Yuan, 1992). The reason for their departure is simple: in the mountain townships they earned only 30 percent of the Taiwan per capita income; in the plains townships they earned about 40 percent (Liu, 1992). Once they arrived in the cities they faced both active and passive discrimination (Goldstein, 1986). Due to stereotyping by the Chinese, all aborigines were thought of as lazy, dirty, irresponsible drunkards (Hwang, 1992), and were thus relegated to those jobs fit only for unskilled laborers (Goldstein, 1986). Under such conditions establishing social relationships with the Chinese is difficult. Many migrants were easily intimidated by city folks due to their poverty and lower educational background (Hwang, 1992). Those aboriginal males who came to Taipei City alone to work in the construction industry had trouble finding housing. As a result they were forced to live in substandard quarters on the construction sites and became urban nomads as they moved from one project to another (Yuan, 1992). Those who brought families with them faced the task of finding housing in a market of ever-rising rents. The municipal housing office could be of little help – the discussion on housing below will show that the municipality has a waiting list of 40 000 Taipei families wanting units in public housing facilities (Yuan, 1992).

Assuming that the aborigines found adequate housing and work, and were able to establish some type of relationship with the greater Chinese population, they then faced the dangers of assimilation. This commonly involved the loss of traditional religious and recreational outlets, the erosion of knowledge of their languages, some intermarriage, and the acquisition of a materialistic outlook (Hwang, 1992; Yuan, 1992). As is common among other aboriginal peoples in similar situations, many of the migrants resorted to two extreme coping activities: drinking and suicide (Liu, 1992).

As was the case with prostitution, both governmental and private agencies have developed programs designed to help the aborigines cope more successfully with the twin challenges of discrimination and assimilation. For its part the city has established a separate administrative office to implement aboriginal programming set by the national and provincial governments. A private organization, the Taipei City Aboriginal Community Development Association, was founded in November 1990. The Association has two main activities. One is to inform aborigines living in Taipei City of the municipal government's programs for which they are eligible. These programs include emergency financial assistance, support for vocational training, scholarships for students from low income families, and business start-up loans. The second activity is to promote tribal culture. Specific programs to this end include summer camps for youths from the Ami and Bunun tribes and embroidery and garment-making classes (Yuan, 1992). In addition the Association sponsors tribal ceremonies, such as coming of age rites, in order to preserve traditions and encourage tribal youths to remember their tribal ties in spite of competition from modern urban diversions (Yuan, 1992). Finally, the Presbyterian and Catholic Churches in Taipei have established aboriginal affairs committees. Although the specifics of their programming for the aborigines in Taipei have not been reported, in general the churches try to offer material assistance as well as spiritual comfort and guidance (Yuan, 1992; Liu, 1992).

The elderly

In Chapter 4, four main conclusions were presented in regard to the population of Taipei. First, it was shown that the population is ageing and will continue to do so as net migration stays low or becomes negative. Second, dependency ratios are increasing, especially when computed for the over-65 population. Third, sex ratios are badly distorted in Taipei. Fourth, a large population of elderly males, many of whom are single, is rapidly emerging in Taipei. Additional factors contributing to the number of at-risk elderly include the increase in the number of divorced and widowed individuals. Altogether in 1990 there were 253 755 males over 50 years of age and 219 467 females over 50 years of age who were either single, divorced, or widowed and therefore in possible need of non-family assistance. These seemingly simple demographic situations taken together become a social and political problem – what services should be provided for the elderly and how should they be provided? The need for the government even to consider these questions is a strong indicator of the impact of modernization on the Chinese family structure. In Taipei families can no longer maintain even the barest semblance of the idealized extended, or joint family system found in the past. Such a family typically would be patrilocal, and consist of a husband and wife, all unmarried children, all married sons and their wives and children; at times there have been as many as five generations living together under one roof (Baker, 1979; Lang, 1946). Such living arrangements would be hard to imagine in Taipei for two reasons. First, a single-family house or apartment large enough to accommodate such an extended family would be quite expensive. Secondly, given the migration patterns of Taipei, it is hard to imagine that all of the members of such an extended family would be in close enough proximity even to think of living together. The net result is a growing cohort of individuals separated from their families who would find it increasingly difficult to manage on their own.

The city government has responded to the problem of a growing elderly population with three main programs. Adult day care, available from 9 a.m. to 5 p.m. at a cost of US$400 per month, is provided. Those who use this service get breakfast and lunch, regular physical examinations, and entertainment (*Republic of China Yearbook*, 1993). In addition 3000 community centers have been built where cultural and recreational programs for the elderly are available. The centerpiece of the city's response to the increasing needs of a growing elderly population is a series of five nursing homes able to accommodate 863 residents. The program has expanded from a free-standing geriatric facility in Sungshan called Fraternity House for the elderly without families to a seven-center network including four additional nursing homes, an orphanage and a medical clinic. Residents of the nursing homes live cost free and receive a small monthly allowance of US$38 to cover incidental and personal items (*Republic of China Yearbook*, 1993). It appears that the majority of the residents in the Fraternity system are part of the 1949 migration from the mainland. Most of them are men who have never married and have limited means for survival during old age. Their passing will not, however, appreciably reduce the need for facilities to care for the elderly. Although the national legislature has discussed the suggestion that a system of tax breaks be instituted for families supporting elderly members, it is most likely that both the municipal government and private sector will need to continue building facilities expressly for the care of the elderly.

Poverty

Despite the wealth and prosperity of Taipei, some of its citizens have not participated or shared fully in the fruits of economic development. These individuals can be seen in pedestrian over- and under-passes or on street corners selling gum by the stick, betel nuts, cigarettes, flowers, or pencils. Some of them have plied their meager trades in the same areas for decades, with grandparents, parents, and children participating. Homeless individuals can be seen sleeping near parking ramps or in parks.

There are three reasons it is hard to gauge the exact number of poverty-stricken individuals from the official statistics. First, the published data on the officially poor employ vague, undefined categories. During the 1960s and 1970s, there were three classes of the poor: those with no apparent cash income, those with limited cash income, and those "living at the margin." During the 1980s and 1990s the poor have been classified into two groups: those requiring substantial help ("patronizing households and individuals"), and those requiring limited help ("assisted households and individuals"). Regardless of the system used, the published data do not indicate what cash values are attached to any one category. Secondly, the municipal government has no fewer than *four* assistance programs covering social relief, emergency aid, care for the needy, and medical assistance. Finally, those receiving assistance include not only the poor but the mentally and physically handicapped, infants and orphans, and the elderly. In many cases any one individual can be receiving aid from several sources because of eligibility in a number of programs.

Despite these definitional problems it is possible to describe changes in the numbers and distribution of the poor since the late 1960s. In 1968 there were 48 442 poor in Taipei; 90 percent of them fell into the poorest categories requiring assistance. By 1989 the total number of poor had declined to 11 914; the percentage of truly poor had declined to 76.16. The secular trends are somewhat more complicated than these data would indicate since the lowest recorded number of poor (7192) was recorded in 1981. Since then there has been an increase in the number of those requiring limited assistance.

In terms of the distribution of the poor there have been significant changes (Figures 6.3, 6.4). In the 1970s the poor were mainly in Kuting, Sungshan, and Ta-an *chu*. By 1989 the poor were found mainly in Mucha, Sungshan, and Shuangyuan *chu*. In terms of the poor as a percentage of the total population there have also been significant shifts (Figures 6.5, 6.6). In 1970 Mucha, Shuangyuan, and Kuting *chu* had at least 5 percent of their populations categorized as poor, and only Chiencheng, Chingmei, and Shihlin *chu* had less than 3 percent of their populations in this category. By 1989 only Shuangyuan and Mucha *chu* had more than 0.5

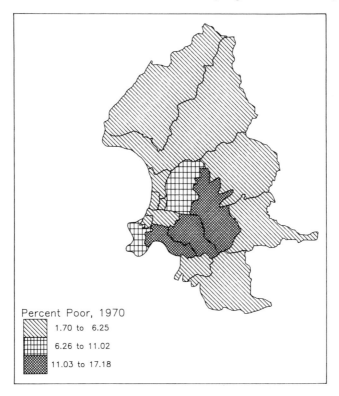

Figure 6.3 Distribution of poor population, 1970

percent of their populations in the poor categories. In essence what has happened is that the old *chu* have witnessed massive declines in the number of poor while the new *chu* have witnessed less dramatic declines. One *chu*, Mucha, actually had a 75.6 percent increase in the number of poor. Location quotients comparing the percentage of poor to the total population in each *chu* show only Kuting, Mucha, Shuangyuan, and Sungshan having values greater than 1 in 1970. By 1989 only Mucha and Shuangyuan had values ranging above 1.

Cutting across these patterns of mixed change is a steady growth in the cost of funding the municipal relief programs. While the percentage of the population needing relief has declined from 2.2 to 0.44, the budget for their assistance has increased some 4299 times from US$626 525 in 1968 to US$27.5 million in 1989. Although the increase may seem alarmingly large, it must be noted that as a percentage of the total municipal budget such welfare costs have actually declined from 2.02 to 0.88 percent. In addition it must be pointed out that some welfare programs and funds are provided by private, and especially religious, institutions. Such institutions include the Buddhist Association of the Republic of China which has

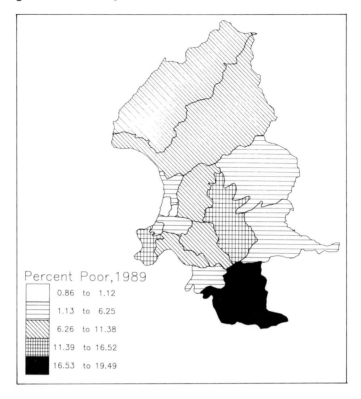

Figure 6.4 Distribution of poor population, 1989

contributed to the city's medical subsidy program and donated two buses to a rehabilitation center, and the Christian Salvation Service which provides safe shelter for unwed mothers. In all there are some 100 religious and fraternal organizations which serve the needs of Taipei's disadvantaged (*Free China Journal*, May 14, 1991, 4; Lee, 1992c; Shen, 1993).

Infrastructure problems

Part of the solution to all of the environmental problems involves the construction of major infrastructure projects. The solutions to two infrastructure problems, housing and transportation, have possible environmental consequences. But these two problems are so important that they require not only separate treatment here, but would be attended to regardless of any environmental gains or losses attending their solutions. The two problems share common origins, two phases in the evolution of their nature and characteristics, the appearance of both public

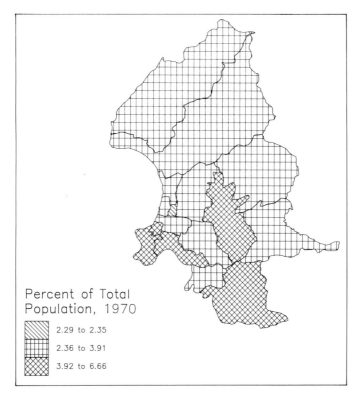

Percent of Total
Population, 1970

2.29 to 2.35

2.36 to 3.91

3.92 to 6.66

Figure 6.5 Poor as a percentage of total population, 1970

and private attempts at their solution, and the unfortunate compromising of optimum solutions by the political process.

Housing

In 1981 Tanzer reported that the rents on Taipei housing had increased, thus bringing an end to an era of reasonably priced housing and ushering in an era of housing scarcity. While it is true that by Western standards rents in Taipei during the 1960s and 1970s were low, it is a mistake to see the housing problem as either starting in 1981 or focusing mainly on the cost of renting. Rather what 1981 marks is a two-fold change in the housing problem. The two changes involve the root causes of the crisis and the solutions to it.

During the 1960s and 1970s there was ample evidence that there was a housing problem in Taipei. Squatter housing was evident in many parts of the city. In some areas, such as section three of Hsin-yi Road in Ta-an *chu*,

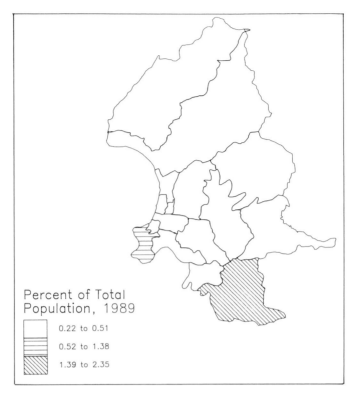

Figure 6.6 Poor as a percentage of total population, 1989

the entire center of what was planned as a broad avenue was taken over as squatter housing. In other areas, which could be found virtually all over the city, individual shacks made of wood could be seen leaning precariously against new apartment buildings, walls surrounding older Japanese style houses, or business establishments. In addition to building housing, squatters sometimes also just occupied abandoned or derelict structures.

Often these squatter housing areas had access to electric and telephone utilities. The larger concentrations developed networks of industrial and commercial activities. Despite the economic vitality of these squatter areas, they had two general drawbacks. In addition to being eyesores they were health and safety hazards. Since cooking facilities were limited in any one squatter unit, meals were frequently cooked out by the side of the house virtually on the edge of traffic lanes (Figure 6.7). Cooking was usually done using a primitive charcoal burner made of what appeared to be large discarded fruit or vegetable cans. At least twice a day, the resulting smoke contributed to a decrease in visibility in the neighborhood and to air pollution. Safety and health hazards were not limited to domestic

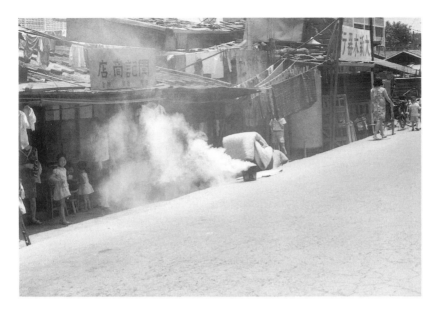

Figure 6.7 Poverty and rapid population growth contributed to the presence of squatter housing, which in turn created safety, traffic, and pollution problems

activities, however. Those squatters engaged in manufacturing contributed to the problems as well. In order to maximize their production space, many craftsmen did their work right out in the street, again virtually in traffic lanes. Although open flames and power equipment were used slight attention was paid to safety precautions. Those whose materials or products required them to work inside had to contend with extremely hot and humid conditions. Throughout the squatter settlements noise pollution was deafening. Since there were no green areas about children frequently played in the streets as their mothers cooked or fathers manufactured goods (Figure 6.8).

The development of squatter housing can be traced to two main causes: poverty and population growth. Especially in the transition period from Japanese to Chinese rule and then after the establishment of Taipei as the provisional capital of the Republic of China, refugees flooded into the city. Although there was some expropriation of Japanese living quarters, and some displacement of Taiwanese, the existing housing stocks were not adequate to accommodate all new residents. Given the economic dislocations of the times, squatter housing was a natural response. A 1963 survey showed that there were some 52 887 squatters living in Taipei (Ambruster, 1976). The government's response to their development had two components: short term and long term. In the short term many squatter areas were tolerated, since neither the national nor the city

Figure 6.8 Lacking any playground, children in the 1960s along Hsin-yi Road created their own play area amidst traffic and commerce

governments had the planning or fiscal resources to provide alternatives. Occasionally particularly blighted areas might be leveled, especially if they were along routes to be taken by important foreign visitors. Once they were leveled the cleared area would be fenced off with 12 foot high wooden fences featuring a basket-weave design painted green. Although the fences gave the appearance of an orderly, maintained environment, litter frequently accumulated behind the fences creating a new eyesore for those who lived in the vicinity. By the mid-1970s this approach led to the removal of about half the squatters (Ambruster, 1976).

In the long term, the government converted the squatter areas to the use outlined in the current city land use plan. The owners of vacant lots where squatters were sometimes found were subject to an added tax so long as the land was not used productively, and this acted as an incentive for removing squatters. For its part the city removed the Hsin-yi squatters when in the mid-1970s funds were finally available to rebuild the road. Another source of squatter removal was urban replotting. In obliterating the squatter areas the city improved the visual landscape considerably. However, in removing the squatters and their economic activities, the city also destroyed homes, jobs, and incomes. Although promises of priorities in obtaining city-owned apartments were made and some compensation was paid (Ambruster, 1976), there appears to have been little follow-up regarding the relocation of the squatters or their long-term economic fates.

The second housing crisis, widely reported during the 1980s and 1990s, involves a shortage of affordable rental and purchase property, especially for the lower and middle classes. There are several ways to document the shortage. For example, according to Taipei municipal government income and expenditure surveys, income between 1975 and 1989 went up by 810 percent, whereas the cost of living went up by 650 percent. However, the cost of housing in that time went up by 892 percent. Only the cost of transportation, communication, education and recreation went up by a larger amount. Alternatively, in 1979 the average price for an apartment in Taipei was 3.6 times the average salary (Lee, 1979); by 1989 the average price had increased to 13 times the average salary (Pun, 1992a). In terms of rental property, the average price for an apartment has gone from $300 in the late 1960s to $1150 in Ta-an and Chungshan *chu*, or $1550 in Shihlin *chu* in 1991. These 1991 rental costs must be compared to the one-third of disposable income standard, or $295, recommended by the municipal government for its employees (*Free China Journal*, Mar. 13, 1989, 3).

Before cataloguing the causes for the shortages and price increases as well as governmental responses to the problem, it is necessary to put the housing issue into the broadest possible perspective. One the one hand numerous surveys have shown that Taipei is now the third most expensive Asian city to live in (*Free China Journal*, Apr. 24, 1989, 3; Sept. 6, 1990, 3), and has gone from the eleventh to the sixth most expensive city in the world to live in (*Free China Journal*, June 5, 1989, 3; *China Post*, Jan. 13, 1991, 8; *Central Daily News*, Dec. 12, 1992, 7). Although the high cost of housing is a factor in Taipei's high cost of living, inflation during the 1970s and the appreciation of the New Taiwan dollar from 40 to the US dollar until 1972 to 26.21 in 1989 also contibuted to increased living costs. In many cases old or inflated prices were never adjusted to the new New Taiwan dollar value, thus driving the cost of living even higher.

Another issue which must be reviewed is the rate of home ownership in Taipei. Since the mid-1970s it has gone from 50.35 percent of all households to 72.36 percent in 1989. So although the price of housing has gone up, the government's policy of encouraging each family to own its own home (*Housing Taipei, 1976–1985,* 1990; Lee, 1977) has made an impact on consumer behavior. Taipei residents also appear to have a high level of expectation in terms of mobility. In the past, Taipei residents changed their homes every 15 years on average. More recently, people expect to change every eight to ten years (Lin, 1989). Price increases may have dampened the ability to move as often as desired and hence part of the shortage may be psychological. It must be noted too that these moves have involved occupation of larger apartments or homes. The average per capita amount of space in each Taipei apartment has increased from 8.2 square meters to 12.26 during the period of price increases. Although part of this increase may have been the result of the decline in the average number of people per household from 5.56 to 5.29, part of the increase is also related to moving to larger and more modern accommodation (Lee, 1977). In terms of cost, it must be remembered that although the cost of renting has increased, the percentage of income spent on rent has remained virtually constant, varying very narrowly between 21 and 24 percent of family income. In terms of supply two factors complicate the evaluation of housing stock. First, the central government assumes that the average dwelling in Taiwan will remain habitable for 70 years (Lee, 1977). Data from the *1975 Sample Census of Population and Housing* (Volume IV, table 25) suggest that around 10 percent of the total housing stock of Taipei would now fall into the age category where replacement should be contemplated. Second, as many as 10 000 empty housing units have been reported in Taipei (Kaye, 1989). Two explanations have been offered for the continued presence of empty units despite increased demand: high prices (Kaye, 1989) and the unwillingness of absentee owners to rent flats originally purchased as investments under the assumption that vacant, unlived-in apartments are easier to resell (Moore, 1989).

To the average Taipei resident seeking to buy or rent living space, the contradictory contextual evidence outlined above has led to a high level of frustration. Taking advantage of the democratization process evolving in Taiwan, two groups organized rallies to vent their frustrations in the hope of pressuring both the national and city governments into dealing more effectively with their concerns and worries. On 26 August 1989, 20 000 people responded to the call by the Homeless Persons Union to participate in a "sleep-in" downtown to protest their housing problems (*Free China Journal,* Sept. 4, 1989, 3). A march through Taipei streets a year later, called by an *ad hoc* organization terming itself "Snails without Shell" drew some 1000 participants. Their dissatisfaction with the slow progress of the government in solving the housing problem was echoed by some 101 other organizations (*Free China Journal,* Aug. 30, 1990, 2).

The municipal government's response to the housing problem can be divided into three parts. Before describing and analyzing the response it must be remembered that none of the three levels of government in

Taiwan – national, provincial, or municipal – has historically played a major role in the building of housing (Lee, 1979). This was reflected by the low priority which housing received in both the budgeting and planning processes. At most public housing constituted some 6 percent of the total housing stock (Shapiro, 1984; Tsai, 1987). An additional reason for ignoring housing and concentrating on economic and industrial development has been traced to the Kuomintang's fears over inflation to which public housing projects may contribute (Tanzer, 1981).

Before the government could develop a public housing policy and implement it, however, it was necessary to define the root causes of the housing problem. Several factors have been blamed for the increase in the price of housing. Expatriates have been targeted for criticism since they seem willing and able to pay whatever prices are demanded, especially for rental properties at the high end of the cost spectrum (*Free China Journal*, Jan. 28, 1992, 8). The decline in the savings rate has also been cited as a cause (*Free China Journal*, Nov. 6, 1992, 5). Increases in world oil prices have also been mentioned as a large contributor to increased housing prices. There are two ways in which oil influences housing costs. First, landlords apparently use increases in fuel costs as justifications for raising rents (*Free China Journal*, Sept. 13, 1990, 3). Secondly, as increased oil costs contribute to inflation, rents or prices of houses go up, thus dampening demand for new units. As no new units are built, the stock of available housing declines, thus driving rents or prices up even higher (Tsai, 1987, 20).

In formulating an approach to the housing problem, however, the government saw three other factors as the main causes of the housing crisis: scarcity of land, speculation, and scarcity of funds. The government's response to the housing problem thus deals with each of these three elements.

In Chapter 5 the impact of land and land policies on the planning process was described. In terms of housing, land scarcity took on six meanings. First, there is an absolute scarcity, in the sense that some 60 percent of the area is not deemed suitable for urban development (*Introduction to Urban Planning Of Taipei City*, 1990). Second, housing must compete with other urban functions for land (Lee, 1979). Third, when land is available it is often fragmented into discontinuous small plots, which are not readily usable for housing (Lee, 1977). Fourth, land resources were frequently mismanaged when the city government sold some of its land holdings in order to make up budget deficits (Lee, 1979). Fifth, national land laws do not permit urban governments to purchase available land from adjacent *hsien* (counties) (Lee, 1977). Finally, the price of land contributed to scarcity. Land costs in Taipei commonly consume one half of the project budget (Lee, 1979). What was most disturbing was the increase in land prices. In formulating its policies the national and city governments used price increases from 1953 to 1976 as the base line. During that period, whereas income increased by 1175 percent and the consumer price index by 280 percent, land prices increased by 13 290 percent (Lee, 1979).

The land scarcity problem was addressed in five ways. As was shown in the discussion on planning, replotting was used to make land use more orderly and to increase the amount of land available. A second strategy was actively to engage in urban renewal. In addition to generally rundown areas, the government targeted the 178 "villages" in Taipei which had been built for military dependents. These military housing areas covered a total of some 181 818 square meters (or some 181.2 hectares) (*Housing Taipei*, 1990). In cooperation with the Ministry of National Defense these areas were razed and new housing built. Reluctantly the government also opened hillsides and slopelands as sites for housing. There have been fears expressed that in so doing the government has opened the way to active use of the Kuantu Plain, described above in the section on environmental problems. However, Mayor Wu indicated that although parts of the Kuantu Plain, reclaimed land along the Keelung River, and some farm lands are earmarked for housing development, the areas under conservation protection will not be opened for construction of public housing units (*Free China Journal*, Sept. 7, 1989, 3). In some cases land was condemned and then taken by eminent domain (Lee, 1979; Yeung, 1991a). Finally, the government tried to avoid using its power of eminent domain and arranged instead joint private–municipal development of land (Yeung, 1991a).

Of the three causes of the housing crisis perhaps no other so enraged the general public than charges of speculation. Two types of speculation were practiced. The first, mentioned above when the context of the housing shortage was reviewed, is simply holding apartments off the market until prices reach a point where the investor is willing to sell. It is estimated that island-wide some 6 670 000 apartments are involved in this practice (*Free China Journal*, Jul. 2, 1992, 6). Second was the practice of trust companies holding land, and then requesting changes in designated site uses. Such changes often permitted the trusts, who reportedly held some 55 percent of all vacant land in Taipei (Tanzer, 1981), to reap inordinate profits when the land was resold. The most infamous case of this involved the Cathay Insurance Company, which bought a plot of land in 1987 for US$989.90 per square foot. It used the land as a parking lot to avoid the tax on unused land. Then just before the two-year grace period on developing the land as specified in city plans was to end, the company requested, and received, permission to change the land use designation from hotels to office buildings. This change in designation was estimated to be worth some US$80 million in extra profit as Cathay Pacific could then sell the land at US$2277.80 a square foot (Pun, 1992b). The public outcry, accompanied by accusations of municipal complicity in approving the land use changes, led to action by the national government to curb land speculation. The national government reform program, hailed as a "second" land reform (Song, 1992), involved revising the Equalization of Land Rights Act so that the tax levied on the sale of property would use actual transaction prices rather than the much lower government-assessed land values. As direct and effective as this approach appeared, when suggested it was so controversial that it led to the resignation of the Finance Minister (Yu, 1992). Opposition to the proposals came from real estate owners and the majority of the members of the opposition party, the Democratic Progressive Party (DPP). The DPP saw the plan as a Kuomintang trick to take away profits from small landowners. The threat of such a tax, however, had important short-term advantages as speculators sold property through fear of modified tax proposals actually being adopted. The net result was a surge in land tax revenue such that it became the biggest source of revenue for the national government in the 1992 fiscal year (Song, 1992). Despite long-term calls for a reform of this type (Lin, 1989; Pannell, 1974; Tanzer, 1981), the fear that debate on the tax would weaken voters' support for the Kuomintang in the December 1992 elections was enough to shelve any plans for reform. The municipal government is not able to deal effectively with speculation therefore until such time as the national government does.

The same dilemma was relevant to the third proximate cause of the housing shortage, shortages of funds. It has long been recognized on the Taipei scene (Tanzer, 1981) that three factors were needed to deal with the shortage of funding for housing: sufficient capital, long-term mortgages, and low interest rate mortgages. The ability of the municipal government to deal with all these issues was hampered by three predominant factors. First, banks in Taiwan in general prefer to deal with real estate developers, not buyers of individual apartments (Tanzer, 1981; Pun, 1992c). Secondly, arranging long-term, low interest mortgages frequently conflicted with policies of the Central Bank of China designed to fight inflation (Pun, 1992a). Thirdly, banking regulations restricted what proportion of a bank's loans could be for real estate, and especially at concessionary rates and terms. When banks felt that the proportion of loans in these restricted areas came too close to legal limits, they cut back on such loans (Pun, 1992c). Despite these impediments, the municipal government was able in 1990 and 1991 to arrange for variable interest loans of up to 20 years. The problem was that the amounts available, US$1.6 billion in 1990 and US$800 million in 1991, were not adequate to fund the demand for such loans, even when a cap of US$80 000 was placed on how much any one family could borrow (Pun, 1992a).

Given its inability to single-handedly deal with all three causes of the housing problem, the municipal government went into the business of

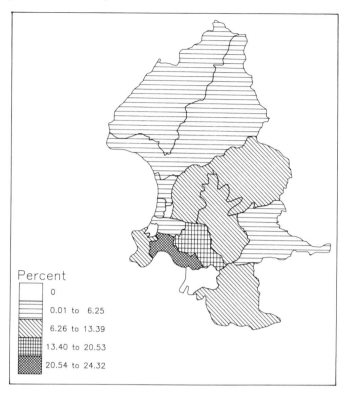

Figure 6.9 Distribution of public housing

building and managing public housing complexes. Figure 6.9 shows the areas where public housing was constructed. Table 6.3 shows the various government organizations which supervised the various programs, and the number of units completed. It is obvious from the distribution of housing units that urban renewal and the rebuilding of old military villages were strong determinants of location. It is also clear that the government has been involved in the housing area for more time than the public discussion of the second housing crisis would lead one to believe. It is also clear that in addition to designing, building, and managing housing complexes the government has used various administrative frameworks, such as joint government/private developer ventures, and self-help, for completing units.

Once the government directly became involved in providing housing it had to establish a means for Taipei residents to become eligible for a municipal housing unit, in the form of a housing lottery. All registered citizens of the municipality who own no real estate may register for available public housing. In general males must be over 25 years of age and females over 22. However, unmarried persons sharing living

Table 6.3 Taipei municipal government housing programs

Dates	Organizational framework	Major projects	Units built
1950–61	Taipei City Residence Construction Council	Joint ventures with private contractors	4 615
1962–66	Public Housing Council of Taipei Municipality	Loans to government employees and military personnel	10 935
1967–73	Public Housing & Community Construction Council of Taipei Municipality	Self-construction Resettlement housing Urban renewal	12 739
1974–75	Housing Department of Taipei Municipality	completed 1967–73 projects	
1976–81	"	Six-Year Plan	28 838
1982–85	"	First Four-Year Plan	8 121
1986–1989	"	Second Four-Year Plan	1 762
1990	"	Fiscal Year Project	5 100
1991	"	Fiscal Year Plan	3 200

Source: After *General Introduction* (1990).

accommodation with at least two persons of third grade relatives may also apply for housing regardless of age (*General Introduction*, 1990). Twice yearly names are drawn from these "waiting" lists. The names of those awarded housing but who do not respond are replaced on the waiting list. As of March 1990 there were 59 168 names on the general housing waiting list, and 13 564 on the loans waiting list (*General Introduction*, 1990). As such it is obvious from Table 6.3 that current projects cannot possibly meet demand in the near future.

This being the case alternative solutions have been tried. For example, self-help housing is a program funded by a special group, such as faculty members at a given school. Blueprints for housing are provided by college faculty or engineers. The key to the success of this approach is cheap land, which is usually available on slopelands (Lee, 1992d). A second approach is to build underground. This approach has been followed by the city as it plans a new underground stadium and new underground transportation and shopping center (Liu, 1989). A third approach has been to abandon plans for projects if the price of land gets too high (*Free China Journal*, Feb. 5, 1990, 3). Fourthly, people are buying houses outside of Taipei and commuting (Pun, 1992e; Moore, 1990). In addition to halving their housing costs (*Free China Journal*, July 5, 1991, 4), commuters avoid pollution and can enjoy neighborhoods with more public space facilities (Pun, 1992e, 1992f). There is a negative trade-off in moving to the suburbs. All infrastructure, and transportation in particular as will be discussed below, is inadequate (Moore, 1990). Real estate securitization, which allows individuals to buy and sell real estate much like stock market securities, is also being debated as a way to raise sufficient capital to finance public and private housing developments (Pun, 1992d). Finally, many couples are willing to live in the three-generational arrangement described above in the discussion of the elderly and meeting their needs. Although surveys show that about 75 percent of young couples are willing to use such arrangements, unfortunately their ideal garden home of some 105 square meters is not considered large enough to accommodate three generations (*Free China Journal*, Apr. 11, 1991, 3).

As is frequently the case, government attempts at solving the housing problem have created new problems, or made housing a scapegoat for other problems. Two examples show how building new housing has generated new problems. At the simplest level, although replacing ageing or squatter housing has eliminated some of the dangers from fires, especially in winter, the replacement buildings are also hazards. When the problems of planning were discussed in Chapter 5 it was pointed out that both legal and illegal businesses are frequently located in basically residential buildings. Fires in restaurants, MTV and KTV studios are implicated in the deaths of several hundred Taipei residents yearly (Lee, 1993). A more specific, and more dangerous, public health situation was found in some units of public housing. In Minsheng New Community some of the supporting steel rods appear to have been contaminated with Cobalt 60. As a result since 1983 residents have been exposed on a daily basis to several hundred times the annual safe limits for radiation exposure (Wehrfritz, 1992). The irradiated rods were apparently produced when contaminated imported scrap was used to produce re-enforcing steel rods for housing construction. The government has adopted several strategies to deal with the problem. All buildings built during the early 1980s are being monitored for radiation. Free medical examinations have been provided and long-term surveys of the residents are planned. The government has considered installing lead plates to block radiation damage. Tearing down the buildings has been requested by the residents, but there appears to be no agreement on the issue of compensation by the government on covering all costs (Song, 1993).

In terms of the housing shortage being embroiled in other issues, three examples can readily demonstrate this. First, just as the government was debating changes in the land law, the then Premier Hau Pei-tsun raised the issue of how ugly the urban housing landscape is. In particular illegal decorations, signage, and window grills were targeted for criticism (*Free China Journal*, Apr. 1, 1991, 3; Lee, 1992b). But these issues are not new (Tsai, 1987), and to raise them in the midst of debates on how to finance housing seems to be a ploy to distract the populace from the really central issues of the housing crisis. Secondly, licensed real estate brokers have taken the crisis as an opportunity to press for tougher laws requiring that all real estates sales be conducted by those who have licenses (Lin, 1989). Finally, the high cost of housing has been blamed for the low crude birth rate in Taipei (Huang, 1993b). This position assumes that since couples see home ownership as a prerequisite for having children, the high cost of housing has thereby depressed the desire of two-income families to reproduce.

Transportation

Transportation problems can also be summarized in a two-stage crisis framework. Before the mid-1970s the basic transportation problem was lack of capacity. For example, in 1968 there were just 3698 cars on the roads, 21 865 motorcycles, and one public bus company running 607 vehicles over 53 routes. The system, however, was simple to use, reasonably efficient and very cheap (Ambruster, 1976). The lack of capacity in the short term did not appear serious. After all, surveys showed (Chang, 1970) that almost half of the trips made on a daily basis were by students going to school, and most of them walked or took the bus. One quarter of the trips were to work, and people took public buses, rode motorcycles, or walked. For recreation, shopping, and visiting relatives and friends people relied on buses, walked, or hailed one of the seemingly ubiquitous taxi cabs which cruised the streets. During the 1950s they could also engage a pedicab. Government agencies and some private companies also provided their employees with a bus service, supplied by either large buses or small vans.

However, as income increased during the 1970s and 1980s the available combination of transportation facilities was perceived as being inadequate. There were two responses to the need to increase the capacity of the transportation system. For its part, the municipal government responded by buying new buses and creating new routes. In particular new buses seemed to appear just before the Kuomintang party congresses opened. When these additional routes seemed inadequate, the city permitted 10 private bus companies to begin operating new routes. As a result, the number of routes increased from 53 in the late 1960s to 205 in 1989; the number of buses increased from 607 to 2862. The citizens of Taipei responded to the lack of capacity by buying motorcycles. As incomes increased further and import restrictions on cars made car ownership more feasible, the public went on a car-buying binge. During the late 1980s and early 1990s some 3000–5000 cars were being added to the streets of Taipei each month! Interestingly, the popularity of motorcycles suffered only a one-year decline. So as more and more cars were purchased motorcycles were being added to the streets at a rate of 7000 a month. The staying power of motorcycles is connected to their relative ease of

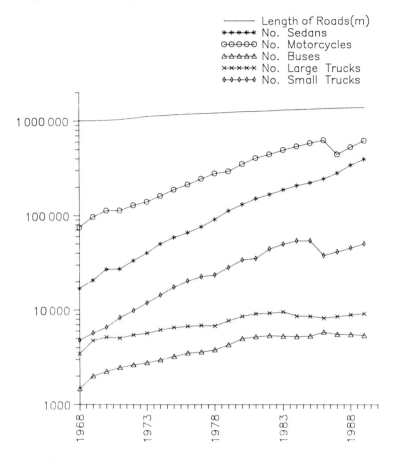

Figure 6.10 Number of vehicles and length of roads

mobility in traffic and the increased popularity of motorcycles among women. The increases in number of vehicles by type are shown in Figure 6.10.

The opening of new bus routes and the public's love affair with motorcycles and cars led to the second transportation crisis: the inadequate carrying capacity of the city's roads and parking facilities. This shortfall in capacity was rendered all the more disturbing since driving in Taipei had become a dangerous experience. Ames and Ames (1972) claimed that Taipei boasted the highest traffic death rate in the world because of driver negligence and lack of driver experience. In terms of traffic flow, the Population Crisis Committee *(Cities: Life in the World's 100 Largest Metropolitan Areas*, 1990) rated Taipei with a score of 2, i.e. the second to worst ranking with an average of speed of 11.5 miles per hour during the rush hour. Business people began complaining of the inordinate amount of time it took to get around the city. One survey showed that it took one hour to go from the Taipei Railroad Station to the Homei Department store two and half miles away. Salespeople were finding that instead of being able to visit four to six clients in the morning and a similar number in the afternoon, they could only visit three to four clients all day (Lu, 1990). Many companies began to feel that they would be better off locating in suburban sites. The human resource costs alone of commuting in Taipei were calculated to be of the order of US$2.2 billion a year (*Free China Journal*, Apr. 22, 1991, 3). Intra-city traffic also began to have an impact on the Sun Yat-sen North–South Freeway. People started using this road as a preferred means of avoiding Taipei city streets. The net result was a decline in the average speed in both the north and south directions of the freeway (Huang, 1993c). Further complicating matters was the fact that Taipei citizens were not the only ones using Taipei streets: some 250 000 workers commute into the city daily from the townships and cities in surrounding Taipei county (Chen, 1992). Finally, the heavy rains so common to Taipei result in flooding and traffic signal failure, thereby further increasing both traffic congestion and driver impatience (*Free China Journal*, Sept. 5, 1988, 1).

The municipal government's response to Taipei's slide towards gridlock has been a five-fold one. First, it has debated three purely administrative means of controlling the situation. A pass system, which would restrict cars without a minimum number of passengers from entering parts of the city, was not only debated, but a trial implementation was underwritten by the national Environmental Protection Agency (*Free China Journal*, Jul. 30, 1990, 3). Strict enforcement of a point system of demerits against a driver's license was suggested. However, full enforcement was not implemented because of lack of police personnel and up-to-date computing equipment to keep accurate records. The fact that any one vehicle may be driven by more than one driver during any given day also complicates full enforcement of existing laws (Tseng, 1991). Finally, the government has begun to insist that traffic codes are systematically enforced for both pedestrians and drivers (Table 6.4). Since jaywalkers are involved in one-third of all traffic accidents, fines of US$14 or up to two hours of traffic safety classes have been meted out to pedestrians. In addition the 11th day of each month has been designated as Traffic Safety Day, where police try to reinforce in the public mind the need to obey traffic laws and thus avoid traffic mishaps (*Free China Journal*, Feb. 19, 1993, 4). Some of drivers' more notorious behavior (Tseng, 1991) such as illegal parking, switching lanes without signaling, running red lights, driving in wrong lanes, using turn lanes to pass other vehicles, and speeding, have been targeted for ticketing. In particular, driving under the influence of alcohol or drugs has been subject to more rigorous investigation, especially during the peak season for such behavior – the month before and after the Chinese New

Table 6.4 Traffic offenses, violations, and fines

Type of offenses	1969	1989
Prohibited turning, backing	24 540	56 480
Illegal parking	29 019	894 895
Blocking roads	11 334	21 186
Failure to obey signs, police	46 879	159 960
Driving in wrong lane	4 488	177 401
Driving without shoes	14 566	159 960
Speeding	5 848	214 734
Total number of reported violations	196 004	2 552 045
Total fines collected (US$)	231 640	11 208 277

Source: *The Statistical Abstract of Taipei Municipality, 1990* (1990).

Year (*China Post*, Jan. 26, 1991, 16; Jan. 27, 1991, 8). Since the campaign began Taipei police have been issuing some 7000–8000 tickets a day for traffic violations and some 1500 tickets for parking violations (Hwang, 1991). As a result of both the increase in the number of vehicles and stricter enforcement of road regulations, the mix of traffic offenses which have been ticketed has shifted (Table 6.4), revenues from fines have increased, and the accident and accident–fatality rates have declined to 10 year lows (*Free China Journal*, June 4, 1991, 4).

In addition to increased fines, the government has tried, with mixed success, to use *economic* mechanisms for dealing with traffic problems. Although the Ministry of Communications was asked to consider raising taxes on cars and licenses, as well as raising tolls and parking fines, politicians have been reluctant to impose higher taxes, despite their successes in Singapore (Chang, 1991; *Free China Journal*, Mar. 11, 1991, 3). Insurance companies have begun exploring the possibility of issuing differential premium policies based on age, gender, driving experience and records (Tseng, 1991). Finally, fare increases for buses and cabs have been granted, although they have been the source of complaints from consumers, bus and cab drivers, and even bus company owners (*China Post*, Jan. 24, 1991, 11). Hopes that higher fares would result in better service and less automobile use have not apparently been realized.

Education has been tried as a means of solving traffic problems, with the municipal government commissioning a well known Taiwan political cartoonist to draw a series of educational cartoons for periodic publication in newspapers (*Free China Journal*, Apr. 1, 1991, 3). Land use and accessibility restrictions have been tried, in Hsimenting, in the hope of reducing the amount of traffic moving through the busy city center (Chang, 1990). In this case traffic-free zones were created when street vendors as well as vehicles were banned from 6 p.m. to 10 p.m. Mondays through Fridays, and from 11 a.m. to 11 p.m. on weekends.

The fifth, and most ambitious approach to the traffic problems involved improving the transportation infrastructure of the city. Five types of improvements have been constructed or are in the process of being completed. Since the planning, construction and use of all six improvements overlap, the discussion first focuses on programs to upgrade or expand existing facilities and then proceeds to review totally new initiatives.

In terms of both impact on the visual landscape and improvement of traffic conditions, one of the most important improvements was the replacement of the Taipei Central Railroad Station (Figures 2.11, 2.13). The first station, built by the Japanese in 1900, covered some 5000 square meters and had by the 1970s become inadequate to handle all the passenger and freight traffic moving through Taipei. So in 1985 construction of a new station was begun on the same site as the original station; on 2 September 1989 the 15 330 square meter station, capable of serving 200 000 riders a day, was officially opened to the public. Altogether there are six above-ground floors. On the ground floor there are 40 ticket counters. The second floor contains shops, restaurants, and boutiques. The remaining above-ground floors are occupied by the Taiwan Railroad Administration. There are four below-ground levels. The first two include the concourse and train track platforms for the railroad. The bottom two contain the same facilities for the Taipei Mass Rapid Transit System (MRTS), to be discussed below.

As convenient and efficient as the new railroad station is for moving people in and out of Taipei, its greatest importance for improving traffic conditions in Taipei is found in the 4420 meters of underground track which was laid, thereby eliminating 13 old railroad crossings to the west and south of the railroad station (Figure 6.11). These crossings were the cause of constant traffic congestion, since every time a train went through the gates came down and traffic stopped, regardless of where in the traffic signal cycle the traffic happened to be. In addition to eliminating these crossings, placement of the tracks underground freed the space previously occupied by the tracks for a multi-lane road with reserved bus lanes (Figure 6.12).

The second existing transportation element which the city has attempted to upgrade is the bus system. Despite low fares (an eight kilometer trip costs around US$0.40), ridership peaked in 1985 at 2.6 million riders per day and has been declining by about 400 000 per day each year since (*Free China Journal*, Mar. 11, 1991, 3). Riders are dissatisfied with waiting and riding time as well as the crowded conditions on the buses (Tzeng and Shiau, 1988). Riding time is frequently slowed down because of the illegal traffic behavior of automobile and motorcycle drivers, in particular curbside parking violations, running red lights, and cutting off maneuvers at corners. Jaywalkers also slow buses down (*Free China*

Figure 6.11 Railroad tracks leading to the Central Railroad Station created traffic problems whenever a train passed

Journal, Aug. 16, 1990, 3). Although stricter enforcement of traffic regulations, as outlined above, should help speed the bus trip, special bus lanes have also been added to some routes to shorten trip time (Hwang, 1991). Televisions have been included in some new buses purchased after 1991 in the hope of making the trip more enjoyable (*China Post*, Jan. 27, 1991, 8). To increase the capacity of the bus system without adding new buses or new routes, double-decker buses were introduced in 1990. The initial six-month experiment on several major east–west and north–south routes proved so successful that the City Bus Administration anticipated purchasing 40 such buses before the end of fiscal 1992 (*Free China Journal*, Aug. 30, 1990, 2). Before the buses can actually run, however, safety standards for buses will have to

Figure 6.12 The placing of railroad tracks underground has opened the crossing areas and permitted a multi-lane road, with dedicated bus lanes. Pedestrian over-passes reduce the chance of accidents

be amended to accommodate the 4.38 meter high buses (*Free China Journal*, Mar. 5, 1990, 3).

Although all of these efforts have the potential for drawing people back to buses, one issue still remains to resolved: the cost of the system. Although the cost per trip is low, the income generated does not cover the full costs. When fare increases were granted in 1991, the increases only covered greater fuel and operating costs and not salary increases for drivers. After cab drivers received a 25 percent fare increase in 1993, bus drivers called a wildcat strike in retaliation on 22 June 1993 from 5 a.m. to 4 p.m. (Pan, 1993). In addition to catching the government by surprise, and inconveniencing riders despite last-minute additions to municipal bus

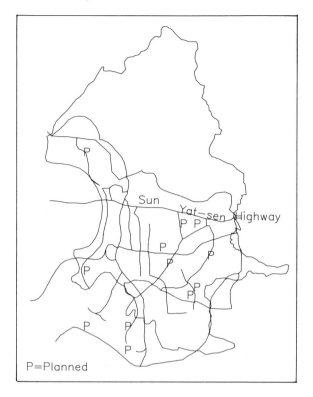

Figure 6.13 Elevated and limited access highways

schedules, the strike left many unresolved issues beyond the problem of price increases. The illegal nature of the strike raised the questions of whether such actions could go unpunished without harming the social fabric of Taipei, who actually precipitated the strike, and why the procedures for strikes outlined in the labor law were not followed.

The third aspect of transportation which the city has worked to improve is the road system itself. Starting in 1968 new roads have been built (Figure 6.10), and major thoroughfares such as Jenai, Tunhua, Chungshan, Aikuo, Peian, Hsinyi, Keelung, Sungchung, Hoping East, Nanking West, and Roosevelt Roads have been rebuilt (*Welcome to the 21st Century*, 1987). By 1987 five elevated highways had been constructed, and a sixth was in use by 1991 (*Welcome to the 21st Century*, 1987, 43; *Free China Journal*, Nov. 5, 1991, 4). Additional elevated roads are planned (Figure 6.13). Of special importance is the one which will join Chungking north and south roads which are presently separated by railroad tracks. Elevated roads are built so that sound barriers minimize noise to the surrounding neighborhoods. New bridges have been built and old ones upgraded. A section of a second north–south freeway will include a Taipei connection of some 3.8 kilometers designed to funnel traffic from Nankang to Mucha (*Free China Journal*, Jan. 26, 1986, 1). Finally, 25 traffic circles, originally built to beautify the city, are to be removed. Many of these circles required eight sets of lights to move traffic, and as a result traffic flows were reduced by 70 percent in their vicinity (*Free China Journal*, May 16, 1988, 3).

As was the case with improving the bus system, road improvements have experienced some problems. Fundamentally the greatest problem is that road building has not adequately kept up with the increase in the number of vehicles (Figure 6.10). Often the new roads are no wider than older roads, and generally lack adequate parking areas (Glenn, 1968). Attempts to build more elevated highways have run into the "nimby" (not in my back yard) syndrome found elsewhere in the world where socially necessary but locally offensive facilities must be built (Hwang, 1991). When elevated highways have been built three problems often result. One is that the neighborhoods are often socially and economically disrupted or devastated. Although such major construction projects do permit major urban renewal to take place, the cost to residents is not only high, but apparently not even considered in the planning and implementation stages. Second, given the space limitations in an urban area, the on and off ramps for the elevated highways are frequently narrower and steeper than desired. As a result, there have been numerous accidents where trucks or buses have slipped off the ramps, causing damage and injuries. Third, the off ramps frequently terminate at already busy intersections, thereby increasing traffic congestion (Figure 6.14).

The fourth component which the city has worked to improve is that of parking. As was the case with housing, the demand for parking far exceeds available supply, and the problem is aggravated by limited amounts of land. The imbalance between supply and demand can be measured in at least three ways. First, a comparison of the number of cars and motor-cycles to the number of available spaces shows that there is a shortfall of some 166 000 spaces for automobiles, and 766 000 for motorcycles (Chang, 1991; Hwang, 1991). Second, surveys have shown that the amount of time it takes to find a parking space has increased from three to almost ten minutes (*Free China Journal*, Dec. 15, 1988, 3). Then the walk from the parking space to work is close to seven minutes! Third, the cost of owning a parking space increased from US$46 000 in 1989 to US$185 000 in 1991 (*Free China Journal*, Aug. 21, 1989, 3; Mar. 11, 1991, 3), thus making the cost of parking greater than the cost of the car itself!

For their part commuters and car owners have adopted a number of strategies for dealing with the shortfall of parking spaces (Chang, 1991; Hwang, 1991). Some workers leave home early enough to arrive at work at 7:30 a.m. If enough people adopt this approach, of course, all that will

Figure 6.14 Off-ramps from elevated highways dump traffic into already congested areas. Pedestrians trying to cross streets frequently add to traffic problems

happen is to make traffic jams occur earlier than they already have. Some drivers will pull into a curb-side car wash and then leave the car all day. Some drivers just park illegally by occupying spaces along yellow curb lanes, by parking on sidewalks, or double parking. The more sophisticated amongst these drivers will even put an old ticket on the windshield. Finally, drivers will leave kids in illegally parked cars while they run into a shop or do an errand. This strategy seems to work as towing truck operators will not baby sit!

For its part the city government has tried to adopt strategies which will both increase the supply of parking spaces and restore order to the streets and sidewalks. To manage, supervise, and implement its strategies the government established the Bureau of Parking management in 1988 (Hwang, 1991). The Bureau has recommended that parking fees and towing/storage fees be increased. Presumably raising fees would discourage people from even considering bringing their cars to work, while raising towing and storage charges will make it more expensive to have your car towed than to park. As it stood in 1991 parking a car in a public lot all day cost US$11, while the cost of towing and storage was US$54.50. Apparently many commuters thought the probability of getting a ticket or being towed low enough to risk not paying to park. The Bureau has plans to install an additional 120 000 curb-side meters (*Free China Journal*,

Mar. 11, 1991, 3). Progress in implementing this is impeded by lack of attendants to service the meters and issue tickets (Chang, 1991). The Bureau has identified some 91 potential sites where additional parking lots can be constructed. Many of these sites are currently occupied by illegal structures (*Free China Journal*, Feb. 27, 1989, 3). Before these parking spaces can be developed, however, the illegal structures must be removed. Although the city would like to demolish the structures, the fiscal arm of the city government rejected a budget request of US$8.9 million in 1989 (*Free China Journal*, Feb. 27, 1989, 3). Since its ability to build new parking facilities itself is thus somewhat limited, as an alternative the Bureau has allowed bids for private development of eligible sites. The Bureau helps to finance land costs by drawing income generated by fees and fines. Private developers are then free to set their own parking fee schedule, and are guaranteed that no street parking will be permitted within a 600 meter radius of the parking lot (*Free China Journal*, Jan. 11, 1990, 3). The Bureau also encourages architects to include basement parking facilities in all new buildings. In exchange for such spaces, taller building heights have been permitted (*Free China Journal*, Oct. 31, 1988, 3). The Bureau's attempts at increasing the number of parking spaces will no doubt be enhanced by the proposal from the nationally owned China Petroleum Corporation to convert many of its gas stations to multi-level facilities which will include parking spaces on upper levels (*Free China Journal*, Oct. 17, 1988, 3). All of these programs to expand the number of parking spaces should be more effective than the longstanding approach to clearing streets – towing illegally parked vehicles and especially motorcycles. This approach, commonly done without warning, seems singularly inefficient since within several hours of a street or sidewalk being cleared of illegally parked vehicles a new crop appears.

The last government program to deal with the traffic problem, the construction of a Taipei Mass Rapid Transit System (MRTS) (Figure 6.15), is the centerpiece of all the government's efforts at improving traffic conditions. The MRTS is expected to absorb some 51 percent of all commuter traffic by the time it is finally completed (Hwang, 1991; Yeung, 1991b). This optimistic expectation is grounded on the assumptions that commuters will find it easier to park at one of the park and ride facilities adjacent to the MRTS stations, that they will use the shuttle buses planned along associated routes, and that they will find the linkages with railroad and regular bus services convenient (Yeung, 1991b). Plans call for a 70 kilometer system running over five lines. Two additional lines – a circle route from Mucha to Neihu and a link from Sungshan airport to the Chiang Kai-shek International Airport in Taoyuan – have been proposed. The entire system, including some 33 stations, is scheduled to be completed by 1999. Six of the stations will be at ground level, ten will be elevated, and the remaining ones will be underground (Strandberg, 1989).

Figure 6.15 Taipei Mass Rapid Transit System

The system will have two types of equipment: on the mass rapid transit parts there will be fully automated train operation, with central monitoring and control. On the medium capacity transit section there will be fully automated, driverless type cars (Strandberg, 1989). The system, which was originally projected to cost some US$3.75 billion and may eventually cost as much as US$17. 5 billion (Chang, 1992), is the largest of the 14 infrastructure projects described in Chapter 1. Funding is to come from four sources: 40 percent will come from national government sources, 10 percent will come from provincial sources, and 29 percent will come from city government funds. The rest will be raised through a special tax (Ge, 1985; Moore, 1987). Building and operating the system is the responsibility of the Department of Taipei Rapid Transit Systems (DORTS).

In implementing the MRTS plan several problems have developed. As with so many projects in Taipei land acquisition is a significant problem and the 1988 legislation authorizing the building of the MRTS included provisions permitting DORTS to pay up to 40 percent more than the official price of land. Special provisions provide for division of underground, surface and air rights between the government and the original landlord. Joint landlord/DORTS ventures are also encouraged (Yeung, 1991b). There have been questions raised as to whether or not politics intervened in both the selection of routes (as seen in the discussion of Kuantu Plain above) and the order in which the five lines should be built (Heikkila, 1987; Poo, 1987). Politics also seems to have played a role in the selection of consultants to DORTS and in the purchase of rail equipment. A British team was replaced by an American–Hong Kong group in an apparent attempt by the central government to provide visible evidence to the United States that serious efforts were being made to redress the large imbalance in US–ROC trade (Strandberg, 1989). When first calls for bids on equipment were made, specifications mandated a 50 percent made in the United States content (Moore, 1988). No wonder then that the first contracts for equipment were awarded to the New Jersey based United Rail Car Company for 132 subway cars at a cost of US$170 million. In fact United Rail Car is owned by the United States subsidiaries of Nissho Iwai and Kawasaki Rail Cars, two Japanese firms (Feron, 1989).

Critics of the project claim that the ridership projections are unduly optimistic. Some feel that when completed the MRTS will have at best provided the level of service that should have been present in the early 1990s (Moore, 1988) and that traffic conditions will not improve. Concern has also been raised about the noise, dirt, pollution, and congestion which will be associated with the MRTS construction (Chang, 1991). Credibility in the ability of DORTS to complete the project on time surfaced several times. Almost at the start, in 1988, the project fell eight months behind schedule due to bureaucratic wrangling and difficulties in acquiring land (Moore, 1988; *Free China Journal*, Nov. 1, 1988, 3). Delays also occurred because DORTS had difficulty finding qualified contractors with appropriate underground construction experience (*Free China Journal*, Nov. 1, 1988, 3). Unanticipated problems over routing developed when excavations in the Yuanshan area of Shihlin uncovered a

7000-year-old site of archaeological significance. Not only was work suspended at the site for three months, but the site of the station under construction was subject to relocation (*Free China Journal*, Mar. 21, 1991, 3). Finally, many critics feel that without increased road courtesy and better enforcement of traffic regulations, any additions to the traffic system will make for only marginal improvements in traffic conditions.

In considering the diverse transportation programs considered or adopted by the city government, five generalizations are immediately apparent. First, both the national and city governments were very slow in considering transportation a problem. The reason for the slow response to the growing problem is usually attributed to a failure to believe that Taipei was going to grow and prosper (Glenn, 1968; *Free China Journal*, Sept. 5, 1988, 1; Yeung, 1991a). Second, planning has suffered both because of the delay in starting and the lack of qualified personnel (Hwang, 1991; Yeung, 1991a). In Taipei a traffic department was established in 1972 but was disbanded in 1974 due to a lack of projects to work on (Hwang, 1991). When it was reconstituted in 1988, a huge backlog of problems had evolved. One of the net results of the lack of planning was a 14-year lapse between the time the MRTS was initially discussed and real planning actually began. Apologists for the way in which this project was handled can point to the historically short-term perspective used in carrying out construction of public works projects. In addition planning during the 1960s and 1970s was usually restricted to the test of directly contributing to economic growth and limited by other budget demands and priorities (Yeung, 1991a). When planning did occur, it was often not coordinated properly (Hwang, 1991). The MRTS is again a good example: the possibility of coordinating its design and construction with the program to rebuild the Taipei railroad station was evident in 1972, when the city government decided to fund some US$250 million worth of construction to put the railroad tracks underground (Yeung, 1991a). Had there been enough qualified personnel, the coordination of projects could have been achieved.

The third generalization is that all attempts to restrict ownership by changing the fee and tax system have failed. Apart from a political failure, this also demonstrates the strength of the car as a social or status symbol (Huang, 1993c). If the car is indeed such an important symbol, it is not clear that the public will abandon the car in favor of the MRTS. Fourth, the vision of how to solve the Taipei transportation system is very limited. For example, apparently no consideration of minibuses was given in any of the planning decisions (*Free China Journal*, Jul. 25, 1993, 3) although they have been a successful part of urban transportation systems elsewhere in Asia.

Finally, transportation planning frequently becomes mixed up in other political issues or priorities having little to do with the immediate problem at hand. Four additional examples of this can be offered. Many delays in getting and accepting the bids are related to the inability of construction firms to guarantee completion on time. Their inability is directly related to the shortage of construction workers (Yeung, 1991a). Although this problem was evident to the national government, there were long delays in permitting foreign workers to come to Taiwan (Selya, 1992). Maximum efficiency and profit in running buses often conflicts with the politically necessary goal of providing cheap and safe late-night transportation for women and students (*Free China Journal*, Apr. 2, 1990, 3). The debate on how best to solve the traffic congestion problem was muddied when one city councillor insisted that any solution must include bike paths. Although a compromise, to put some bike paths along the Tamshui river, was reached, the debate on this luxury in land-short Taipei delayed the passage of important legislation needed to implement other traffic projects (*Free China Journal*, Jul. 19, 1990, 3). Finally, plans to reopen Sungshan airport to international flights will not only create more traffic congestion in the Sungshan area but increase all types of pollution as well. But an additional international airport is required to ensure that access for Taiwan airlines remains open to Hong Kong, Singapore, and Bali in face of pressure from the People's Republic of China to limit access to the Republic of China national carrier, China Airlines (*Free China Journal*, May 14, 1993, 1).

As with some of the environmental and social problems discussed above, the government has not had to act alone in trying to improve the traffic situation. There have been two joint public/private programs designed to help. First, the City Health Department, in cooperation with the taxi drivers' association, plans to train some 70 000 cab drivers in first aid over a three-year period 1993–1996. It is hoped that these cab drivers will be able to offer assistance in the event of an accident and thereby ameliorate the inevitable late arrival on the scene of ambulances because of traffic (*Free China Journal*, Mar. 12, 1993, 4). Second, three radio stations, the Cheng Sheng Corporation, the Taipei City Broadcasting Station, and ICRT (International Community Radio in Taipei), have joined with both the police radio system and a police helicopter in reporting traffic conditions during the morning and evening rush hour (Hwang, 1991; *Free China Journal*, Dec. 24, 1990, 3).

These joint efforts are paralleled by purely private initiatives. Several organizations of retired persons have suggested that retirees be given cameras to take pictures of traffic violators and their vehicles, which could then be used to issue traffic citations. In addition to relieving the police of some of their enforcement duties, such a system would also provide the elderly with an opportunity for exercise, and provide a service which would enhance their self-worth (*Free China Journal*, Mar. 28, 1991, 3). The taxi cab drivers themselves have formed what they call a Green Cross

Traffic Service (Lin, 1990). The objectives of the service include correcting the image of cab drivers as lawbreaking, greedy, rude, unkempt operators of ill-kept, hazardously driven vehicles, as well as assisting the police. They pledge to cooperate with the police by using their cab radios to inform police of accidents, crimes in progress, suspicious behavior, and traffic conditions. In addition the cab drivers are expected to direct traffic 14 days a month at any of the 342 main intersections normally manned by regular police. Membership in 1990 stood at 230 members; a cap of 430 is planned in order to maintain standards. Those who join must be dedicated to safety, courtesy, and be willing to adhere to a dress and behavior code while driving. Only drivers with no criminal charges during the most recent five years, and no traffic violations in the most recent three-year period are eligible to join the service. In 1988 the city formally recognized the value of the service by both granting it tax exempt status and giving it a subsidy of US$3.08 for each hour of service provided by a service member. A third private initiative is some of the programming at the Taipei Children's Museum of Transportation (*Free China Journal*, Sept. 17, 1991, 4). The museum features driving simulation exhibits and a traffic park with miniature Taipei streets and landmarks. Both exhibits are designed to show the importance and usefulness of obeying traffic rules before youths get behind the wheel.

Conclusions

In 1974 Pannell argued that if the land problem in the cities of Taiwan was not solved then in addition to increasing diseconomies, a series of political, physical, psychiatric, and social problems would develop. This prediction appears to have come true for Taipei. Solving the land problem will involve reconciling conflicting political and social values and premises. But it will also require that the "growth at any cost" or "growthism" attitude, which drove much of the early thinking behind the successful economic development of Taiwan, be replaced with an orientation which includes ecological and social values as well. The development of grass roots, public based, organizations committed to these additional values will help to ensure that new economic thinking is applied.

There is, however, an additional, more serious problem, which must also be simultaneously addressed: the necessity of installing a more positive attitude towards obeying the law. Many of the problems outlined in this chapter, and the section in Chapter 5 on planning, derive from a basic disregard for the law. Although some infractions, such as illegal parking of motorcycles, may seem at best harmless and at worst a public incon-venience, others put the health and safety of the population at risk, and inhibit the municipal government from effectively implementing programs to assure the long-term viability of the city. What is required is a change in attitude and behavior on the part of the government, entrepreneurs, developers, and the public. The government should not be satisfied with irregular, albeit periodic, raids or campaigns against illegal behavior. Rather it should provide the police and investigative sections in other government agencies with the resources necessary to enforce the law. Entrepreneurs and developers must take long-term perspectives in making their decisions. What use is there in short-term profit if it leads to long-term problems at the expense of the government and the general public?

Who, after all, should be the ultimate beneficiaries of Taipei's development? The official ideology of the Kuomintang, *San Min Chu I* or Three People's Principles, leaves no doubt that society as a whole should benefit. It is not clear how the attitude that anything which creates additional gross domestic product is *a priori* contributing to the implementation of the government's long-term social and economic goals is derived from *San Min Chu I*. Are not developers and entrepreneurs part of society as a whole? They should be reasonably rewarded for the risks they take, but not at the expense of Taipei's environment and social fabric. For its part the government needs to enact reasonable legislation and then see to it that the laws are enforced. Any other action will undermine the confidence the public has in the emerging democratization of Taipei and Taiwan society.

The alternatives to dealing fully with the land and law problems are easy to predict and unpleasant to contemplate. Already growing disparities in wealth have developed, undermining the credibility of Taiwan's experience with economic development where both growth and equity were possible simultaneously. The source of the gap in wealth is access to real estate. Should the gap widen even further, the political stability of Taipei and Taiwan could be adversely affected. In another vein, one future scenario is a series of boom and bust real estate cycles as developers and Taipei residents constantly adjust to market conditions (Lin, 1989; Tanzer, 1981). By extension such a scenario might include an increasingly agitated populace willing to demonstrate in the streets and to follow political leaders willing to help meet its needs (Pan, 1993). A third future scenario would be the systematic abandonment of Taipei as a center of manufacturing, commerce, and tourism. In fact this process may have already started. Some industry has moved out of Taipei and hotel builders appear to be looking to other sites in Taiwan for future development (Boydell, 1990). Although the search for new hotel sites is also related to the desire of the Taiwanese for new forms of recreation in new locations, the high cost of land is also a driving force. This scenario would not appeal to national political leaders since, as will be documented in Chapter 7, they are anxious to maintain and expand Taipei as an important economic center in order to use Taiwan's economic importance as a lever for expanding the political legitimacy and participation in regional and world organizations of the Republic of China. A fourth scenario involves increasing lawlessness, anarchy, and the necessity to reimpose martial law. While extreme, this scenario might appeal to hard-liners in the Kuomintang, who see political liberalization as both a threat to their power base and the cause of the decline in morals. However, a return to any form of authoritarian rule would no doubt undermine all progress towards resolving the state of civil conflict with the People's Republic of China, and alienate Taiwan from its trading partners.

In short, the long-term viability of Taipei as a thriving, livable urban center, and the successful development of new regional and international roles for Taiwan, depend on solving the land and law problems. In this regard Taipei and Taiwan are not unique: other areas in East Asia have similar challenges to meet (Paisely, 1993). In striving to solve the land and law problems the national and municipal governments need not work alone. Many of the solutions to Taipei's problems have been and can be dealt with through private efforts or joint public–private cooperation. But the goodwill and evolving commitment by private groups to solving public problems must be met with political resolve and integrity by elected and appointed officials.

References

Air Pollution Control in Taipei City (1972) Environmental Protection Agency, Taipei.

Ambruster, W. (1976) Letter from Taipei, *Far Eastern Economic Review* 94, Nov. 19, 70.

Ames, E. and M. Ames (1972) Taiwan's Development Typhoon, *Nation* 214, March 20, 370–372.

Baker, H. D. R. (1979) *Chinese Family and Kinship*. Columbia University Press, New York.

Bierma, T. J. (1985) A Personal Look at Taiwan's Air Pollution Problems, *Bulletin–Illinois Geographical Society* 27:2, 18–27.

Boydell, M. (1990) Hotel Builders Leaving Taipei, Turning to Resort Development, *Central Daily News, Supplement*, Apr. 22.

Bullough, V. C. (1976) *Sexual Variance in Society and History*. University of Chicago Press, Chicago.

Buruma, I. (1985) Red Lights and the Heavy Shadow of Hypocrisy, *Far Eastern Economic Review* 127, Mar. 21, 56–7.

Central Daily News (1991) Singapore Can. Taipei Should Be Able To, Jan. 8, 7.*

Central Daily News (1992) Taipei Sixth Most Expensive City in the World, Dec. 12, 7.*

Central Daily News (1993) Separate Neighborhood Building Sites: Two Apartment Buildings Collapse in Taipei, Mar. 2, 7.*

Chang, C. (1975) My Twenty Years in Taipei, pp. 493–499 reprinted in English in P.-y. Chi, ed., *An Anthology of Contemporary Chinese Literature, Taiwan: 1949–1974, Vol. 1*, National Institute for Compilation and Translation, Taipei.

Chang, C. (1983) An Inside View of the Taipei City Police Force: Too Many Missions Weigh Down the Long Arm of the Law, *Free China Review* 33:9, 50–52.

Chang, S.-d. (1970) Land Use and Intraurban Travel in Taipei, *Proceedings, Association of American Geographers* 2, 40–45.

Chang, S.-d. and F-.t. Tang (1978) Urban and Environmental Problems in Taiwan, pp. 101–148, in *Sino-American Workshop on Land Use Planning*, National Science Council, Taipei.

Chang, W. (1990) Hsimenting Goes Pedestrian, *Free China Journal*, Jan. 18, 3.

Chang, W. (1991) Taipei Parking Blues, *Free China Review* 41:3, 26–28.

Chang, W. (1992) True Grit: The Making of the MRT, *Free China Review* 42:11, 1992, 29–37.

Chen, C.-s. (1957) *Taipei*. Fu-Min Geographical Institute of Economic Development, Research Report No. 79, Taipei.*

Chen, C.-n. (1992) Extended Commuting and Migration in the Taipei Metropolitan Area, *Journal of Population Studies* 15, 161–182.

Chen, D. W. (1988) AIDS – A Modern Hydra, *Free China Review* 38:10, 48–51.

China Post (1989) Motorcycle Checks Kick Off Today, Jul. 3, 12.

China Post (1991a) 211 Reported 'Ice' Users in Taipei, Jan. 12, 12.

China Post (1991b) Taipei Ranks 10th Most Expensive City in MOEA Survey of World Cities, Jan. 13, 8.

China Post (1991c) Drivers' Group Opposes Rush Hour Surcharge, Jan. 24, 11.

China Post (1991d) Bus Fare Increases Anger Drivers, Jan. 24, 11.

China Post (1991e) Drink Driving Crackdown, Jan. 26, 16.

China Post (1991f) City Buses to Have TVs Installed, Jan. 27, 8.

China Post (1991g) Taipei Police Nab 94 Drunk Drivers, Jan. 27, 8.

China Post (1991h) Taipei's Mayor Leaves for Singapore, Jan. 29, 12.

Chiu, J. (1992) Feared Hand of AIDS Touches Taiwan Society, *Free China Journal*, Mar. 3, 5.

Cities. Life in the World's 100 Largest Metropolitan Areas (1990) Population Crisis Committee, Washington.

DeVries, B. (1989) Air Pollution from Traffic Sources in Taiwan and Taipei Basin, pp. 687–728, in *Taiwan 2000: Balancing Economic Growth and Environmental Protection*, Steering Committee, Taiwan 2000 Study, Institute of Ethnology, Academia Sinica, Taipei.

Enloe, C. (1989) *Bananas, Beaches, and Bases. Making Feminist Sense of International Politics*. University of California Press, Berkeley.

Fan, Y. H. (1977) Flood (sic), New Towns, and the Development of Northern Taiwan Region, *Science Reports* 9, 87–93.*

Fan, Y. H. (1985) A Framework for Evaluation of Slope Land Development, *Science Reports* 12, 123–140.*

Feron, J. (1989) Made in New York: Taiwan's First Subway Cars, *New York Times*, Sept. 27, C1.

Free China Journal (1986) Freeway to Free Taipei Traffic, Jan. 26, 1.

Free China Journal (1988a) Three Not Enough of a Crowd in Taipei, May 16, 3.

Free China Journal (1988b) Taipei Traffic Posse Rides, Sept. 5, 1.

Free China Journal (1988c) Taipei's Ozone 2 Peaks Daily EPA Study Says, Sept. 22, 3.

Free China Journal (1988d) CPC Plans Parking Lots, Oct. 17, 3.

Free China Journal (1988e) Architects May Solve Parking, Oct. 31, 3.

Free China Journal (1988f) Taipei's Trains on Line by 1997, Nov. 1, 3.

Free China Journal (1988g) Exhausting Job, Nov. 28, 3.

Free China Journal (1988h) Taipei Drives On, Dec. 15, 3.
Free China Journal (1989a) Taipei Fights Youth Crime, Jan. 9, 3.
Free China Journal (1989b) New Parking Lot Ploy, Feb. 27, 3.
Free China Journal (1989c) Housing Expenses, Mar. 13, 3.
Free China Journal (1989d) Taipei Land Prices High, Apr. 24, 3.
Free China Journal (1989e) Like Brigadoon, Taipei is Sinking into the Mists, May 11, 3.
Free China Journal (1989f) Taipei Rental Said Too Steep, Jun. 5, 3.
Free China Journal (1989g) Parking Costs More than Cars, Aug. 21, 3.
Free China Journal (1989h) Homeless Seeking Homes, Sept. 4, 3.
Free China Journal (1989i) Housing Woes are Examined, Sept. 7, 3.
Free China Journal (1989j) Well Drillers Sinking Land?, Sept. 11, 3.
Free China Journal (1989k) Taipei's Patience Asked During Construction Era, Oct. 30, 3.
Free China Journal (1990a) Taipei Seeking Parking Lot Bids, Jan. 11, 3.
Free China Journal (1990b) Taipei Land Sky High, Feb. 5, 3.
Free China Journal (1990c) Double-Deck Buses Due, Mar. 5, 3.
Free China Journal (1990d) Operators Claim Night Owl Bus Fare too Skimpy, Apr. 2, 3.
Free China Journal (1990e) Space Made for Pedal Pushers, Jul. 19, 3.
Free China Journal (1990f) Traffic Pass System Set to Ease Congestion, Jul. 30, 3.
Free China Journal (1990g) Buses Groan to a Halt, Aug. 16, 3.
Free China Journal (1990h) Taipei's Downtown Costly Digs, Aug. 30, 2.
Free China Journal (1990i) Taipei is Garbed in Expensive Glass, Sept. 6, 3.
Free China Journal (1990j) Landlords Here Mindful of Tensions in Mideast, Sept. 13, 3.
Free China Journal (1990k) Poll Indicates Public Favors Crime Crackdown, Oct. 18, 3.
Free China Journal (1990l) Traffic Surveillance Airborne in Taipei, Dec. 24, 3.
Free China Journal (1991a) High Tax Takes Aim at Curbing Vehicle Growth Problems Here, Mar. 11, 3.
Free China Journal (1991b) Hooray! An Empty Seat, Mar. 11, 3.
Free China Journal (1991c) Unearthed Relics Win Out Over Transit Digs, Mar. 21, 3.
Free China Journal (1991d) Retirees Eager to Use Cameras on Lawbreakers, Mar. 28, 3.
Free China Journal (1991e) Premier Lashes Out at Spread of 'Ugliness', Apr. 1, 3.
Free China Journal (1991f) Serious Comedy, Apr. 1, 3.
Free China Journal (1991g) Old Ways are New Housing Trend, Apr. 11, 3.
Free China Journal (1991h) Traffic Woes Said Costly, Apr. 22, 3.
Free China Journal (1991i) Taipei Religious Groups Show Love Through Money, May 14, 4.
Free China Journal (1991j) Accident to Vehicle Ratio Down, Jun. 4, 4.
Free China Journal (1991k) Wanna Home? Pay Nine Years Wages, Jul. 5, 4.
Free China Journal (1991l) Transportation Museum Puts Emphasis on Youths Following Rules of Road, Sept. 17, 4.
Free China Journal (1991m) Commuter's Connection, Nov. 5, 4.
Free China Journal (1992a) High End Housing Blooms, Jan. 28, 8.
Free China Journal (1992b) Land Bill Fitted with New Teeth, Jul. 2, 6.
Free China Journal (1992c) Housing Out of Reach, Nov. 6, 5.
Free China Journal (1993a) Pedestrians Must Obey Laws, Feb. 19, 4.
Free China Journal (1993b) Taxi Drivers to the Rescue, Mar. 12, 4.

Free China Journal (1993c) Noise Nuisance Controls, May 4, 4.

Free China Journal (1993d) Taipei Sungshan Airport to Accommodate International Flights, May 14, 1.

Free China Journal (1993e) Commuters Bear Brunt, Jul. 25, 3.

Free China Review (1991) Growth Outruns Policy, 41:8, 12–18.

Ge, S.-m. (1985) Relief on Way for Traffic Bound Taipei, *Free China Journal*, Dec. 1–7, 4.

General Introduction (1990) Housing Department of Taipei Municipal Government, Taipei.

Glenn, W. (1968) Growing Like Topsy, *Far Eastern Economic Review* 61, Aug. 8, 280–289.

Goldstein, C. (1986) Crumbling Culture of Taiwan Aborigines. *Far Eastern Economic Review* 132, May 29, 46–9.

Guide to the Department of Environmental Protection (1984) Department of Environmental Protection, Taipei.

Heikkila, E. (1987) Establishing Routing Priorities for Taipei's Rapid Transit System, *Industry of Free China* 68:5, 15–22.

Heikkila, E. (1988) Taipei Going Underground to Avert Traffic Crisis, *Far Eastern Economic Review* 139, Feb. 25, 42–3.

Hobson, B. M. (1987) *The Politics of Prostitution and the American Reform Tradition*. Basic Books, New York.

Housing Taipei, 1976–1985 (1987, reprinted 1990) Housing Department of Taipei City Government, Taipei.

Hsien, R. (1981) The Effect of Family Pathology on Taipei's Juvenile Delinquents, pp. 213–229, in *Normal and Abnormal Behavior in Chinese Culture*, A. Kleinman and T.-j. Lin, eds., D. Reidel, Boston.

Hsu, S., Chen, Kuo-yen and Yau, Yat-man (1988) A Study of Rainfall Intensity and Urban Surface Run-off in Relation to Flooding Problems in Taipei, *Geographical Studies* 12, 15–60.*

Huang, H. (1993a) Police Prostitution Sweep Will Not Solve the Problem, *Free China Journal*, May 7, 6.

Huang, H. (1993b) Housing Crisis as the Root of Procreation Shortfall, *Free China Journal*, June 15, 6.

Huang, H. (1993c) The Appeal of Private Cars Brings Traffic to Standstill, *Free China Journal*, June 11, 6.

Huang, S.-l. (1989) Integrating Storm-Water Management Concept for the Development of the Kuantu Plain in the City of Taipei, *Landscape and Urban Planning* 18:1, 37–53.

Hwang, J. (1991) Sliding Towards Gridlock, *Free China Review* 41:3, 4–13.

Hwang, J. (1992) United We Stand, *Free China Review* 42:6, 40–43.

Industrial Wastes Survey (1971) Taipei Area Sewerage Planning Committee, CIECD, Taipei.

Introduction to Urban Planning of Taipei City (1990) City Planning Department, Bureau of Public Works, Taipei.

Kaye, L. (1989) Sleep-in for Housing: A Teacher Protests Against Housing Costs, *Far Eastern Economic Review* 145, Sept. 7, 42.

Lang, O. (1946) *Chinese Family and Society*. Yale University Press, New Haven.

Lee, R. F. F. (1991) Bird Project Targets Pollution, *Free China Journal*, Dec. 6, 4.

Lee, R. F. F. (1992a) Environmental Respect Theme of Bird Life Park, *Free China Journal*, Feb. 26, 4.

Lee, R. F. F. (1992b) Chromatic Housing to Beautify Urban Landscape, *Free China Journal*, July 24, 4.

Lee, R. F. F. (1992c) Holiday Feast for Taipei Homeless, *Free China Journal*, Jan. 31, 4.

Lee, R. F. F. (1992d) Home Seekers Take Task in Hand, *Free China Journal*, May 1, 4.

Lee, R. F. F. (1993) Autonomous Managing Key in Buildings Rights, *Free China Journal*, March 5, 1993, 4.

Lee, Z. N. (1977) An Evaluation of the Public Housing Policy of the Republic of China, *Industry of Free China* 47:1, 15–25.

Lee, Z. N. (1979) Land Problems of Housing Development in Taiwan, *Industry of Free China* 51:1, 16–23.

Lin, C.-w. (1989) Realty Pros Seek Controls, *Free China Journal*, Feb. 27, 7.

Lin, C.-w. (1990) When Cross is Green It is Safe to Cross, *Free China Journal*, Jan. 8, 3.

Lin, D. (1992) 'Panic Disorder' On Rise in Taipei Streets, *Free China Journal*, Sept. 4, 4.

Lintner, B. and H.N. Lintner (1992) Immigrant Viruses: AIDS Moves Freely Over the Thai-Burma Border, *Far Eastern Economic Review* 155, Feb. 20, 3.

Liu, P. (1992) Striking a Better Balance, *Free China Review* 42:6, 16–19.

Liu, W.-l. (1989) Subsurface Project Begins, *Free China Journal*, Nov. 23, 3.

Lu, I.-y. (1990) Corporations Join Exodus to Suburbs, *Free China Journal*, Jan. 25, 3.

Meng, J. (1984) The Spatial Organization of Crime Phenomena in Taipei, *Geographical Studies* 8, 91–110.

Modak, P. M. and B. N. Lohani (1985) Optimization of Ambient Air Quality Monitoring Networks, Parts I, II, and III, *Environmental Monitoring and Assessment* 5:1, 1–53.

Moore, J. (1987) Traffic Relief in Sight, *Far Eastern Economic Review* 144, Sept. 24, 83.

Moore, J. (1988) Rumbles in the Subway, *Far Eastern Economic Review* 145, Dec. 1, 176–77.

Moore, J. (1989) No Ceiling: Taipei's Soaring Real Estate Prices Spark Street Protests, *Far Eastern Economic Review* 146, Oct. 19, 65.

Moore, J. (1990) Moves Afoot to Slow Frenzy, *Far Eastern Economic Review* 147, May 29, 54.

New Image of Taipei (1988) Department of Information, Taipei City Government, Taipei.

1975 Sample Census of Population and Housing, Taiwan-Fukien Area, Republic of China (1976) Census Office, Executive Yuan, Taipei.

Overall, C. (1992) What is Wrong with Prostitution? Evaluating Sex Work, *Signs: Journal of Women in Culture and Society* 17, 704–24.

Paisely, E. (1993) South Korea. Wounded Tiger, *Far Eastern Economic Review* 156, June 24, 22.

Pan, W.-h. (1993) Commuters Bear Brunt of Strike by Bus Drivers, *Free China Journal*, July 2, 6.

Pannell, C. W. (1974) Urban Land Consolidation and City Growth in Taiwan, *Pacific Viewpoint* 15, 111–122.

Peng, L. (1967) Long Term Variations of Temperature and Precipitation at Taipei, *Science Reports* 4, 125–136.*

Peng, L. (1968) Persistence and Probability of Rainfall Occurrences at Taipei, *Science Reports* 5, 107–114.*

Poo, D. (1987) A Critique of Professor Heikkila's Paper, *Industry of Free China* 68:5, 23–26.

Population Crisis Committee (1990) *Cities: Life in the World's 100 Largest Metropolitan Areas. Statistical Appendix.* Washington, D.C.

Pun, A. (1992a) Home Buyers Cheer US$8000 million in Aid, *Free China Journal*, July 2, 3.

Pun, A. (1992b) Public Outcry on High Prices Prompts Action to Curtail Real Estate Speculation, *Free China Journal*, July 17, 8.

Pun, A. (1992c) Long Term Mortgages Encouraged, *Free China Journal*, Oct 30, 3.

Pun, A. (1992d) 'Securitization' offers cost-free building, *Free China Journal*, May 12, 4.

Pun, A. (1992e) Stage Set for Preconstruction Housing Sales, *Free China Journal*, Apr. 7, 8.

Pun, A. (1992f) Taipei Restructures, Shifts to Suburbs, *Free China Journal*, June 12, 4.

Reanda, L. (1991) Prostitution as a Human Rights Issue, *Human Rights Quarterly* 13, 202–28.

Republic of China, 1988. A Reference Book (1988) Highlight International New York Inc, New York.

Republic of China Yearbook, 1993 (1993) Kwang Hwa Publishing Company, Taipei.

Reynolds, H. (1986) *Economics of Prostitution.* Charles L. Thomas, Springfield, Illinois.

Rubin, G. (1984) Thinking Sex. Notes for a Radical Theory of Sexuality, pp. 267–319, in C. S. Vance, ed., *Pleasure and Danger. Exploring Female Sexuality*, Routledge & Kegan Paul, Boston.

Schinz, A. (1989) *Cities in China.* Gebruder Borntraeger, Berlin.

Selya, R. M. (1975) Water and Air Pollution in Taiwan, *Journal of Developing Areas* 9:2, 177–202.

Selya, R. M. (1992) Illegal Migration in Taiwan: A Preliminary Overview, *International Migration Review* 26:3, 787–805.

Senftleben, W. (1986) Tourism, Hot Springs Resorts, and Sexual Entertainment. Observations from Northern Taiwan – A Study in Social Geography, *Philippine Geographical Journal* 30:1 and 2, 21–41.

Sewerage Development in Taipei City (1978, 1991) Sewerage Engineering Department, Bureau of Public Works, Taipei.

Shapiro, D. (1984) Building for Privatization, *Asian Business*, Nov., 38–40.

Shen, P. (1993) Group Helps Disabled Step into Light of Day, *Free China Journal*, June 1, 5.

Sheu, C.-j. (1990) Non-syndicated Organized Crime in Taipei, Taiwan, *Police Studies. International Review of Police Development* 13, 151–3.

Shih, T. T., J. C. Chang, M. L. Chen and C. H. Tseng (1989) A Synthetic Study of the Dynamic Environment of Taipei Basin, *Geographical Research* 15, 1–72.*

Shih, T. T., J. C. Chang, M. H. Shen and C. C. Lim (1990) Slope and Land Use of Slope Land Around Taipei Basin, *Geographical Research* 16, 1–32.*

Shrage, L. (1989) Should Feminists Oppose Prostitution? *Ethics* 99, 347–64.

Smith, D. C. (1981) An American in Taipei, *Free China Review* 31:3, 18–20.

Song, S.-f. (1992) Land Revenues Filling Up Coffers, *Free China Journal*, July 14, 3.

Song, S.-f. (1993) Radioactivity Checks for Steel Products, *Free China Journal*, Feb. 9, 8.

Strandberg, K. W. (1989) Taipei, Taiwan, ROC: Mass Transit At Last, *Mass Transit* 16, 42, 44.

Taipei-Keelung Metropolitan Regional Plan (1968) Urban and Housing Development Committee, Council for International Economic Cooperation and Development, Taipei.

Tanzer, A. (1981) End of a Taipei Rents Bargain, *Far Eastern Economic Review* 111:10, Feb. 27, 79–81.

Truong, T-d. (1990) *Sex, Money, and Morality. Prostitution and Tourism in Southeast Asia*. Zed Books, London.

Tsai, H.-h. (1987) Public Housing Development in the Republic of China on Taiwan, *Industry of Free China* 68:4, 19–28.

Tseng, O. (1991) Auto Insurers in A Crunch, *Free China Review* 41:8, 48–53.

Tzeng, G.-h. and T.-w. Shiau (1988) Multiple Objective Programming for Bus Operation: A Case Study for Taipei City, *Transportation Research* 22B:3, 195–206.

Underwood, L. (1993) Garbage Wars, *Free China Review* 43:8, 40–49.

Wang, B. (1989) Small Island, Big Problems, *Free China Review* 39:6, 5–11.

Water Supply in Taipei (1990) Taipei Water Department, Taipei.

Wehrfritz, G. (1992) Living Dangerously. Geiger Counters Discover Irradiated Apartments, *Far Eastern Economic Review*, 164, Dec. 10, 13.

Welch, J. (1991) Developers Eye Taipei's Virgin Land, *Free China Review* 41:8, 32–39.

Welcome to the 21st Century (1987) Department of Information, Taipei City Government, Taipei.

Wester, L. (1988) Vegetation Change in the Guan Du Marsh, Taipei, 1978–1985, pp. 415–426 in: *Detailed Planning of Guan Du National Park*, City Hall, Taipei.

Wong, J. C. Y. (1987) *Inundation Hazards and Adjustments in Western Taipei Basin*. Chinese University of Hong Kong, Department of Geography, Occasional Paper 90, Hong Kong.

Wong, K.-y. (1986) The Trend of Climate Change in Taipei and Its Urban Climatic Characteristics, *Geographical Research* 12, 87–101.*

Wu, C.-l. (1987) Perception and Adjustment of Environmental Pollution: A Case Study of Nankang and Neihu, Taipei, *Geographical Research* 13, 193–248.*

WuDunn, S. (1990) Taipei Journal. War on Crime Makes Hero of Hated General, *New York Times*, Oct. 29, A4.

Yang, M. (1945) *A Chinese Village. Taitou, Shantung Province*. Columbia University Press, New York.

Yang, W. C. (1982) The Problems of A Below Sea-level Area in Taipei Basin/ Taiwan, *Beitrage zur Hydrologie* 3, 291–313.

Yau, Y.-m. (1985) The Study of Spatial Distribution, Number of Exceedances, and Design Value of SO2 in Winter in Taipei, *Geographical Research* 11, 127–144.*

Yeung, I. (1991a) This Land is My Land, *Free China Review* 41:8, 4–11.

Yeung, I. (1991b) A Slow Start to Rapid Transit, *Free China Review* 41:3, 20–28.

Yu, S. (1992) ROC Finance Ministry Witnesses Changing of the Guard, *Free China Journal*, Oct. 23, 1.

Yuan, Y. (1992) Migrate, Assimilate, or Integrate, *Free China Review* 42:6, 4–15.

7
Taipei as a center of culture

Don't bother with Taipei ... it's a limited city with very little to offer.
(Peterson, 1974)

Taipei citizens work hard. The vibrant economy described in Chapter 3 imposes a heavy work schedule upon all its citizens. Taipei citizens also live hard. The evolution of Taipei into a world city has exacerbated the long list of environmental and social problems which were described in Chapter 6. These problems impose harsh burdens on its citizens. How then do residents of Taipei relax and renew themselves? In a *Far Eastern Economic Review* survey of Asian affluents, 64 percent of Taiwan respondents indicated that they wanted more leisure time (*Asian Affluents* 2, 1992). However, it appears that many in Taipei share the view of Peterson's friend whose advice on visiting Taipei is quoted above. Furthermore, such perceptions of Taipei have even entered the professional social science literature (Brunn and Williams, 1983). Teenagers in Taipei especially believe that there is not much to do. What is available tends to be limited by difficulties in accessibility and the amount of time available for recreation and leisure (Chen, 1989).

Peterson's critique seems mild when compared to the evaluation provided by Ambruster (1976). He cites common complaints raised by visitors to Taipei: tickets for events, especially first-rate movies, are hard to get; the Taipei City orchestra is said to be worse than many American high school orchestras. But surely these complaints are just remnants of the early days of Taipei's evolution! The governments of both the city and the Republic of China wish this were the case. They are both concerned that surveys show that for many citizens of Taipei and Taiwan all too often leisure time is spent either staring idly at TV screens or going out to entertainment centers and returning home well after midnight. Hence the call from the Directorate General of Budget, Accounting, and Statistics for greater awareness of cultural activities in order to improve the quality of life in Taipei and Taiwan (*Free China Journal*, Jan. 28, 1991).

In this chapter the leisure-time activities open to the residents of and visitors to Taipei are described and analyzed. The overall framework for the discussion is Redfield's (1956) division of cultural activities into great and little cultures. Components of the great culture are valued and perpetuated by the elite. They tend to be formally transferred from generation to generation in schools or temples. In contrast the little tradition is usually the domain of the majority, the unreflective. Its activities are not formally taught and usually evolve through the ongoing lives of village cultures. Of course the dichotomy is imperfect. There is often a degree of syncretization, where little traditions evolve into great ones. Furthermore, the two traditions interact as a part of the wider social structure of a culture. The little tradition, although often officially denigrated or deprecated, is effective in providing popular outlets and in creating new traditions. Using this dichotomy permits not only a ready means of cataloguing what opportunities exist for recreation, but also a sensitive measure of recreation as a means of political expression.

Great culture activities

Without a doubt the four crown jewels of the great culture in Taipei are the National Palace Museum, the Chiang Kai-shek Memorial Complex, the National Central Library, and National Taiwan University.

The National Palace Museum

The National Palace Museum is located in the Waishuanghsi area of Shihlin (Figure 7.1). This site was selected in no small part for security reasons. The main exhibition hall backs onto a mountain into which some 4000 burglar-proof storage chambers have been hewed. The concern for security for the some 600 000 paintings, porcelains, bronzes, rubbings, and tapestries has two origins. First, the museum opened in 1965, a time when tensions between the Republic of China and People's Republic of China were felt to be very high, and there was a concern that the museum collection would be a military target. Secondly, the museum collection is considered stolen property by the People's Republic of China. The original Palace Museum Collection, which started with activities of the Song dynasty Tai-tze Emperor (960–976) to encourage literature and the arts, was located in Beijing. During the period 1924–1926 the Nationalist

Figure 7.1 National Palace Museum in Shihlin is set against a hill for security reasons

government sorted and organized the collection. In 1931 the entire collection was packed in some 20 000 cases and moved to Nanking to prevent the treasures from falling into the hands of the Japanese. The collection was further moved to other sites during the Japanese and Civil War. At the end of the latter war in 1949 some 4800 cases were shipped to Taiwan.

At any one time the museum has some 16 000 works of art on display. In order to display the entire collection, exhibits are rotated every three months. In addition to the 42 322 square feet of display space, the museum has a library containing some 200 000 books, 154 cases of Mongolian, Tibetan, and other Buddhist sutras, and some 400 000 Ching dynasty court documents. The museum complex also includes the outdoor Chih Shan gardens which are based on Song dynasty designs. In addition to the indoor and outdoor exhibits and library, the museum's activities include a series of general and scholarly publications. All these activities are aimed at fulfilling the museum's mandate as a subordinate agency of the Executive Yuan, to preserve Chinese art and culture.

Chiang Kai-shek Memorial

The Chiang Kai-shek Memorial (Figure 2.15), which was dedicated on 5 April 1980, is sited in a 62 acre park directly opposite the new National

Figure 7.2 National Concert House, a part of the Chiang Kai-shek Memorial, features traditional Chinese architectural elements

Central Library in the southeast part of the Chengchung district. The complex includes a memorial building, containing a 25 ton bronze statue of the late President, and the National Theatre and National Concert House. As might be expected, the opening of the theatre and concert house in October 1987 was accompanied by some start-up problems. Three problems were especially troublesome: a lack of clear identity and mission, financial shortfalls, and structural problems. The lack of identity and mission was as much a political as a cultural predicament, since legislation formally recognizing the two buildings as official government organizations had been delayed. Despite average 76 percent box office sales on all events, the complex has accumulated in the first five years of its operation a US$36 million deficit. Since the management of the complex is committed to a seat price structure which is affordable to local residents, alternative sources of private and foundation funding are being sought. The structural problems involved complaints about the acoustical characteristics of the performance halls themselves. The acoustical problems arose because of the selection by Madame Chiang Kai-shek of an exterior fashioned on the traditional style of the Ching dynasty, and an interior based on Western opera house style designs (Figure 7.2). The Chinese "straw hat" design placed the highest point in the two buildings in their centers, while the acoustical requirements of the Western opera house place the apex closer to the rear of the hall.

Regardless of these problems, there is general agreement on two points. First, halls able to accommodate theatre, dance, and music were sorely needed in Taipei. The older halls used for these purposes, mainly the Sun Yat-sen Memorial in northeastern Ta-an district, and the Old City Hall, in Chengchung district, were not up to modern standards in terms of size, seating, or facilities for performers. Second, the new halls have provided a rich diversity of performances. The diversity includes local groups and soloists, such as the Cloud Gate Dance Theatre, the National Symphony Orchestra, the Taipei Concerto Soloists, the well known Taiwan pianist Fou Tsong, and foreign groups and soloists including the New York Philharmonic, the Alvin Aily American Dance Theatre, the Meister Consort, Sir Yehudi Menuhin, and José Carreras. Some concerts have even featured artists from the People's Republic of China, such as Yu Li-na, who appeared on the same program as her son Li Chien, who lives in Taipei. The halls have thus helped to put Taipei on the itineraries of major performers and groups. The popularity and heavy use of the halls has unfortunately at times meant that some visiting groups, such as the Cincinnati Symphony Orchestra, have had to use the older Sun Yat-sen Memorial Hall. In addition, the opportunities to perform have spawned new preparatory groups, this ensuring that Taipei audiences of future generations will have concerts, recitals, and dances.

The National Central Library

The National Central Library (Figure 2.16), located across the street from the Chiang Kai-shek Memorial, as with the National Palace Museum had its origins on mainland China. The original library was founded in Nanking in 1933 and moved to Chungking during World War II. From 1949 to 1986 it occupied a site in the Taipei Botanical Gardens. The collection contains some 1.4 million volumes, and the new building has space for a total of 2.5 million. The library houses special holdings such as the Chiang Kai-shek Memorial Collection, the Chinese Studies Collection, the Government Documents Collection (including materials from Taiwan's Japanese Period, 15 different countries, and a number of international organizations), and the Rare Books Collection. The library also contains collections incorporated from other Taiwan based libraries. Of special note in this regard are the Taiwan Provincial Library's Southeast Asian and Australian materials and the volumes of the former Library of Southern Japan. Some 2000 readers use the library and its services daily. In addition to seating for 1300 readers in its research and reading areas, the Library has a 202-seat conference hall, a 540-seat lecture hall, and exhibition galleries.

National Taiwan University

National Taiwan University, the largest and most prestigious institution of higher learning in Taiwan today, is the successor to the Taihoku Imperial University established by the Japanese in 1928. Located in south-central Ta-an district, the university has 2257 faculty, 1207 staff, and 16 500 students. Its seven colleges house 47 departments and 53 graduate institutes. Some of its facilities, such as the Medical School and University Hospital, are located off campus. Its libraries hold some 1.3 million books and 19 134 periodical titles.

These four cultural institutions stand at the apex of a large system of supporting and collateral institutions. The National Palace Museum, for example, is merely the best known of the many museums in Taipei. Other worthwhile collections are found in the Armed Forces Museum, the National Museum of History, the Taiwan Provincial Museum, the Folklore Museum, the Postal Museum, and the Butterfly Museum, and the newer Taipei Fine Arts and Peitou Folk Art Museums. In turn, all these museums lend support to a series of galleries which focus on either auctions or sales of works of both local and Western, especially European, artists (Karp, 1992). The changes in location of these private galleries are sensitive indicators of which neighborhoods are considered either wealthy or attractive to the wealthy.

In terms of education, National Taiwan University is just one of 13 public and 11 private junior colleges, colleges and universities operating in Taipei (Table 7.1). Some of these, such as National Taiwan Normal University, were originally founded by the Japanese, as was National Taiwan University, and subsequently reopened under the supervision of the Ministry of Education. Still others, such as National Chengchi University, were transplanted from the mainland in 1949. Finally, there are educational institutions which were founded after 1949 to meet the demand for higher education. In general all of the institutions are on the fringes of the *chu* in which they are located and form a circular ring within the city. Since educational facilities are notorious consumers of space, these locations reflect past land use decisions and patterns; their sites were either available government lands or marginal lands which could be converted to this urban use. By the 1990s all of the universities and colleges found themselves in congested, densely occupied areas.

In addition to these 24 institutions of higher education, there is one free-standing government-sponsored research institute, Academia Sinica. Set up in 1928 in Nanking, it too was moved to Taipei in 1949, although most of its personnel and equipment were left behind on the mainland. During the 1950s Academia Sinica was reconstituted at a campus-like site in Nankang *chu*. There are 15 institutes which cover mathematics, physics, chemistry, earth sciences, information science, statistics, botany, zoology, biological

Table 7.1 Institutions of higher learning in Taipei

National Taiwan University
National Chengchi University
National Taiwan Normal University
National Yang Ming Medical College
National Taiwan Institute of Technology
National Art College
Taiwan Provincial Taipei Teachers' College
Taipei Municipal Teachers' College
Soochow University*
College of Chinese Culture*
Taipei Medical College*
Ta-Tung Institute of Technology*
Mingchuan Junior College*
National Taipei Junior College of Technology
National Taipei Junior College of Nursing
National Taipei Junior College of Commerce
Taipei Municipal Junior College of Physical Education
Shih-Chien Home Economics Junior College*
Tehming Junior College of Commerce*
Shihjei Junior College of Journalism*
China Maritime Junior College*
China Junior College of Technology and Commerce*
China Junior College of Technology*
Guangwuu College of Technology*

Key: * Private

chemistry, history and philology, modern history, ethnology, economics, American culture, and the Three Principles of the People (*San Min Chu I*). Two additional institutes are in the planning stage: biomedical sciences, and atomic and molecular sciences. Academia Sinica functions as the highest academic institution in the Republic of China and has two basic missions: to conduct research within its own institutes, and to aid and coordinate research at other institutes and universities.

All of these institutions of higher education and research are at the top of an elaborate educational hierarchy. It is important to remember this because quite frequently when one meets someone in Taipei and aks their occupation the response is "student." No doubt this response is a reflection of both the high esteem which the Chinese traditionally afforded to scholars (Lin, 1983), and the notion that prestige within Taiwan society is most commonly correlated with levels of education (Marsh, 1968).

The bottom of the hierarchy consists of three levels: pre-school (kindergarten) education, nine-year compulsory education divided between elementary and junior high schools, and then senior secondary education, commonly divided between senior high and senior vocational high school. Table 7.2 shows the numbers of each type of school in Taipei. Junior and

Table 7.2 Types of schools in Taipei

Kindergartens	484
Elementary	138
Vocational	26
Junior high	68
Senior high	26

senior schools are segregated by gender. Some schools have gone to a co-ed format, such as the Ta-an and Chinhua senior schools. Instruction even in these co-ed schools, however, is still segregated. Admission to elementary and junior schools is by registration; parents register their child at the closest neighborhood school. Admission to senior schools is by examination. Although this system would suggest that there is a relationship between the distribution of school-age children and the location of schools, this is not the case. To be sure, schools are planned and built so as to accommodate changes in population (personal correspondence, Lin Chao-hsien, July 10, 1991). However, schools with either good reputations or with outstanding facilities attract more students than necessarily live in the neighborhood. This is the result of a parent simply changing the household registration of the student to that of a relative or friend living within the school district. As a result of this system, good schools frequently have to go to double shifts, while other schools may have unused classrooms. The inconvenience to students and the diseconomy to the city are evident to anyone who has ever had to take a bus at rush hour. The diseconomies and the questionable wisdom of registering students in schools outside their parents' districts have been examined in both a short story (Chang, 1975) and a geographic analysis (Tseng, 1978). In addition to the public schools there are five foreign schools – serving the American, French, German, Japanese, and Korean communities.

Formal schools in Taipei are paralleled by a set of informal educational opportunities. Cram schools (*bushiban* in Chinese), sometimes referred to as supplementary schools, first made their appearance in Taipei in 1953. Their popularity declined somewhat with the abolition of the junior high school entrance examination. By 1990 there were 808 of them operating. Designed both to supplement public schools with extra-curricular topics and to provide intensive tutoring for students preparing for either high school or university entrance examinations, the cram schools usually specialize in a subject area such as foreign languages, sciences, business, or fine arts. There are mixed motivations for attending a cram school (Lee, 1993a). From the parents' perspective, in addition to ensuring mastery of materials, the cram schools also function as baby-sitting or childcare centers. The need for such a function reflects the growing tendency towards two-income families and the need for a safe haven for children until a parent is done with work. From the students' perspective fear is a significant element: cram school classes are frequently taught by the very same public and/or private school teachers a student has for school, although this practice is illegal; the fear is that many teachers will hold a bias against a student who does not attend the extra courses they offer off campus. What is of special interest is the location of these schools. According to Tsai (1990) the schools cluster in a six to eight block vicinity of the Central Railroad Station. The same area is the location of both eating places and amusement attractions. The cram school locations reflect a two-fold locational attraction: accessibility due to the convergence of numerous bus routes on the area near the Central Railroad Station, and agglomeration since students commonly combine attendance at the cram schools with a stop for a snack and with socializing. High rents and the need for urban renewal in the area may require a shift in the location of the schools.

For those not wanting to attend cram schools, coffee shops provide a haven for quiet study (MacGregor, 1984). In addition to providing coffee and snacks these facilities rent study space to students. Not surprisingly, the coffee houses are clustered around National Taiwan and National Taiwan Normal Universities. These coffee houses are very much products of affluence and their inclusion within a subcategory of great tradition stands in stark contrast to coffee houses in Taipei during the 1960s. These earlier coffee houses, located in basement shops near the Shihmenting entertainment zone, were perceived, by students, parents, and the police, as outlets for rebellious and disrespectful behavior. This perception was no doubt reinforced by the large number of Western students who frequented them.

In terms of library resources, the National Central Library again is symbolic of the recreational use of reading in general. In addition to the National Central Library the municipal government maintains a library system consisting of a new main library and 26 branches. The municipal government also operates one mobile library unit. Total holdings for the city library system include some 1.2 million volumes. In addition to the municipal library there are specialized private libraries such as the Library of Chinese Dietary Culture, and the Little Sun Children's Library. The latter library has attracted considerable attention since it charges a minimum yearly fee of US$463 for browsing privileges (Song, 1990a). Despite the high fees, the library appeals to parents who are concerned over the quality of children's programming on television.

Not all reading is done within the formal educational or library environments. Literally hundreds of outlets for buying books exist in Taipei. These stores arrange themselves hierarchically in terms of distribution and number and type of books available (Chen and Chen, 1983). Many small street vendors either specialize in books or include books in their inventories. Most commonly these vendors, who can be found on street corners or in pedestrian over- and under-passes, sell newspapers, magazines, dictionaries, reprints of the Chinese classics, as well as modern novels and government reports. Most districts feature stores which specialize in general reading materials and schools supplies. More serious readers requiring specialized or critical editions would shop along Heng yang Street in Chungcheng district. Here the venerable old printing houses from mainland China, such as the Commercial Press and the Chung Hwa Book Company, relocated after 1949. An additional source for specialized and technical materials is the book stores found around the colleges and universities in Taipei. Those looking for more attractive and modern stores specializing in general works will shop in stores along Tunhua South Road. This latter location reflects a major shift in the location of many older book stores. During the 1960s and 1970s the center of the retail book trade for both new and used books was along Chunjou Street opposite the Botanical Gardens and Historical Museum. However, as the neighborhood first deteriorated and then experienced rebuilding these book stores relocated to the more fashionable, newer areas along Tunhwa South Road (Chang, 1989; Liu, 1992b).

Foreign, and especially English titles are available as well. Stores specializing in this type of reading matter tend to locate along Chung Shan North Road. Although the number of these stores diminished when the United States military ended its advisory group, the remaining stores are as infamous and interesting as their forebears. The stores' mixed reputations derive from the notorious pirating of books. Taiwan has long had a reputation for not honoring copyright law, especially when it comes to intellectual property rights. As such the newest items on the New York Times Best Seller list as well as important non-Chinese works on Chinese history are readily available. Although the government of the Republic of China has made commitments to enforce the international copyright laws, pirated books continue to be available. Their attractiveness, however, has diminished as their prices have increased because of the appreciation of the New Taiwan dollar against the United States dollar.

Taipei residents are able to use reading as a recreational outlet in no small part owing to the concentration of the publishing industry in the city itself. Some 2304 publishing and printing establishments employing 21 886 workers (representing 37.3 and 43.8 percent respectively of the total Republic of China printing industry) are located within Taipei. Within Taipei, printing is heavily concentrated in the Shuangyuan, where 37 percent of all printing activities are housed. The rest of the industry is more evenly spread out among the remaining districts, although Chingmei, Nankang, and Neihu each have less than 1 percent of the printing establishments. In addition to books the printing industry supplies Taipei with 2684 magazine titles and 31 daily newspapers. Of the 31 newspapers,

29 are Chinese language papers and two are English language papers, 24 publish morning editions and seven publish evening editions. Some concern has been raised that two privately owned papers, the *United Daily News* and the *China Times*, dominate the newspaper market accounting for two-thirds of daily circulation. Owners of both newspapers are members of the Kuomintang Central Committee, thus giving the impression that the editorial policies may merely echo official party dictates. However, in reality each owner has a different political orientation within the Kuomintang and different ties to party and government officials, and thus different concerns. Furthermore, given the size of the two papers it may well be the case that they help to ease official party and government restraints on editorial choices for all newspapers (Goldstein, 1985a). Nevertheless, Taipei residents do enjoy a wide range of options not found in many world cities when it comes to choosing a daily newspaper.

Little culture activities

Little culture activities and recreational outlets which the elite tolerate and often eventually elevate to great culture status include eating and shopping, tea houses, and the zoo, and there are also activities which the elite frowns on and would like to see eliminated or better controlled such as night clubs, beer and dance halls, brothels, TV, MTV, video parlors, and religion.

Many of the little culture activities were slow in developing and their absence may have contributed to the poor reputation cited at the beginning of this chapter. Part of the delayed development was actually dictated by the government. During the 1950s when both the economic and political prospects for the Republic of China looked very bleak, austerity was imposed. Thus no night clubs or dance halls were permitted (Glenn, 1968). However, by the 1960s prosperity had created an environment where little culture outlets developed on their own. Part of this new environment included the presence of the U.S. military, the growth of tourism, the migration of women to the district of Peitou, and the general expansion of the economy and services (Connolly, 1969; Glenn, 1968).

Eating and shopping

At first glance the inclusion of eating and shopping amongst little culture activities seems misplaced. Are these two activities not more like necessities? While there is no denying that much shopping, especially for food before the development of modern grocery and convenience stores discussed in Chapter 3, fell into the category of daily necessities bordering on drudgery, it is also possible to see eating and shopping as recreational activities. First of all, eating is rarely done alone; perhaps nothing puts panic into the heart of any Chinese restaurateur than to have a lone Westerner appear for a meal: the tables are always sized and set in multiples of two or three. Shopping is also frequently a group activity, albeit involving informal, spontaneous groups. For teenagers especially, the two activities are frequently combined: while out shopping, or actually browsing since one is not obligated to buy anything while shopping, a stop is made for some form of refreshment.

In terms of eating, Taipei is frequently compared to Hong Kong in attempts to decide which city offers more varieties and better quality of Chinese food (Joseph, 1970; Zich, 1977). Regardless of the eventual outcome of the comparison, one thing is clear: Taipei does feature a wide range of regional Chinese cuisines, including both vegetarian and more exotic specialities. In the latter category are included shops located in Hwashi Street in Wanhwa section, featuring live snakes, often poisonous. The diner literally picks the desired snake and handlers then prepare either a blood drink or meal. The wide variety of Chinese food obviously reflects the flight of the Chinese from the mainland in 1949. During the 1960s the broad regional representation was augmented by more international fare. Restaurants featuring British, French, German, Indian, Indonesian, Italian, Japanese, Thai, and Vietnamese menus have opened. Sometimes these restaurants are freestanding and very mobile: as tastes in food and neighborhoods shift the restaurants frequently change menus or locations. Other times these restaurants are found in the newer hotels, which often feature a coffee shop for breakfast, as well as separate Western and Chinese restaurants. In 1984 the range of choices expanded with the opening of a McDonald's franchise in Taipei. McDonald's was quickly followed by other fast food companies such as Baskin and Robbins (advertising "31 Treats"!), Kentucky Fried Chicken, Pizza Hut, Ponderosa Steak Houses, and the Japanese Steak House Yoshinoya. These restaurants frequently locate on main streets (i.e. Chung Shan North Road, or Nanking East Road), upscale neighborhoods, or around the Central Railroad Station. The fast food restaurants became such instant hits, especially with teenagers, that they have been termed "franchised hangouts" (Chen, 1989).

The presence of Western fast food outlets has put considerable pressure on small restaurants to upgrade both the cleanliness of their operations and the quality of their food. These small restaurants, which are literally ubiquitous, include three main types. One type is operated out of a portable kitchen, commonly mounted on some type of wagon. These "restaurants" offer a variety of popular local breakfast and lunch dishes.

Often they offer some specialty such as spiced bean curd, cold drinks, roast meat sticks, pressed dried squid, or fresh cut fruits. A second type may operate out of either a portable or permanent kitchen, but located on a side street so as to afford the diner a table and stool or chair to sit on. A third type is located in vest pocket type store fronts with no seating (and hardly any work room for the cook/sales staff). All small restaurants have been implicated in the endemic presence of type B hepatitis in Taiwan in general and in Taipei in particular. Some 15–20 percent of the population in Taipei are chronic carriers (Hwang *et al.*, 1983; Johnstone, 1988). The restaurants are implicated because of the unsanitary methods used in food handling and service. For example, food handlers frequently did not wash their hands as they served different foods, washed dishes, and went about their daily routines. Dishes in these small restaurants were often washed in large basins of water placed near the edge of the sidewalk, near the sewers which were often open. Little soap was used, and the water was not only cold, but polluted. Although vaccination is one way to reduce the incidence of hepatitis, better food handling, such as wearing rubber gloves or using plastic bags as gloves, would help break the chain of transmission. Instead of washing dishes disposable styrofoam and plastic eating ware could be used. In fact all these changes have been adopted by smaller restaurants, either owing to pressure from the government or competition from the Western fast food chains. In terms of quality, these small restaurants seem at least to be giving more attention to the appearance of their offerings.

One additional widespread reaction to the Western fast food presence has been the development of family oriented all-you-can-eat restaurants. Although often located in large hotels, several chains with restaurants in multiple locations have also opened their doors (Liu, 1992a).

In terms of shopping, Taipei offers a wide range of buying opportunities. As described in Chapter 2, one of the dominant architectural forms in Taipei is the shophouse. In older neighborhoods this form provides a front of specialty shops along virtually every main street. In newer office and residential buildings this form is often incorporated into the design so that retail shops are found at street level (Figure 7.3). In addition to these ubiquitous shops, local food markets run by the city government also feature non-food items. In general these shops are narrow speciality stores, although occasionally one can find the same space being occupied by more than one entrepreneur with resulting combinations of goods or services which often seem strange (at least to the Western eye), such as shoes and toys, or clothing and paper supplies. A further qualification of the narrow speciality designation involves shops which manufacture and sell a product. During the 1960s and 1970s such shops would offer tatami mats, wood products, and clothing. A more modern variation of this type of shop would be picture framing.

Figure 7.3 Even in purely residential developments, first-floor space is still devoted to retail or office activities

As discussed in Chapter 2, land use patterns do not necessarily follow the Western pattern; so too for intra-urban distribution of retail and wholesale specialities. Broadly speaking, however, older shopping areas such as those found in Wanhwa feature more traditional, cheaper goods, while newer neighborhoods such as the Tunhua North Road area feature more upscale, designer type goods. This latter type of goods tend to shift their location as the definition of fashionable and upscale as applied to neighborhoods changes. In addition the area to the south of the Central Railroad Station does contain streets or clusters of some retail and wholesale specialization. The only other notable area with a concentrated retail function is the Haggler's Alley (China Bazaar) described in Chapter 5 (Figure 5.2).

These ubiquitous shopping locations are supplemented by two additional types of outlets. First, there are Western style department stores. These have clustered around the Shihmenting area. The department stores have two main characteristics which distinguish them from other retail stores found elsewhere in Taipei: variety and price. In general department stores carry a large range of goods in contrast to the one-good speciality shops. The department stores feature a one-price policy, so that the bargaining often found in older stores is not possible. One store in particular, the Today Department Store, has perhaps pushed the variety of wares to the ultimate level: in addition to the normal range of goods found in a department store it features several floors of entertainment opportunities including puppets, singers, concerts, plays, and even Beijing opera!

Secondly, shopping is supplemented by the presence of an informal retail sector which was described in Chapter 3. Their near ubiquitous locations, irregular hours, and frequently off-beat merchandise make them favorite places to shop.

After eating and shopping Taipei residents often find some respite and renewal by visiting a tea shop. According to Chang (1983) there are five types of tea shops operating in Taipei. The first type caters to connoisseurs, who being knowledgeable and fastidious about tea utensils, tea leaves, and tea-compatible pastries come to drink, discuss and criticize tea. The second, and most numerous, type of shop seeks to attract both connoisseurs and ordinary pleasure seekers. Therefore the ambiance in these tea shops is a bit lighter than in the first type, yet they also provide a cozy and relaxed atmosphere. The third type is like a European coffee house, only it serves tea! The fourth type focuses on sales of tea and tea utensils. Seating accommodation is provided merely for the convenience of customers wishing to try before they buy. In the last type of tea house tea is actually secondary to other commercial activities such as sale of art or artifacts. In general the fancier tea shops are located in whichever neighborhood is currently passing as upscale; but one can find tea houses in older neighborhoods, the more rural parts of Taipei, and close to universities (Reid, 1984).

Taipei Zoo

The last of the little culture activities viewed with favor by the elite is the zoo. Originally established in February 1915, by the Japanese government, in September 1986 the zoo was moved from its old site rich in archaeological materials in Yuanshan to a 182 hectare one in Mucha. The zoo collection includes some 500 mammals, 800 birds, and 250 reptiles. The design and construction of the new zoo facilities was one of the 12

233

large development projects financed by the central government during the 1980s. Like many modern, world-class zoos, the Taipei Zoo has multiple goals: to provide an opportunity to see animals and to participate in programs designed to ensure the continuation of endangered species.

Unsanctioned little culture activities

Some little culture activities are frowned upon by the authorities and elite. Occasionally such activities are short lived, such as the fad of motorcycle racing in busy streets which swept the city in the late 1980s. These activities, often reflecting a combination of boredom and alienation, can be controlled by better enforcement of existing laws. However, activities such as night clubs, beer, dance, and wine halls, and brothels, have a long history and are therefore more difficult to control.

Night clubs and discos

In general the government has tried to control these activities in order to keep crime out via limitations on the number of establishments permitted. Night clubs and discos, first permitted in 1986 under the guise of promoting tourism (Royal, 1989), are a natural extension of the "sugar daddy" bars found on Shuangchang Street near the President Hotel during the Vietnam era, and in fact occupy the same sites as the old bars (other sites have been taken over by restaurants specializing in foreign cuisine) (Reid, 1984). The patrimony of the past "sugar daddy" days is also found in typical disco names: Kiss, Touch, Day and Night. In addition to the Shuangchang area discos are also found in large hotels such as the Hilton, Lai Lai Sheraton, Mandarin, President, and Imperial. They have proved very popular with young people despite a US$15 cover charge. On the average Friday or Saturday night 2000 people will spend time at each of the discos. Many bars and discos also feature karaoke singing. Karaoke clubs, known as KTV in Taiwan, are very popular. For example, it is estimated that in 1992 some 386 KTVs served more than 12 million customers (Huang, 1993).

Wine houses

Wine houses, also known as girlie bars, are officially not brothels. Rather, one buys drinks and has the opportunity to buy drinks for some of the young ladies working there; in return the girls, often just out of high school, are expected to sit and talk with their host. Not uncommonly though, after a man has purchased the requisite number of drinks for the girl, the couple do indeed slip away from the wine house, with the girl returning later alone.

Brothels and prostitution

Taipei does host a formal, thriving brothel industry. Taipei police records show that there are 29 brothels in Taipei employing 199 prostitutes. For many travelers to Taipei, brothels, along with drinking, are *the* main attraction. Guide books mention them, and in one travel article a hierarchy of brothels was suggested (Herr, 1968). The negative consequences of prostitution have been major themes in modern Taiwanese fiction. From the perspective of the government, the industry is best supervised via a strict system of registration. According to official police records there are 3732 registered prostitutes in Taipei (Li, 1992). In addition it has been estimated that there may be as few as 47 188 or as many as 83 393 additional unregistered prostitutes in Taipei (Li, 1992).

Each registered prostitute not only has to register with the police, but once a month is subject to a physical examination in order to control the spread of venereal diseases. Despite such monitoring venereal diseases remain a significant public health problem. Since screening and treatment began in 1953 the number of cases in Taipei has been on the increase and the percentage of all cases reported in Taiwan found in Taipei has increased. For example, the number of new cases of syphilis discovered rose from 1473 in 1975 to 3386 in 1990. These cases rose from 29.98 percent to 41.8 percent of all cases reported in Taiwan. Similarly, the percentage of new cases of gonorrhea found in Taipei rose from 69.4 to 85.3 percent. Virtually all other venereal diseases reported in Taiwan occur in Taipei. Interestingly, when special clinics were established for high risk areas, Taipei was not an area selected for a clinic. The private market does provide treatment, however: signs on doctors' offices quite nonchalantly mention the availability of treatment for venereal diseases, especially in areas near brothels and bars such as Peitou and Chungcheng.

As an industry, prostitution actually has two separate components (Senftleben, 1986). First, as mentioned above, there is legalized prostitution, which in addition to being regulated is spatially confined to the Yuanhuan and Wanhwa areas. Secondly, there is underground prostitution, which includes such activities as street walking, call girls, and striptease. These activities are found on streets, especially near Taipei New Park, hotels, barber shop and massage parlors, girlie bars, clubs, Western style pubs, dance halls, discos, cabarets, theatre restaurants, tea houses, and music halls. The intensity and locations of these activities have been somewhat fluid. For example, the end of the Vietnam War, and the resulting loss of Taipei's rest and recreation designation, severely cut back on girlie bars, clubs, and Western style pubs. Similarly, the decline of Peitou *chu* and its hot springs as centers of prostitution can be traced to both the end of the Vietnam War and a conscious decision by the Taipei City Council in 1979 to prohibit the continued practice of prostitution there.

Beer houses

Beer houses are another recreational outlet frowned on by the government and the elite (Sutherland *et al.*, 1987). As a landscape phenomenon, the beer house appeared rather suddenly in the spring of 1985 and quickly spread not only in Taipei but all over the island. In Taipei two main clusters of beer houses quickly developed: one in Tienmu along Chungshan North Road section 7, and a second along section 4 of Jen-ai Road, the upscale and affluent commercial and residential neighborhood in northeast Taipei. As the number of beer houses grew to 69 in 1986, a dispersed set of locations also emerged. The increase and popularity of the beer houses can be attributed to the entrepreneurial spirit of the Taiwanese, an increase in leisure time and disposable income, and a longstanding fascination with things new and Western, i.e. the same variables which have made American fast food chains such a success.

Residents living near the beer houses objected to their presence because of the noise generated by the crowds, episodes of vandalism, and displays of public urination. For its part the government was disturbed by the growth of the beer houses for three reasons. First, they are illegal, i.e. unlicensed, and as such do not pay any taxes. Second, although Taipei land use is very mixed, the beer houses are located on land designated for other uses in planning documents. Third, sanitary conditions in kitchens and bathroom facilities were not up to standard. The government therefore attempted to crack down on beer houses, by tearing them down and fining their owners. What developed in the short run was a variation on the "hide and seek" or "cat and mouse" approach to control: no sooner would the government tear down a beer house than it would relocate elsewhere. In the longer run, the government did officially license some establishments, especially when some owners argued that their presence did not violate land use plans or regulations. Further effort by the government may be unnecessary as it appears that the beer houses are a hot weather phenomenon. At the end of each summer many of them close permanently.

Television

Television is reported as the most popular form of recreational activity (*Free China Journal*, Feb. 16, 1989). Color television ownership seems to bear this out: by 1990 virtually every Taipei home had at least one color television set. In addition to an educational television service, there are three television channels available in Taipei. China Television is owned and operated by the Kuomintang; the Chinese Television service is owned and operated by the Ministries of National Defense and Education; Taiwan Television is owned and operated by the Taiwan provincial government (Goldstein, 1985b).

Television is categorized as a little culture activity because of programming content. Programming on all three of the "commercial" stations is heavily weighted to news, sports, and what can best be described as soap operas. The story lines on the soap operas are variations on a limited number of plots or settings: historical, *kung-fu*, or contemporary. During the 1970s one popular soap opera program featured puppets. The basic three programming areas are supplemented by American cartoons and some prime time shows, as well as movies. However, the limited choices available have led to individuals buying and illegally installing dish antenna to pick up cable television. The central government in 1991 drafted, but by 1992 had not passed, a cable television law. Many hotels feature Japanese cable television, which often features American news and prime time shows dubbed in Japanese.

MTV

Since cable television is not available, MTV in Taipei is a uniquely Taiwanese institution: 115 of the 500 MTV studios are located in Taipei (Chira, 1988; Sallinger, 1991). Despite its use of the American video channel title, MTV is actually a unique recreational outlet used by teenagers. An MTV outlet is basically a video rental establishment which rents not only the video tape, but a quiet, furnished room, complete with television, VCR, and furniture, in which to watch the video. The average MTV outlet has between 20 and 30 viewing rooms; seating capacity in each room varies between two and twelve. Viewing rooms have a range of furnishings – beanbags, couches, tatami mats and frequently feature air conditioning, high quality equipment, and free soft drinks. MTV studios insist on a safety standard of 2.5 meters distance between the television and the seats. Public morals are maintained with doors to the rooms which have no locks but do have a window. First introduced in 1982, the service quickly went through three phases. Initially, the television and video equipment were located in large rooms, and were part of makeshift coffee shops, often featuring only one viewing area. These first MTV studios catered mostly to foreigners. The second generation studios added feature full length movies and earphones. In the third phase individual viewing rooms were made available. The lobby of the third generation MTV studios often features a coffee shop.

Teenagers were first attracted to MTV because of the poor quality of television programming and movies. Movie theatres often select films carelessly, and showing schedules are quite inflexible. In addition a seat must be reserved in advance. The movie theatres themselves are not an ideal viewing environment: frequently they are dirty, with poor air quality due to smoking, and quite noisy due to children crying. As such MTV studios are refuges from dirt, noise, and pollution. They are also refuges from parental and school pressures, and dirty and crowded streets.

Parents and the government are not as enthusiastic as the teenagers are. From the parental perspective, there are worries over the fact that not all MTV centers follow the window and lock rules, thus making sexual intimacy and drug use possible. The government has the same concerns it had with the beer houses, with one additional problem. As with the beer houses, the MTV studios are frequently not licensed, and are usually located in large office buildings near major transportation nodes (as are the cram schools), or in apartment blocks. Regardless of their location, their presence violates zoning regulations. There is also a fear that safety regulations are either violated or ignored. This fear is a real one: it has been estimated that every year more than 100 patrons of illegally located businesses die in accidental fires (Lee, 1993b). One additional concern which differentiates MTV from other frowned-upon outlets involves copyright. As with books, video tapes are pirated. Furthermore the use of the MTV logo is not licensed. Hence the entire MTV phenomenon presents an impediment to better trade relations. The government has tried both to control the studios and placate United States trade and film representatives by prosecuting MTV operators. The results have been mixed. In one landmark case, the judge ruled that showing a video in an MTV center does not constitute a "public showing"; however, he did fine an operator for not seeking permission to show copyright videotapes and for using private, pirated editions. For their part, MTV owners have tried to legitimize their operations by restructuring their establishments as private clubs, complete with fee (set at US$6.00 in 1989), and membership cards. Many closed when they were unable or unwilling to use properly copied and licensed videotapes.

Video parlors

Video parlors or arcades are relatively new diversions, first appearing in the late 1980s. There are two types of arcades. First is a Japanese import, *pachinko*, a modified version of something called the Corinthian game, a sort of vertical pinball machine without flippers (Chow and Liu, 1988; Christopher, 1983). By 1988 some 300 *pachinko* houses had been established in Taipei. The larger houses have large television screens at street level and stereo speakers so that passers-by can be lured in. Second are the electronic games which have come to replace pinball machines. As with food and shopping there is a wide range of opportunities to play the video games. At the low end of the spectrum are individual machines literally parked on the sidewalk, or directly outside a small retail establishment. At the high end there are spacious, well lit halls with curtained windows so that passers-by cannot look in. Such halls often feature refreshment stands. Regardless of the setting of the video arcades, they open early and close late. In terms of location the freestanding machines are found wherever retail activities are found. Not surprisingly there is a heavy concentration of larger, fancier, more elaborate video arcades in the same areas where MTV and *bushiban* (cram schools) are located, i.e. to the south and west of the Central Railroad Station. Other arcades are found in areas with large teenage populations and where large crowds pass on the way to and from work.

Religion

Religion is included as a part of unsanctioned little culture activities for three reasons. First, many activities in the 399 officially registered temples and churches are not religious in nature (see Table 7.3 for the types of religious temples or churches). For example, temples are places where people gather to study religious texts, to eat and socialize, as well as to bring food and incense offerings and to seek answers to future events through divination. An example of this was the proliferation in 1990 of some 1200 commercialized home altars, most of which were concentrated in Peitou, Sungshan, and Shihlin *chu*. While appearing to cater to the religious needs of Taoist believers, most of them claimed to represent prophets of Taiwanese or Chinese folk gods who could assist worshippers in selecting winning numbers for the Hong Kong Mark Six numbers game. After some 120 complaints about these private temples were registered, the government proceeded to investigate them based on the noise and air pollution generated by the chanting of sutras and burning of incense. Regulation of such activities was to be left to officials of the Environmental Protection Agency, once the extent of the problem could be assessed and a schedule of proper fines constructed (*Free China Journal*, Feb. 15, 1990, 3). Secondly, although large temples are obvious on the landscape and therefore easy to supervise, there are literally dozens of temples which are no more than store front operations or wayside niches

Table 7.3 Types of religious institutions in Taipei, 1990

Religion	Number of houses of worship
Buddhism	90
Taoism	104
Islam	1
Shiuan Yuan	2
Hsiaism	2
I-Guann Daw	1
Catholicism	19
Protestantism	176
Bahai	1
Tenri Kyo	1
Judaism	1

which are hard to identify and supervise. The same holds true for the numerous small altars found in offices and homes. Thirdly, the government has frowned on ritual performances which form the core of popular religious activities (Rohsenow, 1973; Weller, 1985, 1987). The ritual performances often involve lavish festivals, which the Kuomintang government felt were antithetical to the 1940s and 1950s goals of "suppressing insurrection and being frugal." Such antipathy was not new, however: even under the Japanese administration of Taiwan attempts were made to suppress expressions of popular religion. In addition to the Kuomintang's concern about the costs of feasts and festivals, government opposition also stemmed from embarrassment at the rituals and their seemingly superstitious foundations, and the concern that the popular religious movements would become vehicles for celebrating and developing Taiwanese autonomy and identity (Weller, 1987). In fact the temples have been identified as potential centers of community development (O'Hara, 1967). In addition to police checks, anti-festival propaganda, and newspaper articles aimed at embarrassing festival sponsors and participants, the government has resorted to co-opting festivals as a means of suppressing them. For example, the Lantern Festival at Lungshan Temple in Wanhwa (Figure 7.4), which marks the close of the Lunar New Year holiday season, is actively publicized by the government as a part of its tourism promotion activities. In fact the government has gone so far as to proclaim the days before and after the Lantern Festival as Tourism Festival Week (Nerbonne, 1985). Alternatively the government has promoted those religious and quasi-religious activities it favors. Good examples of officially sponsored quasi-religious activities would be *taichi* (shadow boxing), the Dragon Boat Races (celebrated as part of Poet's Day) and the biennial celebration of the birthday of Confucius (which falls on 28 September).

Figure 7.4 Lungshan Temple in Wanhwa is famous for its Lantern festival. In addition to serving a religious function the temple provides important social services to older local residents

Tickets to the ceremony are in such short supply that the government also distributes tickets to the dress rehearsal for the ceremonies. It is not at all clear whether or not government concerns for temples functioning as centers of actual opposition activities are well founded since, for example, few of the 90 Buddhist temples have any affiliation with formal organizations, and frequently the temples had no resident monks or nuns (O'Hara, 1967). The distribution of temples may have played a role in the government's concern: there was a heavy concentration of temples of all sizes in the old city districts with some small ones outside the city, and very few in new areas or communities. This same pattern persists today with some 57.3 percent of all the houses of worship located in the old districts of Chungshan, Chungcheng, Ta-an, Tatong, and Wanhwa.

Unclassified activities

Two recreational activities are too new to have attained the status of either great or little culture. These are professional sports and recreational gardening.

Professional sports

In the Taipei context, professional sports really means baseball (Wu, 1992). Taiwan in general, and Taipei in particular, has actively supported Little League baseball since 1948 when the Taipei City Department of Education designated three primary schools as "baseball schools." Professional baseball in Taipei dates from 1983 when the owners of the Brother Hotel in Taipei established their own team, complete with high salaries for top players. The government initially resisted the move to professional baseball fearing the impact it might have on amateur teams (most of which were sponsored by government-run organizations or corporations). However, by 1989 three more private companies had established teams and professional baseball was a reality in Taiwan.

There are two serious problems confronting the development of professional baseball. First is a serious shortage of qualified players. Several teams have recruited managers and players from Panama, Japan, and the United States (Kossler, 1992). There are two main difficulties in even recruiting players: the relatively low pay offered in Taiwan, and the decline of Little League teams. For example, Chinese players would rather play in Japan, where the top salary of US$80 000 paid to Taiwanese baseball players is the bottom of the pay scale. Second, there is a lack of modern playing facilities in Taipei and the other four cities (Hsin-chu, Taichung, Tainan, and Kaohsiung) with baseball teams. For example, the Taipei Municipal Baseball Stadium, located on the site formerly occupied by the United States Military Advisory Group support facilities complex on Chungshan North Road, section 3, is not only too small to permit enough seats to be sold to generate a profit for team owners, but its location is close to the Sungshan airport, with resulting noise pollution, and is associated with traffic problems. The municipal government is committed to constructing a new stadium similar to the "Big Egg" in downtown Tokyo. The main question is where to locate it. A sports complex including a 20 000-seat baseball park, a 20 000-seat track and field arena, and a 6000-seat gymnasium with tennis center has already been approved for the Tienmu area in Shihlin district (Chiu, 1992). Alternative sites such as the Kuantu Plain or the present site of the municipal field have been suggested. Whichever site is finally chosen, Taipei government officials want to ensure that accessibility will be maximized for the entire Taipei population. Lack of adequate playing facilities has handicapped the other major sport to capture the popular imagination – basketball. For Taipei the problem is that the main basketball stadium was destroyed in November 1988 when exploding firecrackers burned a hole in the roof of the China Sports and Culture Center. It took two years to decide what do to with the burned-out shell.

A new 11 000-seat structure, with a parking lot for 700 cars was scheduled to be completed by 1993.

Although baseball and basketball have captured popular attention, the elite has adopted other sports. Tennis and golf are especially popular. Advertisements for golf courses are carried by buses. But the golf links are not accessible, being located in Shihmen dam area, south of Taipei City, in Hsinfeng in Hsinchu *hsien*, and in Lungtan in Taoyuan *hsien*.

Recreational agriculture

Recreational agriculture is a new activity which has the potential for eventual adoption by the elite, since at a minimum it reinforces and restores the link between land and people which has been at the very foundation of Chinese civilization. Unfortunately for many citizens of Taipei, that link has been broken as the city has grown. Recreational agriculture takes three basic forms: growing plants at home, harvesting, and cultivation in prepared plots (Lin, 1989; Song, 1990b). In the discussion on the economy of Taipei these three forms were described. It was noted, for example, that many farmers now run nurseries for the direct sale of trees and plants to Taipei house and apartment dwellers. As a result, many Taipei apartment houses are somewhat disguised by the dense foliage growing on balconies. Although there are no exact data on the extent of recreational agriculture, the concept has proved to be so popular that the national government's Council of Agriculture is planning to set up some 25 leisure farm plantations around the island. For the citizens of Taipei there is little need to travel outside the city for either the second or third type of recreational agriculture since the new districts of the city contain sufficient areas to support these activities. In addition, given the bus system of Taipei City, the Taipei sites have the added advantage of being more accessible.

Conclusion: what is missing?

Despite the perception on the part of Taipei citizens that little is available in terms of recreational outlets, Taipei does provide a rich variety of leisure-time activities beyond television. Yet there is one main gap in the array of opportunities – a lack of open green spaces and parks. This lack is frequently cited in inventories and surveys of the tourist potential in the Taipei area (Tzeng and Lee, 1989). Historically the lack of green space has been attributed to a combination of population pressure and limited living space resulting in public spaces being seen as expendable luxuries (Chen,

Figure 7.5 In replotting small areas are made available for vest pocket parks

1956). One result was that before the sidewalks of Taipei were paved, children literally played in the streets (Figure 6.8).

The Taipei municipal government is justifiably proud of the increase in green space/park areas over the past 30 years from 31.04 hectares (76.69 acres) to 343.02 hectares (847.58 acres). Numerous parks, varying in size from vest pocket playgrounds (Figure 7.5) to large recreational complexes, have been created. In fact the Taipei City government has worked hard to increase the amount of park land available. For example, it has gone so far as to reject proposals for the development of the site set aside for city park number 7, when the developer allocated less than 60 per cent of the area to green space. Similarly, when 140 red cedars along Ai kou West Road were designated to be torn up in order to prepare the area for construction of the Mass Rapid Transit System, the mayor insisted that these 99-year-old trees be transplanted to a nursery for later replanting in their original places. And when the 35-year-old historic Taipei International House on Hsin-yi Road, section 3, was razed in 1992, the site was designated for development into a wooded park, even though it is located in the heart of a desirable neighborhood. Private developers no doubt would have been more than willing to build apartment and retail complexes (Lee, 1992).

Through government efforts there has therefore been an absolute increase in park land. However, the area per capita has declined, despite the 1988 goal of increasing per capita park land to 2.8 square meters (*Welcome to the 21st Century*, 1987). In fact this goal represents a scaling

Figure 7.6 New Park, built by the Japanese, is the only large green space in the CBD

back of earlier hopes to increase park land to 5 square meters per capita by 1992 (*New Image of Taipei*, 1988). The development of private health clubs has been seen as a private attempt to create more opportunities for exercise and recreation (Friedman, 1991).

In terms of park use, beyond the crowding which develops, their use is not maximized for several reasons. First, some large areas, such as the walks within the Chiang Kai-shek Memorial, are made of concrete and the green and planted areas are not really designed for romping or playing (Figure 2.15). Second, even when parks have been designed for play, such as New Park (Figure 7.6), the design and maintenance of equipment are not only not conducive to play but at times dangerous. Third, some large areas such as the Yangmingshan National Park, which alone is 55.8 hectares (135 acres), are inaccessible: it can take upwards of an hour by bus to get there. To compensate for the lack of accessibility the Taipei City Bus administration runs an additional 60 special buses to take visitors to the area during the height of the flower (around Chinese New Year) and butterfly (in July) seasons. During these times 50 000 people a day can visit the park. Inaccessibility can also derive from lack of publicity. For example, just east of the new Taipei Central Railroad station there is a small park housing a Sun Yat-sen Historic Events Memorial Hall. This delightful park is hardly used. Finally, apart from the physical constraints and safety concerns of park land use, there is also the question of a perception that play (and recreational activities) in public areas are not appropriate activities as they distract children from study (Schak, 1972). Furthermore mothers are worried that in playing with children outside the family their children will pick up bad habits and moral values. Finally, mothers are concerned with the physical safety of their children. It is not clear whether or not the attitudes of mothers have shifted as the economy of Taipei has matured and the ranks of the middle class increased. Empty playgrounds still abound. And often it is grandparents who take small children out for an opportunity to feed fish in the ponds in New Park or the Sun Yat-sen Memorial. Both observations suggest that although planners and foreign observers decry the lack of play and park land, even if the area increased and accessibility was improved, parents and children would still seek recreational outlets in front of the television set.

References

Ambruster, W. (1976) Letter from Taipei, *Far Eastern Economic Review* 94, Nov. 19, 70.

Asian Affluents 2 (1992) Far Eastern Economic Review, Hong Kong.

Brunn, S. D. and J. F. Williams eds. (1983) *Cities of the World. World Regional Urban Development*. Harper and Row Publishers, New York.

Chang, C. (1975) Twenty Years in Taipei. Translated by J. McLellan, in P-y. Chi, ed., *An Anthology of Contemporary Chinese Literature, Taiwan: 1949–1974, Vol. 1*. National Institute for Compilation and Translation, Taipei.

Chang, C. (1983) Tea Time in Taipei. Tapping the Ambience of Distance Years and Places, *Free China Review* 33:7, 57–63.

Chang, W. (1989) Upscale Bookstores Thrive, *Free China Journal*, 17 Aug., 7.

Chen, C.-s. (1956) *The City of Taipei*. Research Report Number 71, Fu-Min Institute of Economic Development, Taipei.

Chen, D. W. (1989) Franchised Hangouts, *Free China Review* 39:8, 40–42.

Chen, K.-c. and H.-m. Chen (1983) Location of Bookstores and Consumer Behavior in Taipei, *Geographical Research* 9, 1–19.*

Chira, S. (1988) Video Madness in Taiwan: Little Rooms With Big Screens, *New York Times* July 22, 2.

Chiu, J. (1992) Planners Cooking Up Recipe for Constructing 'Big Egg' Stadium Here, *Free China Journal*, Jan. 28, 5.

Chow, E. and B. Liu (1988) Pachinko Hot New Entertainment Form in Taipei, *Free China Journal*, Dec. 8, 6.

Christopher, R. C. (1983) *The Japanese Mind*, Fawcett Columbine, New York.

Connolly, M. (1969) Taipei Theatre, *Holiday* 45, Nov., 16, 18.

Free China Journal (1990) Gambler Gods Unwelcome, Feb. 15, 3.

Free China Journal (1991) Leisure Life Spent Idly, Survey Finds, Jan. 28, 3.

Free China Journal (1989) Taipei Residents Prefer TV, Feb. 16, 3.

Friedman, S. (1991) Pump That Iron, *Free China Review* 48, Jan., 58–63.

Glenn, W. (1968) Growing Like Topsy, *Far Eastern Economic Review* 61, Aug. 8, 280–89.

Goldstein, C. (1985a) Dominance of Taipei, *Far Eastern Economic Review* 130, Dec. 26, 24–9.

Goldstein, C. (1985b) Everyone's Medium, *Far Eastern Economic Review* 130, Dec. 26, 30.

Herr, M. (1968) Taipei: Wicked Cities of the World, Part II, *Holiday* 43, Apr., 46–9, 113, 115, 117, 128.

Huang, H. (1993) Taiwan Residents Singing Up Storm at Karaoke Clubs, *Free China Journal* 4 May, 6.

Hwang, L. Y., R. P. Beasley, C. S. Yang, L. C. Hsu and K. P. Chan (1983) Incidence of Hepatitis A Infections in Children in Taipei, *Intervirology* 20: 2–3, 149–154.

Johnstone, B. (1988) Pioneers Set to Banish Hepatitis B Scourge, *Far Eastern Economic Review* 139, Feb. 25, 42–44.

Joseph, R. (1970) Taipei: The Chinese Experience, *Travel and Camera* 33, 81.

Karp, J. (1992) New Capitals of Art – Buyers Flock to Hong Kong, Taipei, *Far Eastern Economic Review* 155, Oct. 22, 55–56.

Kossler, M. (1992) Foreign Players Adjust to Taiwan Pro Baseball, *Free China Journal*, Oct. 16, 5.

Lee, F.-f. (1992) City Razes International House, *Free China Journal*, Apr. 7, 4.

Lee, R. F. F. (1993a) No Free Time for Anxious Students, *Free China Journal*, Jan. 19, 4.

Lee, R. F. F. (1993b) Autonomous Managing Key in Building Rights, *Free China Journal*, Mar. 5, 4.

Li, W.-h. (1992) *Estimates on the Size of the Singing Girl Problem*, Ministry of Interior , Taipei.

Lin, C.-h. (1991) Commissioner, Bureau of Education, Taipei Municipal Government, Personal Correspondence, July 10.

Lin, C.-j. (1983) The Republic of China, pp. 104–135 in R. M. Thomas and T. N. Postlethwaite, *Schooling in East Asia*, Pergamon, New York.

Lin, C.-w. (1989) 'Take Your Pick' Mushrooms, *Free China Journal*, Mar. 2, 3.

Liu, D. (1992a) Taipei. All you can eat heaven for gourmets, *Free China Journal*, Apr. 28, 5.

Liu, D. (1992b) Socially Conscious Bookstores, *Free China Journal*, May 19, 3.

Marsh, R. (1968) The Taiwanese of Taipei: Some Major Aspects of Their Social Structure and Attitudes, *Journal of Asian Studies* 27, 571–84.

MacGregor, P. (1984) Special Coffee Houses are Student Study Havens, *Free China Review* 34:9, 52–54.

Nerbonne, J. J. (1985) *Guide to Taipei and all Taiwan*, Caves Books, Taipei.

New Image of Taipei (1988) Department of Information, Taipei City Government, Taipei.

O'Hara, A. R. (1967) A Factoral Survey of Taipei's Temples and Their Functions, *Journal of Social Science* 17, 323–37.

Peterson, S. W. (1974) Ilha Formosa, *Travel* 14, May, 32–37.

Redfield, R. (1956) *Peasant Society and Culture. An Anthropological Approach to Civilization*, University of Chicago Press, Chicago.

Reid, D. P. (1984) *Taiwan*, Prentice-Hall, Englewood Cliffs.

Rohsenow, H. G. (1973) Prosperity Settlement: The Politics of Paipai in Taipei, Taiwan. PhD Dissertation, University of Michigan.

Royal, W. (1989) Dancing Heads. Disco Lights. *Free China Review* 39:8, 44–45.

Sallinger, J. (1991) MTVs: Privacy Amid the Crowd, *Free China Journal* Mar. 11, 6.

Schak, D. C. (1972) Determinants of Children's Play Patterns in A Chinese City: the Interplay of Space and Values, *Urban Anthropology* 1, 195–204.

Senftleben, W. (1986) Tourism, Hot Springs, Resorts, and Sexual Entertainment, Observations from Northern Taiwan – A Study in Social Geography, *Philippine Geographical Journal* 30:1 and 2, 21–41.

Song, S.-f. (1990a) Is Reading a Luxury Item? *Free China Journal* Aug. 23, 3.

Song, S.-f. (1990b) Rent-a-Plot. City Dwellers Toy in Dirt, *Free China Journal* Aug. 20, 3.

Sutherland, C., J. Williams and C. Mather (1987) Beer Houses: An Indicator of Cultural Change in Taiwan, *Journal of Cultural Geography* 6, 35–50.

Tsai, W.-t. (1990) The Study of the Districts of Supplementary Schools in Taipei, *Geographical Research* 16, 63–90.*

Tseng, W.-t. (1978) The Spatial Structure of School-Age Children and Compelled Schools of Taipei, *Geographical Research* 4, 213–58.*

Tzeng, G.-h. and M.-h. Lee (1989) Spatial Attribution of Tourism Resources and Spatial System of Recreation Demand in Northern Taiwan, *Geographical Studies* 13, 247–70.*

Welcome to the 21st Century (1987) Department of Information, Taipei City Government, Taipei.

Weller, R. P. (1985) Bandits, Beggars, and Ghosts: The Failure of State Control Over Religious Interpretation in Taiwan, *American Ethnologist* 12, 46–61.

Weller, R. P. (1987) Politics of Ritual Disguise. Repression and Response in Taiwanese Popular Religion, *Modern China* 13, 17–39.

Wu, E. (1992) Baseball Fever, *Free China Review* 42:8, 30–39.

Zich, A. (1977) Taiwan: World's Greatest Chinese Restaurant, *Holiday* 58, Mar., 40–1.

8
Conclusions: Taipei as a world city: past, present, and future

The main premise of this study of Taipei as a world city has been that world city status was achieved through the serendipitous juxtaposition of a series of unique historical, political, and economic events. It is not reasonable to assume that the impact of such a fortuitous constellation of events will last forever, or that they will be able to sustain Taipei as a world city even into the near future. In this chapter the status of Taipei as a world city up to 1989 will be qualitatively and quantitatively described, and the national government's plans for perpetuating Taipei as an important economic, cultural, and political center enumerated.

Taipei as a world city

The easiest method of assessing Taipei's status as a world city is to compare its characteristics to the checklist of world city traits enunciated by Friedman and Wolff (1982). The data for the comparison are in Table 8.1. For 9 of the 15 characteristics Taipei unequivocally fits the description of a world city. For all characteristics, however, some commentary is warranted.

The four characteristics which are the most dubious involve international financial issues. Taipei being a home for transnational corporations is labeled questionable for two reasons. First, there are very few Taiwan companies which are included in the Fortune International 500. From 1980 to 1989 the number of Taiwanese companies on the list has increased from one to four. For many years the state-owned

249

Taipei as a world city

Table 8.1 World city traits displayed by Taipei, 1989

Trait	Presence
Home for transnational corporations	Questionable
Safe place for investment of surplus capital	Questionable
Producer of products for world market	Questionable
Role as an ideological center	Shifting
Relative strength as world market	Questionable
Control of urban life	Yes: Nation-state mode
Planners involved in change	Yes
Industrial employment changing	Yes
Service economy restructuring	Yes
Informal sector present	Yes
Social restructuring – class polarization	Shifting
City scape of citadel of glass and steel	Yes
Physical restructuring in progress	Yes
Environmental problems	Yes
Political conflicts	Yes

Chinese Petroleum or China Steel Corporations constituted all or half of the list. The other two positions were held by Formosa Plastics, Nan Ya Plastics, or Tatong Electronics. The small number of Taiwanese companies reflects the continued preference of all Taiwanese entrepreneurs for small, family owned and operated companies. Secondly, since 1952 Taiwan entrepreneurs have invested both within Taiwan and elsewhere. Outward investment has particularly accelerated since the late 1980s when the appreciation of the NT dollar and increases in labor costs in Taiwan made local Taiwan industry non-competitive. Taiwan entrepreneurs have taken their industrial investments to Southeast Asia, including Vietnam, the People's Republic of China, the United States, Latin America, and Europe. From government statistics it is impossible to identify which of these Taiwanese firms has their headquarters in Taipei. But to the extent that Taipei serves as a surrogate for the Taiwan economy, Taipei can be considered as a home for transnational corporations.

In terms of Taipei being a safe place for investment of surplus capital, there are three reasons to equivocate. First, it is true that the government of the Republic of China has been very successful in attracting foreign investment. For example, in the period 1952 to 1989 the government approved 5312 foreign investment applications totaling some US$10.9 billion dollars. Some 35 percent of the investments and 15 percent of the capital were made by overseas Chinese; the remainder was from foreign investors in general. However, since the late 1980s the number and value of such investments have declined. Secondly, in terms of the location of these investments within Taiwan, for 1971 40.07 percent of the overseas Chinese investments, totaling 56.52 of overseas Chinese funds, were invested in Taipei City; for other foreign investments the statistics are 31.62 percent of all investments totaling 33.77 percent of the capital. By 1976 the attraction of Taipei for both groups had declined. Overseas Chinese investors had put 38.42 percent of their investments, and 50.88 percent of their capital, in Taipei. Foreign investors were present in Taipei 32.25 percent of the time, with 37.7 percent of the foreign capital. Unfortunately it is not possible to describe the later pull of Taipei City to all types of foreign investors accurately since these data were not included in the 1981 and 1986 industrial and commercial censuses. Thirdly, in terms of the banking and equities markets, limits have been placed on the role which foreigners can play. This situation is in the process of being changed.

One would expect Taipei to play a significant role as an investment center for two reasons. First, the Republic of China holds the 12th largest stock of gold reserves and the largest stock of total reserves in the world (*International Financial Statistics*, 1993; *Financial Statistics*, 1993). In addition five Taipei banks, Bank of Taiwan, International Commercial Bank, First Commercial, Hua Nan Commercial, and Changhwa Commercial, are among the world's largest 500 banks. However, through the 1980s at least, it is questionable whether or not Taiwan was truly an international banking and investment center.

Similar arguments hold for producer of products for a world market, and relative strength as a world market. It is true that Taiwan has one of the strongest exporting economies in the world. For example, in 1989 Taiwan exported some US$67.4 billion worth of goods and imported some US$50.5 billion worth of goods. As such, Taiwan ranked as the world's 16th leading exporter and 11th leading importer. But there is no way reasonably to differentiate exports and imports from Taipei *per se* in these data.

There are two variables on the checklist for which Taipei appears to present a shifting emphasis. Given the history of the Chinese civil war which ended in 1949, Taipei is an ideological center. For many years the Nationalist government had a strongly anti-communist outlook and foreign policy. It was one of the founding members of the Asian Pacific Anti-Communist League in 1954 and the founder of the World Anti-Communist League in 1967, whose headquarters were located in Taipei. The demise of communism in Eastern Europe and the former Soviet Union, as well as Taipei's decision to trade openly with communist countries (Selya, 1992), have reduced Taipei's role as a center of anti-communist activity and publication. In fact, in 1990 the World Anti-Communist League changed its name to the World League for Freedom and Democracy and relocated its headquarters to Seoul, Republic of Korea. However, it could be argued that the use of the political thoughts of Sun Yat-sen, in the form of *San Min Chu I*, as the basis for developing

Table 8.2 Percentage changes in number of establishments of manufacturing, 1954–1986

Product	Change
Food	−40.19
Clothing	30.23
Metals	−36.29
Printing	697.23
Wood	−32.22
Chemicals	350.00
Machinery	280.00
Transportation	−38.94
Electrical/electronics	956.80

Sources: Computed from *Taipei Municipal Statistical Abstract*, various years; *Industrial–Commercial Census, Taiwan-Fukien Area, Republic of China*, cited years.

the Taiwan economy is a distinctly ideological position. Further, deeply ideological debates regarding the future of the Republic of China dominate policy debates in the Legislative *Yuan* (branch) of the central government.

The second shifting trait is that of social restructuring and class polarization. In Chapters 2 and 3 the ethnic and income bases of residential segregation were shown to have had a long history. Evidence presented suggested that at least ethnicity as a basis for segregation had declined by the 1980s. However, in Chapter 6 the discussion on housing clearly implied that a new and potentially disruptive basis for segregation has emerged. What is not clear is whether or not political debate on the growing housing issues has reached the level of class warfare rhetoric used to describe this particular world city trait (Friedman and Wolff, 1982).

For the remaining nine traits there appears to be a very tight fit, although it is sometimes difficult to measure quantitatively the extent of the fit. In terms of control of urban life, there is an elite with a decisively nation-state, not urban, orientation. In Chapters 5 and 6, the difficult role of planning and planners was described. Planners are frequently in short supply and feel that the public does not understand the need for planning. The same can be said for the elite when plans do not fit their *laissez-faire* methods. In Chapter 3 the shifts in manufacturing and services were described. In terms of shifts in the types of manufacturing activities, food, metals, wood, and transportation have declined, while clothing, printing, chemicals, machinery, and electronics have grown (Table 8.2). The new mix reflects Taiwan's changing labor costs, growing environmental concerns, and evolving role as a major economic power. The same can be said of the service sector (Table 8.3). As with shifts in manufacturing, it is

Table 8.3 Shifts in number of service establishments, 1981–1986

Type of service	No. 1981	No. 1986	Percentage change
Wholesale trade	10 403	11 786	13.29
Retail trade	34 521	44 189	28.01
Foreign trade	16 883	19 284	14.22
Finance	624	871	39.58
Foreign banks	25	32	28.00
Insurance	93	200	115.05
Brokerages	5 462	1 465	−73.18
Legal	610	680	11.48
Accounting	167	305	82.63
Consulting	410	720	75.61
Engineering		214	
Investment		9	
Management		320	
Data processing	89	192	115.73
Advertising	1 033	1 089	5.42
Design		64	
Other		1 801	
Social	2 322	3 238	39.45
Mass media	689	1 183	71.70
Medical	1 683	2 255	33.99
Cultural	884	713	−19.34

Sources: Industrial and Commercial Census cited years.

somewhat difficult to find the appropriate data to demonstrate the changes. For manufacturing long-term data on the number of manu-facturing establishments are the least subject to changes in census definitions and coverage. For services, as the economy has grown more complicated and more sophisticated, the number of service categories specified in the census has grown. But it is not until the 1981 census that data permit a clear sense of just how comprehensive services in Taipei have become. When describing both manufacturing and services the presence of an informal sector was mentioned. This sector continues to thrive despite the municipal government's attempts to control or eliminate it. The latest phase in architectural development, as described in Chapter 3, features stunning new buildings featuring the universal world city materials of glass and steel, albeit with an increasingly Chinese flavor. The need to revise the city plan, described in Chapter 5, can best be interpreted as evidence of a city undergoing spontaneous physical restructuring. In Chapter 7 the origins and interconnections between a wide range of environmental problems were described. The issue of political conflict appeared not only in the discussion of government and planning but in the materials on solving all the environmental, infrastructure, and social problems of Taipei.

Government plans for Taipei's future

In enumerating the national government's plans for Taipei it is important to remember that there is no evidence that any member of the government has ever heard of the concept of a world city; nor is there any evidence that the phrase world city has been used in describing Taipei's future. What is clear is that the national government is keenly aware of the need to take action to ensure the continued political legitimacy of the Republic of China as an independent political entity. Any actions *vis-à-vis* Taipei that will contribute to that goal will by definition contribute to Taipei's future as a world city.

The actual plans fall into two categories. First, both the national and municipal governments seek to attract institutions and activities which will keep the name of Taiwan, the Republic of China, and the city of Taipei in a bright, positive, international spotlight. In addition to actively engaging various cultural groups with international reputations or outstanding visiting art exhibits, as discussed in Chapter 7, five specific subject areas have been solicited. In terms of attracting activities with a strong political overtone, Taipei has succeeded in having several United Nations related organizations, such as the International Organization of Migration, the Asian Vegetable Research and Development Centre, and the Food and Food Technology Center of the Asian and Pacific Region, establish their regional headquarters in Taipei. Taipei has hosted an annual meeting of the conference of governors of Southeast Asian central banks. Similarly an annual conference of the Inter-American Center for Tax Administrators has been held in Taipei. The government periodically invites world leaders to visit Taipei for consultations. Taipei has applied to the GATT, demands equality at meetings of the Asian Pacific Economic Cooperation Forum, and is considering applying for readmission to the United Nations. However, the largest political outreach has been by participating in the Sister Cities program. Taipei has ten sister cities – Atlanta, Georgia; Cleveland, Ohio; Guam; Houston, Texas; Indianapolis, Indiana; Los Angeles, California; Marshall, Texas; Oklahoma City, Oklahoma; Phoenix, Arizona; and San Francisco, California. This is the largest number of sister cities for any one city anywhere (*Directory of Sister Cities, Counties, and States, by State and Country*, 1990).

A second subject area is that of sports. Taipei submitted an application to host the Asian Games in 2002. Based on the Asian Games application it plans to submit an application to host a world's fair, even considering holding its own, independent fair entitled the 21st Century Taipei Exposition if its bid fails. Taipei started sponsoring in 1989 an international marathon. Its popularity has grown to the point where in 1992 the race attracted some 12 000 runners from 25 countries.

In the area of science, in addition to hosting conferences sponsored by the Republic of China's National Science Council, Taipei has been the site of international science meetings, such as the third annual Pacific bio-technology conference in 1992. In order to enhance its economic status Taipei has sponsored its own international trade fairs, such as the Taipei International Fair, the International Electronics Fair, and the International Construction Show, and hosted fairs sponsored by national and international associations, such as a Philippines Philatelic show, and the International Book Exhibition. Finally it has attracted non-political professional and fraternal conventions and meetings such as those of the Lions International, the World Trade Center Association Board, and the American Society of Travel Agents. One international event, the Miss Universe Contest, fits none of the above categories. Taipei did host the contest in May 1988, although the appropriateness of a beauty pageant in an area with such prudish attitudes towards women did make the event somewhat culturally anomalous. It does, however, suggest just how far Taipei and Republic of China leaders are prepared to go in order to keep Taipei in the view of world leaders and trend setters.

Attracting these various types of activities has required that Taipei make the city attractive. As such the city and national government have encouraged the building of international class hotels and actually built convention and meeting spaces, such as the Taipei World Trade Center complex (Figure 8.1), which in addition to the Trade Center includes a special international convention center featuring twelve meeting rooms, five dining halls, and easy access underground parking, the International Trade Building and a 1000-room Grand Hyatt hotel (Peng, 1991).

The second major category of activities is much more ambitious, for two reasons. First, it goes beyond activities featuring periodic visits or activities to permanent ones. Secondly, it requires basic structural changes in Chinese law, and by extension in ways of conducting political and economic activities. The proposal which is being especially pursued is to make Taipei a major financial hub. The proposal does have a precedent, in the form of the successful development of the Taipei World Trade Center as a part of the Hsin-yi Sub-center special land use district.

The idea that Taipei should become an international financial hub was first aired as part of the publicity for the Six-Year National Development Plan (*Free China Journal*, Oct. 8, 1990). By June 1991 the decision had been made to pursue the goal. The first public step was for the Premier (Hau Pei-tsun) to address a special meeting of bankers, officials, and academics to solicit their views and proposals (*New York Times*, June 25, 1991). The governor of the Central Bank of China was then charged with developing a plan. The plan was to assume that Taipei would gradually emerge as a regional financial center, first serving Tokyo, and then

Figure 8.1 The Taipei World Trade Center is the centerpiece of commercial development in the Hsin-yi project

expanding to serve Hong Kong and Singapore (*Free China Journal*, Dec. 6, 1990). All discussions and plans have assumed that Taipei has identifiable advantages which would make it attractive as a financial center. These advantages include the size of the foreign reserves held by the national government, the availability of a trained, educated workforce, a strategic location, a rich cultural life, a lively night life, and access to outdoor recreation such as golf, water sports, and mountain climbing (*Free China Journal*, Dec. 6, 1990; Chen, 1993; Lin, 1991). However, Taipei's pollution and unkempt streets were also cited as problems which must be overcome if foreigners are to be attracted to Taipei (Chen, 1993; Lin, 1991).

Although a complete draft of a formal plan has not been publicly circulated, there are three general problematic areas which must be addressed if Taipei is to emerge as hoped. First, the internal banking and financial systems must be liberalized; second, they must be internationalized; and third, adequate infrastructure must be built (Lin, 1991; Shieh, 1992b).

Liberalization of the banking and financial systems is necessary because as of the early 1980s they were basically the same system as that introduced by the Japanese at the beginning of the twentieth century. The reason the systems had not been changed is that the government was so worried about inflation and an imbalance in trade it deliberately took a very conservative approach to managing banking and finance (Yin, 1989). Liberalization fundamentally means deregulating the systems to permit free trade in gold, new financial products such as futures and options, and securitization (Shieh, 1992a,b; Lin, 1991; *Free China Journal*, Nov. 22, 1990; *New York Times*, Jul. 5, 1991). Internationalization involves attracting international brokerage houses to Taipei (Shieh, 1992b), easing restrictions, removing limits on foreign banks such as limits on loan periods to less than seven years, restrictions on branch banking, and limits on loan portfolios, making the New Taiwan dollar an international currency, expanding the foreign currency market, creating and expanding a foreign exchange call-loan market.

Four types of infrastructure have been specifically singled out as preconditions for successful liberalization and internationalization. First, a building to house international financial institutions must be built. Although the private market could provide ample office space, the concern is for appropriate facilities, in an appropriate location, at a price which foreigners will find reasonable (Shieh, 1992a; *Free China Journal*, Nov. 22, 1990). Secondly, telecommunications and transportation facilities must be improved. This includes not only the installation of the latest in technology, but also reducing rates, especially for long distance and overseas telephone calls (Shieh, 1992a; *Free China Journal*, Nov. 22, 1990). Thirdly, the legal framework must be modernized. On the one hand this refers mainly to banking regulations (Lin, 1991). However, it also includes the more problematic issues of land acquisition, bureaucratic red tape, inadequate copyright protection, tax evasion, insider trading, and underground investment and futures companies (*Free China Journal*, Oct. 8, 1990; Mar. 5, 1993). Finally, the knowledge and skills of financial officers in particular, and the service workforce in general, must be improved (Lin, 1991; Shieh, 1992a).

Although the national government has only begun to implement all the changes outlined above, the idea of Taipei as an international or regional hub has generated other programs with the potential for enhancing Taipei's role as an international financial center. For example, Citibank has decided to make Taipei its regional headquarters for its credit card operations (*Free China Journal*, Jan. 31, 1992). Thus over the next few years Taipei will be the designated location for processing Citibank's records and materials for Taiwan, Japan, Republic of Korea, and Hong Kong. As market conditions warrant, Malaysia and other Southeast Asian countries will be serviced from Taipei. This new operation will require the Chinese officials to consider how they currently manage the credit card market in Taiwan, including Citibank's Taiwan credit card operations. American Telephone and Telegraph has decided to make Taipei its regional communications center. The British firm ICI and the Dutch firm Philips have also decided to make Taipei regional administrative hubs.

Negotiations are under way with Federal Express, Bayer (Germany), Bull Computers, Microsoft, and DEC to locate Asian administrative facilities in Taipei (*Free China Journal*, Mar. 5, 1993).

Conclusions

The success of the leadership of the Republic of China in exploiting the initial advantages of Taipei strongly suggests that they were able to set in motion circular and cumulative processes (Myrdal, 1957) which then led to the evolution of a vibrant, thriving world city. The same conclusion seems to be applicable to the goal of adding finance to Taipei's world city functions. The same type of bold, forward-looking policies and initiatives which steered Taipei and Taiwan to rapid economic development must be implemented if Taipei is successfully to solve its land and legal problems and continue in an expanded role as a clean and livable regional and world center.

References

Chen, D. (1993) Taipei Must Clean Up its Act to Attract Business, *Free China Journal*, July 16, 6.

Directory of Sister Cities, Counties, and States by State and Country (1990) Sister Cities International, Alexandria, Virginia.

Financial Statistics, Taiwan District, Republic of China (1993) March. Central Bank, Taipei.

Free China Journal (1990a) Taiwan Seen as International Trade, Financial Center, Oct. 8, 2.

Free China Journal (1990b) Taipei to be Financial Hub, Nov. 22, 7.

Free China Journal (1990c) Plan to Make Taipei Financial Center, Dec. 6, 2.

Free China Journal (1992) Citibank Evalulates Taiwan as Best Spot for Asian Credit Card Center, Jan. 31, 3.

Free China Journal (1993) Economic Council Head Promotes Regional Hub Goal, Mar. 5, 3.

Friedman, J. and G. Wolff (1982) World City Formation: An Agenda for Research and Action, *International Journal of Urban and Regional Research* 6:3, 309–424.

International Financial Statistics (1993) August. International Monetary Fund, Washington.

Lin, C. C. S. (1991) Toward the Emergence of Taipei as an International Financial Market, *Economic Review* 262, 1–9.

Myrdal, G. (1957) *Economic Theory and Under-Developed Regions*. Gerald Duckworth, London.

New York Times (1991a) Taiwan's Financial Plan, June 25, D13.

New York Times (1991b) Bank Reform in Taiwan, Jul. 5, D2.

Peng, T. C. (1991) Taipei International Trade Center, *Free China Journal*, Aug. 31, 5.

Selya, R. M. (1992) Taiwan Turns "East": Trade Between the Republic of China, the USSR, Eastern Europe, and Vietnam, *Asian Profile* 20:4, 281–295.

Shieh, S. C. (1992a) The Outlook for Taipei as a Regional Financial Center in Asia, *Economic Review* 266, 1–10.

Shieh, S. C. (1992b) Financial Liberalization and Internationalization: The Development of Taipei as a Regional Financial Center in Asia, *Economic Review* 269, 6–15.

Yin, N. (1989) Rejuvenating the Financial System, *Free China Review* 39:1, 5–7.

Index

Index

Index

Ta-an district (*cont.*)
  as projected industrial area 32
  as residence for foreign nationals
    114
  dependency ratio in 111
  migrations patterns 107–8
  population in 103
Ta-tao-chen 21–3, 28, 29, 34, 37
  as part of central business district
    30
  as social area 118
Taipei Art Museum 44
Taipei Basin xv, 31, 153
  climate in 55–6
Taipei Area xv
Taipei City, Administrative status of
    122–4
  as host to two governments 4
  as special municipality 32
  districts of xv–xvi
  hydrology xv
  location of xv
  topography xv
Taipei City Aboriginal Community
    Development Association 178
Taipei Women's Rescue Association
    176–7
Taipei World Trade Center 255
Taipei Zoo 26, 81, 233–4
  new location of 46
Tainan City, Compared to Taipei City
    27
Taiwan Economic Miracle 8
Takokan River xv, 21
Tamshui River xv, 21
  as tidal river 153
Tatun mountains xv, 53
Tatong district xv
  as potential area for manufacturing
    118
  as social area 118
  as industrial area 33
  birth rate in 95
  death rate in 96–7
  elderly population in 97
  illegal factories in 64, 65
  manufacturing in 70–3
  migration patterns 107
  population 103
    growth of 90, 92–3
    ratio to physicians 101–2
Taxes 136–7

Three Principles of the People *see* San
  Min Chu I
Tihua Street, as historic district 47
Topography, as constraint to
    population 102
  as constraint to urban development
    163–4
Transportation, government programs
    to improve 197–210
  non-government programs to
    improve 209–10
Tunghua North and South Roads, as
    shopping areas 37
Tongho Temple, preservation of 48–9

United Nations, loss of seat at 5–6
United States Military Advising and
    Assistance Group 5
  as factor in growth of
    manufacturing 70
Urban Planning Law 138–9

Vegetation, natural, changes in 166
Vietnam War 12

Wanhwa 28, 29, 39, 235–6
  as historic district 47
  as shopping area 84
Water Pollution 155–6
Water Supply 154–5
Wildlife Preservation 164–7
Wu Poh-hsiung 125, 151, 190

Yangmingshan Administrative District
    xvi
Yangmingshan National Park, access
    to 246
Yenping district, xv
  as area preferred by Mainlanders
    118
  birth rates 95
  death rates 96
  hospitals, location quotient for 101
  illegal factories in 65
  manufacturing in 70, 73
    location quotient for 72
  migration patterns 107, 108
  population, density 104–5
    growth of 90–2
Yenping North Road 84